Evelyn Meynard

RE-IMAGINING MODERN ARCHITECTURE

EMILIO DUHART

1940–1970

TABLE OF CONTENTS

FOREWORD

Fernando Pérez Oyarzun

Fernando Pérez Oyarzun–Chilean architect, academic, and researcher. He graduated as an architect from the Pontifical Catholic University of Chile in 1977 and obtained his doctorate in architecture from the Escuela Técnica Superior de Arquitectura of Barcelona in 1981. He was director of the School of Architecture (1987–1990) and Dean of the Faculty of Architecture, Design, and Urban Studies of the Pontifical Catholic University of Chile (1990–2000). He received the Chilean National Architecture Prize in 2022. Between 2019 and 2023, he was director of the Museum of Fine Arts of Santiago.

Published in April 1966, the third issue of AUCA magazine included a dossier dedicated to the United Nations building in Santiago (later the CEPAL headquarters) designed by Emilio Duhart. The cover of the magazine featured a large photograph of the assembly hall helicoid and a smaller one of the entire building, which illustrated the precision of its design and the cloistral regularity of its layout. Additional content was dedicated to a competition sponsored by the Chilean Embassy in Buenos Aires, the family home of the architect Gonzalo Mardones Restat, and a project by Javier Gutiérrez for Ciudad Sandino—a rural settlement of fifteen thousand inhabitants in Cuba—illustrating the professional and cultural context of that time. The UN building was considered the highlight of Duhart's career.

Accompanying the dossier was an interview, a format introduced by the magazine to encourage the architectural criticism it claimed was nonexistent in Chile. The architect was asked a series of questions that addressed the construction's technical virtuosity and possible operational problems while still acknowledging the quality of the building and its significance in national architecture. Admiration for Duhart's career and talent—including the fact that he had worked with Gropius and Le Corbusier—was interspersed with a critical view regarding decisions the interviewer considered gratuitous and formal.

The photograph of the cone, enveloped by the spiral staircase that ascends to a viewing terrace overlooking the valley of Santiago, clearly expressed the culminating moment that the building represented in Duhart's career and in Latin American architecture. This image depicted the bas-reliefs on the walls that run along the staircase and allude to milestones of Latin American history. References to history and geography, the city and the house, were thus fused in a building both monumental and domestic, where Duhart desired to bring his experience and skills into play. Additionally, the UN headquarters in Latin America was constructed in a city that, according to Adrián Gorelik in *La ciudad latinoamericana* (2022), was considered the Geneva of Latin America due to the numerous international organizations that located their headquarters in Santiago in the 1960s.

Three years after the AUCA interview, Duhart was invited to meet with students from the Pontificia Universidad Católica de Chile School of Architecture. When asked about the UN building, he responded bitterly that he preferred not to talk about it. Various problems with the clients, partly caused by the death of Secretary General Dag Hammarskjöld (an enthusiastic supporter of the project) and the arrival of U Thant (more critical of it), seemed to have obscured the Chilean architect's moment of glory. Soon after, Duhart emigrated to France in 1970, never again to return to Chile except to receive the National Architecture Award in 1977 and an honorary doctoral degree from the Universidad Católica in 1994.

At once fascinating and tragic, this appealing character is the subject of Evelyn Meynard's *Re-Imagining Modern Architecture: Emilio Duhart, 1940–1970*. Duhart is undoubtedly one of the most significant architects of the second half of the twentieth century in Latin America, as demonstrated by the inclusion of the UN building in the 2015 exhibition "Latin America in Construction: Architecture 1955–1980" at the Museum of Modern Art in New York. A practitioner and educator, cultivated and sophisticated, his knowledge of a wide variety of subjects earned him the dislike of many of his colleagues. His professional work covered all scales, from the domestic sphere to urban and regional planning, and his work was known both in Chile and abroad. In recent years, there has been increased interest in his work and studies continue to multiply. However, Meynard's research is perhaps the first conducted from a distance—in a North American academic environment. This structural rather than circumstantial fact allows us to value her contribution to the understanding of Duhart's life and work. The author's Chilean origins and fluency in Spanish have facilitated her access to the multiple and varied sources required for this research. Additionally, her long-term residency in the United States along with the work she has carried out in the intellectual environment of the Parsons School of Design in New York is the backdrop to her unprecedented contribution to the knowledge of this architect.

Duhart's biography is characterized by very diverse cultural and geographical references, which enriched his personality and marked his intellectual and professional trajectory. Such experiences likely also introduced cultural tensions that were difficult to resolve and, despite his unquestionable success, made it difficult for him to fully adapt to Chile. One must imagine what it means to have been born and to have spent his early years in a remote rural town in southern Chile, where his family had emigrated to, and to have gone to school in France. His subsequent return to Santiago to study architecture at the Universidad Católica, far from his family environment, must have been equally challenging. Although Duhart's command of Spanish was perfect, he always retained a slight French accent in conversation. His later studies at Harvard and in Paris, his contacts with Gropius and Le Corbusier, and his proximity to architects such as Ieoh Ming Pei and Ernest Kump were all difficult for his contemporaries to assimilate. Chile provided him with important opportunities, among them his affiliation with Sergio Larraín, Dean of Architecture at the Universidad Católica and among the country's most prominent architects. He also enjoyed challenging commissions and completed projects that achieved great notoriety, collaborating with celebrated figures such as Christian de Groote and Roberto Goycoolea—both National Architecture Award laureates—and later Alberto Montealegre, a renowned architect, professor, and author of a monograph on Duhart's work.

However, it seems his expectations in his birth country were not fully met, so he opted to return to France, where he worked as a lecturer and practitioner. Although his work was not as relevant there as it had been in Chile, he received important rewards, such as the National Order of Merit in 1982. His retirement in Ustaritz, in the French Basque Country and place of origin of his family, seems to have closed a circle that took him from one rural environment to another, having witnessed and participated in some of the most significant architectural undertakings of the twentieth century. All this is not only a fascinating personal story but a reflection of complex social phenomena that traversed the twentieth century and significantly affected architecture and its culture.

Meynard clearly articulates that the purpose of her book is to rescue Duhart from relative obscurity. Although there have been several studies on the architect, including various dissertations written in Chile and abroad, global knowledge about his trajectory has been mostly limited to the Chilean cultural sphere. Within this project of recovery, the author has structured her book as a critical biography that interweaves the architect's voice with descriptions of his historical context. It is her express wish to follow in the architect's footsteps, so that his ideas emerge organically before the readers, allowing them to reconstruct his trajectory. This highlights a primary feature of this work's originality: a biography on Duhart of this nature has not existed until now. The broad outlines of the architect's life were known, but they had never been addressed in detail or contextualized in this manner.
In the last part of the book, Meynard analyzes the architect's entire body of work. An extensive bibliography and numerous notes and references attest to the seriousness and depth of her research.

The initial chapters are dedicated to Duhart's formative period, which concludes with his studies at the Universidad Católica and his graduate studies at Harvard University. Among the young architect's early works, Meynard considers his architectural degree project, which she analyzes in detail, and his first professional commissions both in Chile and the US. Particularly noteworthy is how the author relates the Chilean cultural environment—including the early presence of local artistic avant-gardes—to Duhart's childhood and adolescence, from his early years in Cañete to his schooling in France and university studies in Chile. In particular, the examination of his years in the US sheds new light on the academic and cultural context of Duhart's training as well as the development of his early professional networks.

Although there is a chapter specially dedicated to evaluating his work, the biography constructed by Meynard intertwines the facts of the architect's personal life with his projects and academic activity. This is evident in the sections covering the years between his return to Chile, his association with Sergio Larraín García Moreno in 1945, and his departure to France in 1970. The bulk of his work—both in collaboration with Larraín and as an independent architect after 1958—appears there. Two works of very different scales that received international attention frame this period: his home on Vaticano Street, built in 1948 and included in the MoMA exhibition, and the UN building in Santiago. The account of his Parisian interlude in 1953—when Duhart worked for a time in Le Corbusier's studio—deserves special mention, not only because it clarifies the circumstances that led him to the mythical workshop on Rue de Sèvres, but also because of the relationships he established with Le Corbusier and the work he was commissioned to do there.

The analysis devoted to Duhart's work has, paradoxically, a robust theoretical inclination. As Meynard examines his works, the architect's ideas about the themes of his projects emerge. The author recognizes the difficulty of interpreting a body of work that is not formally homogeneous and depends on the circumstances of the commission and the evolution of the architect's sensibility and experiences. She contrasts Duhart's ideas with those of contemporary theorists, which allows them to be situated in a broader context. Some references are recurrent, such as those of Kenneth Frampton on the importance of the geographical and cultural location of the architecture. Meynard suggests that a significant part of Duhart's contribution is associated with his ability to adapt and modulate certain principles, materials, and project strategies to the specific circumstances of his commissions. The fact that he did so with rigor and passion is what endows Duhart's work with such exceptional quality.

With *Re-Imagining Modern Architecture: Emilio Duhart, 1940–1970*, Meynard has fulfilled her aim to rescue the architect from certain international and contemporary oblivion by resituating his trajectory in a rich and nuanced context. In presenting him to a wider cultural audience, the picture she paints takes on a new meaning. Strictly speaking, it is not just a matter of settling a debt with Duhart and with a professional trajectory that traveled beyond the boundaries of Chile. Duhart is at the center of those comings and goings, tensions, understandings, misunderstandings, and misconceptions that characterize what we usually refer to as modern architecture. To understand him better is also to comprehend a network of personal and institutional relationships, as well as a motley set of convictions set against various historical, political, and economic situations that were complex and ultimately tragic. This resulted in a remarkable but controversial body of work, which has nevertheless helped shape the form, quality, and density of our daily life as we know it today. Meynard's account and analysis of Duhart—his life and work—are a vital contribution to the history of modern architecture. We are reminded, in this way, that architecture is not just the feat of a group of talented and influential masters but something much more collective and collaborative. Contemplating this evolution from an individuality like Duhart's and from a cultural milieu such as the Chilean one, which in some sense was broadened by the architect, allows us to visualize this panorama with an oblique view and an unexpected angle for which we can only be grateful.

Translated from Spanish by Michele Faguet

PREFACE

Isabel García Pérez de Arce

Isabel García Pérez de Arce is the Director of the Archivo de Originales of the Faculty of Architecture, Design, and Urban Studies of the Pontifical Catholic University of Chile. She is a researcher and curator in visual arts and architecture. García Pérez de Arce was the Director of the Center for Documentation of the Arts of the Centro Cultural La Moneda in Santiago (2006–2010). She has worked on curatorial projects since 2004, including for the São Paulo Biennial (2008), the Chile Triennial (2009), the Museo Nacional Centro de Arte Reina Sofía, Madrid (2010), and the Metelkova Museum of Contemporary Art, Ljubljana (2014).

In a conference held at the School of Architecture of the Catholic University of Chile in July 2024, Evelyn Meynard described what motivated her research on the architect Emilio Duhart by citing the words of the American philosopher Timothy Morton: "We never hear the wind itself … only the wind in the door, the wind in the trees. … We see the footprint of a dinosaur left in some ancient rock. [But the wind and the animal are no longer there.] … The sum total of all the … events by which an object inscribes itself on other objects is a history … since *history* can mean both events and recording."

When the author explains her interest in developing a biographical history of Duhart, she suggests that it not only means establishing the trajectory of a great architect but also approaching the material imagination inscribed in his architecture for the future. The idea of memory as trace becomes evident in the archive, the Fondo Documental Emilio Duhart H. (FED), where documents and records materially shape his architectural work, revealing his biography and thought.

It is interesting to think that the construction of a philosophical work can also be initiated from materiality, as Didi-Huberman suggests: it is like thinking about the workshop of a mechanic or the studio of an artist or artisan, irrespective of their specific practices and disciplines. In the studio, one works and thinks with one's hands. In this way, a narrative work of documentary reconstruction is initiated from the materiality where the work of a philosopher, a historian, or a theoretician resembles that of an architect.

When we research an architectural archive and its distinct documentary typologies on paper, such as planimetry, drawings, and sketchbooks, perhaps the image of the twentieth-century architect's studio comes to mind—that is, an architect who still designs and thinks with pencils, hands, and drawings, circling around a table and sketching lines on an architectural plan. The use of this method of representation brings us closer to the architect's relationship with orientation in a specific topography and transports us to a time prior to the concrete realization of the building, revealing a process analogous to it.

On the other hand, defining an archive is not only about grouping together different categories of projects and materials, but also understanding the material that makes up each of these documentary pieces and its relationship to the constructed object. In some way, the techniques of planimetry and their translation into the construction of an architectural model are similar to the relationship between sewing patterns and the fabrication of a garment. In this sense, the research also implies a reading based on physical records, which is related to handwork: to engage with the archive is to work with the hands.

Meynard's research on Duhart's planimetric documents involves a rigorous visual and comparative analysis of both the international archives that document his projects and the FED (Archivo de Originales, Centro de información y documentación Sergio Larraín García-Moreno, Pontificia Universidad Católica de Chile). This study reveals the Chilean architect's experience, from his time in Le Corbusier's studio to the production of his own projects in Santiago. In this way, the author offers a thorough reading of the conceptual theoretical translation of the canonical precepts of modern architecture applied by the architect to local regionalisms.

Archival research and the use of its contents implies opening, unfolding, enlarging, and contrasting documents, immersing oneself in a haptic practice far removed from the research of twenty-first-century architectural projects designed with digital tools, obliging us to engage with a process of analysis and interpretation that is different from the digital realm. This tangible dimension of architecture is what Meynard's research alludes to, providing us with vestiges of the evolution of Duhart's architectural techniques and definitions throughout his life.

Her analysis illuminates the stages and thinking implicit in his architectural work, allowing us to identify patterns and methods, and to ascertain the ideas and decisions made during the design of these projects, as well as the exploration of unexpected combinations of traditional and modern materials and techniques, which respond appropriately to climate, geography, integration with the natural landscape, and the revival and valorization of ancestral cultural traditions in the structural and material elements of the architectural project.

Throughout the history of architecture, representation has been of vital importance: it is where a project is born, that is, the origin of a sequence of stages, technical methodologies, and the applied thought on which the project is based. The representations of architecture, like architecture itself as a cultural object, give us an account of the social and cultural values behind that construction. In the CEPAL project (1960–1966), argues Meynard, the architect's creative architectural process is conveyed by his ability to conceive and design the spaces and structures of this building with a profound and creative understanding of materiality. These concepts involve both the selection of specific materials and the exploration of their properties and potential uses, both aesthetic and functional, in the landscape.

This book expands upon the historiographical and theoretical readings of Duhart's work while developing new research procedures, methodologies, and interpretations related to representation and archiving. It includes the oral testimony of the architect Alberto Montealegre (who worked with Duhart on the CEPAL project) about the drawings and documents that he had in his possession before donating them to the Archivo de Originales over twenty years ago. This new information yielded important revelations about the motivations and execution of the bas-reliefs on the Caracol, a building that forms part of the CEPAL building complex. Montealegre describes the handprints on this building and shows the large format drawings he created to develop the basic wooden stencils that served as matrices for the workers and carpenters who realized the bas-reliefs on the building facade.

The bas-relief drawing representations were simple graphics executed on delicate tracing paper, conceptually developed by Duhart to be engraved on the exterior of the building's General Assembly Hall (the Caracol building.) This set of symbols suggests a possible narration of cultural and historical progress in Latin America and the Caribbean. They not only reflect the landscape and architectural design solutions related to pre-Columbian architecture, but also the architect's decision to represent the cultural identity of Latin America and the Caribbean in political terms, thus symbolizing the cooperative relations that CEPAL promoted at the time of its inception in Chile.

Identifying the bas-relief drawings in the FED archive, used to create engravings and handprints on the building, also implies an analysis of the building as a body. A silent body, as Montealegre says in an interview I conducted with him in August 2024, "a mute Caracol that had to be given a voice … [the] building had become a monumental structure, a bit dead, a bit mute. These curves ... are an important influence on Emilio's architecture at that moment, at that time. In his brutalist architecture, Le Corbusier had produced several bas-reliefs in reinforced concrete, for example, his iconic Modulor of a man with one arm raised."

The voice of the architect is channeled through these forty-eight drawings, most of which were made by Montealegre from both the universal history books that were scarce at the time in Chile, and Duhart's own ideas of representation. José Pérez de Arce, a researcher and expert on pre-Columbian cultures, analyzes these drawings in order to understand the idea inscribed in their representation from a contemporary perspective.

Reading a trace, reading a symbol and a representation from the archive produces a new history. In this case, the work of opening these matrices of bas-relief drawings, reorganizing them in terms of their literalness, and comparing them with the original bas-reliefs on the building involves an interesting exercise of analysis through observation and the relationship between representation and architecture. According to Meynard, these archives show us how Duhart established ways to design, represent, and build based on these transfers and the creation of innovative concepts of modernism, adapted to the Chilean context in the projects he realized there.

The nonprofit architectural conservation organization DOCOMOMO has warned that the architectural legacy of modernism, of which the CEPAL building forms part, is currently at risk of disappearing. Its technological innovation, the transformation of the functions for which it was designed, added to the current cultural climate, obliges us to document and preserve the ideas behind this manner of constructing and designing, as it is well known that architects' sketches transmit the essence of their projects. These representations provide us with images that express the processes of the sensible and conceptual experimentations and reflective positions in relation to history and geopolitics.

Translated from Spanish by Michele Faguet

Figure 1: Emilio Duhart Harosteguy, photograph, circa 1950.

INTRODUCTION – A RESCUE FROM INTERNATIONAL OBSCURITY

As expressed by Kenneth Frampton, "Heidegger conceives of architecture as having the capacity not only of expressing the different materials from which it is made but also of revealing the different instances and modes by which the world comes into being."[1] The urban and architectural environment is explained through multiple histories that elucidate a complex fabric of meanings. In Chile the progressive advent of architectural modernity occurred, among many other factors, through the work of several architects who belonged to the elite, and who had either access to information, were able to travel to Europe, or both. Initially, knowledge about modernity was acquired outside the academic classroom as it represented independent interests and endeavors. Many architects contributed to the introduction of the aesthetic of the new twentieth century, but as formulated time and time again in academic circles in Chile, it is the second generation of modern architects that fought for a consistent modernist output that had to be pure, rational, and devoid of ornament. The trajectory of many of them is undoubtedly significant; however, Emilio Duhart represents one of the most transcendental cases, for his relevance and historical impact on the local scene.

1 Kenneth Frampton, *Studies in Tectonic Culture: The Poetics of Construction in Nineteenth Century Architecture* (Cambridge-Massachusetts: MIT Press, 1995), 23.

The present interest in focusing on Duhart's work and trajectory is to unveil a microcosmos of how things operated in the world in the early phases of the modern movement when its forces became such an all-encompassing worldwide phenomenon. Duhart's journey touched issues of travel, migration, education, and class, topics that played central roles in the dissemination of modernism around the world. Under this light, his life represents an interesting template that could be analyzed in comparison to other cases around the world.

Emilio Duhart Harosteguy (1917–2006)—a Chilean architect, urban planner, and academic—is considered the preeminent practitioner of modern architecture of the twentieth century in his native country. However, despite Duhart's acclaim in Latin America based on his iconic CEPAL Building, his career remains virtually unknown in the international arena. Professionally active between 1941 and 1992, he was part of a generation of architects that saw the progressive emergence of modernism, from the late 1930s onward, and witnessed it falling out of favor during the late 1960s.

His trajectory includes a master's degree with Walter Gropius at Harvard's Graduate School of Design, work at Le Corbusier's atelier in Paris, academic positions, and many first-of-their-kind modernist structures built in Chile. In this book, these projects will collectively be given detailed consideration and analysis in the ways they express his architectural principles and philosophy.

The specific intellectual trajectory of Emilio Duhart, with his first encounter with modernism in Chile, and subsequently with his close contact with the international leaders of the movement, Gropius and Le Corbusier, in addition to the many crucial figures he became acquainted with, represented the base from which his career was initiated. However, the processing of his early acquisition of ideas and principles came to fruition when the architect came in contact with a peripheral geographical area, Chile, where the bulk of his projects were realized. The application of this fusion was consummated in this distant-from-the-center kind of reality. This circumstance prompted his interpretation of the modernist vocabulary, leading him to translate the modern architectural language into the Chilean context. It is the products of this amalgam that this book is interested in exposing.

The extent of Duhart's work is considerable: of them, more than one hundred and twenty projects created in Chile are part of his archive currently housed at the Universidad Católica de Chile in Santiago.[2] His architecture, prominently featured in the capital and provinces, exhibits a cohesive modernist imprint. His portfolio includes corporate, educational, industrial, and administrative projects, urban planning, private residences, and "unités d' habitations," hotels, churches, and the international airport in Santiago. Duhart intensely pursued a distinct local quality through modernist expression, contrasting with the rigid Beaux-Arts precepts taught in architecture schools during his student days.

Internationally Duhart is mostly known for his CEPAL Building (1960–66) in Santiago, which many architects and historians consider to be the best example of modern architecture in his native country. In the international literature about modern architecture in Latin America, this later project is omnipresent, cited as a relevant example of one of the foremost illustrations of modernism in the subcontinent for its excellence in formal and conceptual achievements.[3]

However, from early on, Duhart's talent was occasionally detected by critical international players in the field, which led him to be showcased in 1955 in the MOMA exhibition *Latin American Architecture since 1945* with his Casa Duhart, built in 1946. Later, in October 1961, the Museum of Modern

2 Veronica Esparza Saavedra, "Emilio Duhart Harosteguy, Un Arquitecto Integral: 1935–1992," (PhD diss., Universidad Politécnica de Cataluña, 2015), 27. Before being housed at the Pontifical Catholic University of Chile, the archive was in the hands of the family and a number of documents were lost when the premises where they were stored was flooded. This explains why the number of projects in the archive is more limited.

3 To name some examples: Miquel Adriá. *White Mountain: Architecture in Chile.* Santiago: Puro Chile & Germany: Hatje Cantz, 2010; Valerie Fraser, *Building the New World: Studies in The Modern Architecture of Latin America 1930–1960.* London-New York: Verso, 2000; Paul F. Damaz, *Art in Latin American Architecture.* New York: Reinhold Publishing, 1963; Francisco Bullrich, *Nuevos Caminos de la Architectura Latinoamericana.* Barcelona: Blume, 1969; Leopoldo Castedo, *Latin American Art and Architecture.* New York; Praeger Publishers, 1969.

Art in Río de Janeiro organized an art exhibition called *14 Chilenos* (fig. 2). Emilio Duhart was the sole architect represented among visual artists, with 28 photographs, two models, and 25 drawings. More recently, in 2015, Duhart was included in the MOMA exhibition *Latin America in Construction 1955–1980* with his CEPAL Building. Additionally, during his lifetime, his work was featured in numerous articles in architectural magazines in Chile and in France. In the early 1940s, three US magazines also highlighted his work. The *Architectural Forum* issue of September 1943 and the *Arts & Architecture* issue of January 1944, published his *Designs for Postwar Living Competition* project with I.M. Pei, and the *Arts & Architecture* issue of October 1944 highlighted the San Quintín Fishing Base as "A Commercial Fishing Village in Chile." Nevertheless, none of this sporadic attention triggered the production of a comprehensive purview of his body of work at the disposal of the international architectural field, be it in a publication or an exhibition format.

The structure of the book revolves around two fundamental pillars. First, the inquiry exhaustively searches for the architect's voice, in numerous documents, interviews, magazines, books, drawing annotations, and so on, to formulate his evolution through his own perspective, complementing it with a wide range of relevant historical facts to provide context. Second, the narrative meticulously follows the architect's steps to allow the progression of his thoughts to emerge naturally in the text, employing a linear historical narrative to clearly delineate the trajectory of Duhart's singular and independent beliefs about architectural modernism. This constitutes the best proof of his capacity for personal re-elaboration of the international tenets of modernism, tailored to the specificity of the Chilean background of the early twentieth century.

This book does not include the work that Duhart did during his later years after he left the country to move to Paris in 1970. This relocation might have been temporary at first, but it turned permanent presumably because of the political upheaval and ensuing economic difficulties, especially with the advent of the dictatorship of Augusto Pinochet (1973–1989). The work the architect did in France is outside of this book's specific interest; the present examination exclusively concentrates on the projects he realized in Chile.

This book will bring to the fore an essential selection of the portfolio of this pivotal figure in Chilean architecture, establishing a chronicle that argues for Duhart as a true forerunner in Chilean modernist architecture of the twentieth century, considering Duhart's translation of modernism into an idiom indexed by the circumstances of Chilean culture.

Figure 2: Isabel Murtinho, Tuni Murtinho, René Sasson, Jorge Moreira, Emilio Duhart, Luiz Gonzaga do Nascimento e Silva, and unidentified person visiting the exhibition *14 Chilenos* at the Museu de Arte Moderna do Rio de Janeiro, photograph by José Santos, October 19, 1961.

PERIPHERAL HISTORICAL RECONSIDERATIONS

Only during the final quarter of the twentieth century did the recording and methods of writing a "world history" in design and architecture start incorporating more inclusive radical new directions.[4] Nevertheless, history had already occurred despite historians not having paid attention to it. Such exclusions led to countless untold histories of the peripheries, or only bits and portions of them having been rescued. Moreover, in many cases, these partial or incomplete accounts were only considered because they were either readily available to the researchers or were best suited to the dominant narratives of the centers of power. Re-surveying these accounts might be useful in the rewriting of a more complete and accurate global history.

4 D. J. Huppatz, "Globalizing Design History and Global Design History," *Journal of Design History*, Vol. 28 N°2 (March 2015): 183.

Emilio Duhart was professionally active during the period where historicism had a particular program, and the research or lack thereof on his work was affected by it. He exercised his practice when the hegemonic powers were propagated from the West towards the peripheries with rigid "colonial structures of knowledge and conceptual categories"[5] relating to the construction of history. Additionally, as previously mentioned, his work is much more extensive than what is generally known outside his country of origin. It is under the perspective of these two anchors that a reconsideration of his oeuvre is now necessary.

5 Huppatz, "Globalizing Design History and Global Design History," 186.

In *Architecture in Translation,* Esra Akcan affirms that "cross-cultural conversations have hardly been untouched by the politically charged hierarchies that have shaped the world. They have, thus, been neither smooth nor egalitarian."[6] She adds that "global historiographical and design practices remain … underdeveloped and undertheorized,"[7] advocating for the pursuit of "an architectural culture better equipped for a global future."[8] Because of the West's disregard of the architecture and design history of extensive "peripheral" areas of the planet, a global perspective is a necessity. As stated by Christopher Bailey, "the need to develop a genuinely global field of inquiry has moved beyond being a challenge to becoming a duty."[9] The obligation is to construct a metanarrative of a global history of design in contrast to how the canons of the West have established it

6 Esra Akcan, *Architecture in Translation: Germany, Turquey & the Modern House* (Durham & London: Duke University Press, 2012), 7.

7 Akcan, *Architecture in Translation: Germany, Turkey & the Modern House*, 4.

8 Akcan, *Architecture in Translation: Germany, Turkey & the Modern House*, 4.

9 Christopher Bailey, "The Global Future of Design History," *Journal of Design History*, Vol. 18 N°3 (Autum 2005): 233.

during past centuries, where the core mechanism for such approach was the "Hegelian presumptions that Europe maturing into the West represented a model for modernity and progress [a precept which] became present in the writings of most historians."[10] History-making was and still remains a tool for reaffirming colonial powers. As a consequence, before the 1960s, the recording of history had a clear agenda based solely on the worldview of European and North American cultures and had an established linearity to be followed under the parameters of modernization and the pre-established final goal of "progress." By not participating in this program, the rest of the world was left in a non-existent or subordinate position related to historicism. The result was that during much of the nineteenth and twentieth centuries, the peripheries had no other alternative but to participate in the larger narrative imposed by the West, complying with rules already established, or otherwise remaining with no history at all.

10 Huppatz, "Globalizing Design History and Global Design History," 186.

Emilio Duhart's story is an example of historical neglect that needs further scrutiny and is also representative of the geopolitical forces at play in the twentieth century within historiography itself. Duhart's case is emblematic of the type of accounts that have not made it into larger histories and instead have been only partially acknowledged. His trajectory has yet to be considered and possibly integrated into larger international currents of information. At the base of such omissions were the all-too-common assumptions of the time that modern architecture from the peripheries was essentially a second-hand gesture. As Jorge Francisco Liernur formulated it, "Latin America was [perceived as] an area of pure derivation or perhaps of the bizarre–and certainly wrong–development of proposals that originated in those provinces of the world it calls its center."[11]

11 Jorge Francisco Liernur, "Forewords" in *Modern Architecture in Latin America: Art, Technology, and Utopia*, eds. Luis E. Carranza and Fernando Luis Lara (Austin: University of Texas Press, 2014), XIII.

On the other hand, another consideration to highlight is the fact that language can be a barrier or a facilitator for the access and dissemination of information. In this regard, "there is a great deal of material documenting design in various places written in languages other than English that is yet to be translated. Indeed, this issue highlights the English language as a dominant factor that has shaped design history and limited our understanding of design in a global context."[12] Emilio Duhart's archive, along with most research material available to study his work is mostly written in Spanish, making his oeuvre inaccessible for those who do not know the language. Under this light, with Duhart's body of work being in the shadows for such a long time and deserving scrutiny, presenting this global view on the architect's professional output could meaningfully encourage inserting his work into more expansive historical narratives.

12 Huppatz, "Globalizing Design History and Global Design History," 189.

The perspective from which one should look at Duhart's work must be fitting to our contemporary cultural circumstances, where, as Liernur emphasizes, "it is no longer possible to continue to emphasize the single directionality of the relationships of meaning … [and we] have … to conceive of culture as a construction of multiple agents and of crossed signals."[13] The aim is to arrive at a just and accurate account of Duhart's work, arguing that it is an adaptation and reprocessing of the main tenets of international modernism which he interpreted in complex dialogues with his local cultural and physical environment. The account aspires to bring to light Duhart's mind as an original processor and transformer of information, as opposed to just a receptor and imitator. In the spirit of Esra Akcan's notion of "architecture in translation," the intention of this book is to present "an alternative … to passive metaphors such as import, influence and transfer–all of which deny agency to the receiving location."[14]

13 Liernur, "Forewords," XIII.

14 Akcan, *Architecture in Translation: Germany, Turquey & the Modern House*, 5.

The perspective of this analysis is also in alliance with the thought expressed by Valerie Fraser when she writes "Latin American architects demonstrated that they understood the rules but did not need to be confined by them; that it was possible to be modern and regionally or nationally specific at the same time."[15] The objective is to provide an instrument for elaborating new histories that could enlighten more comprehensive relational accounts, integrating peripheral narratives into the larger architectural chronicles.

15 Valerie Fraser, *Building the New World: Studies in The Modern Architecture of Latin America 1930–1960* (London-New York: Verso, 2000), 14.

w

THE ARCHITECTURAL CONTEXT

To better understand the broader context in which Duhart's career was immersed, an array of information must be explored. This includes a basic introduction to Chile, specific events going on in architecture at the time in Latin America and the world, and a brief recount of the architectural environment in which the young architects of Duhart's generation were enmeshed.

Figure 3: Emilio Duhart in his office on Av. Plaza Bello, next to a model, photograph, 1947.

A CONTINENTAL ISLAND

Chile is notably different from other countries on the continent located on the Atlantic and Caribbean coasts or near the United States like Argentina, Brazil, Venezuela, Colombia, and Mexico. In this sense, it is at a disadvantage due to its geographical position, size, and territorial morphology. Fluid cultural exchanges were frequently constrained by these conditions. Because of its remoteness, international travel and communication were, until the end of the twentieth century, the wealthy class's luxury alone, producing a generalized condition of cultural isolation.

To the east, the 2,734-mile-long territory is isolated from north to south by the Andes Mountains, an imposing mountain range with maximum heights of 16,000 feet. To the north, it is isolated by the Atacama Desert (994 miles long), the driest desert on Earth, and to the south by the Antarctic continent. The immense Pacific Ocean confronts the entire length of its western coast. Chile is a narrow country that averages 112 miles in width. Due to its length, except for the tropical type, it encompasses all known varieties of climate.

The country is also distinct due to a population mixture different from other continental regions, especially those of Bolivia, Ecuador, and Peru. The north's indigenous population of Atacameño, Aymara, Diaguita, Kolla, and Quechua is scarce and scattered on the mountains, compared to those historically linked with the regions located further north in Peru and Bolivia. Even more sparse are the Kawésqar, and Yagán people of the southern archipelago. However, the most numerous is the Mapuche ethnic group who have historically occupied the country's central-southern regions. These inhabitants were progressively pushed further south by the Spanish invasion initiated in 1541. For centuries the Mapuche population has vehemently opposed colonization, largely resisted integration, and up to the present have not accepted subjugation.

Nevertheless, over the years, the commanding violent tactics of colonization created a mestizo population. Additionally, the constant European immigration influx, which intensified between the middle of the nineteenth and the twentieth century, left the indigenous population on the margins, disenfranchised, and with a devastated ancestral culture. This compendium of cultures, indigenous, mestizos, prevailing Spaniard colonists, and European immigrants of multiple provenances, has resulted in a lack of a cohesive Chilean identity. The eroded sense of cultural unity and identity remains to this day without an integrated culture rooted in its locality.

Most European and Spanish descendants constitute the ruling class, which for the past 500 years has predominantly negotiated cultural exchanges. Duhart, a member of the elite, was an individual embedded in this particular amalgam, as were most of his colleagues. However, he made a concentrated effort to face the architectural field attempting to build bridges between the different constituent factions, albeit with all the contradictions and legacies of the prevalent colonial frame of mind.

Since their independence from the Spanish in 1810, the Chileans stopped looking towards Spain as their primary cultural referent and instead began focusing on France and England. As Liernur expressed, alluding to the entire continent but applicable to Chile as well, without belonging "to the center ... it is one of its extremities, [located on] the edge of the territory for which the Atlantic is an inland sea."[1] During the twentieth century, Europe became by and large the essential cultural reference for the Chilean elite.

1 Jorge Francisco Liernur, *Escritos de Arquitectura del Siglo XX en América Latina* (Madrid: Tanais Editiones, 2002), 31.

As existing in Peru or Mexico, grand-scale endemic pre-colonial architecture is comparatively scarcer in Chile. The Mapuche people were a semi-nomadic community who moved between the sea and the mountains following the seasons, elaborating transitory structures in the process. The small towns of the northern altiplano (highlands), some still existing in a few scattered places, have constructions of dual Hispanic and indigenous origins, with buildings made of molded adobe, straw, and stone. What remains in larger numbers is the architecture of Hispanic roots located in the central valley, between the desert and the frontier delineated by the Mapuche resistance in the south. The typical colonial house of Hispanic origin represented an architecture built with thick adobe walls to make up for the lack of structural support. They were generally finished with white stucco and had a gable roof with clay tile. The houses were built around internal patios and had broad eaves and open-air covered corridors to protect people from the sun and the rain. The trusses, ceilings, and interiors were finished in wood, and floors were usually covered in stone (fig. 4).

A significant amount of the country's colonial architectural heritage has been dramatically affected or destroyed by the seismic activity that plagues the entire territory. The bourgeoisie, always intent on imitating European trends, predominantly built structures mirroring the different transatlantic novelties, and the architects diligently served this class until the advent of modernism.

Figure 4: Cuna de Prat Sanctuary in Ninhue, Chile, 1995.

MODERNISM IN LATIN AMERICA – A SHORT LIVED NOTORIETY

While Duhart was professionally active in Chile, between the early 1940s and the early 1970s, some distinct conditions were being developed concerning architecture in Latin America. These conditions are essential to call attention to insofar as Duhart's work is part of a broader context being established. To some extent, they explain it as a constituent of more significant merging events.

Under this perspective, it is pertinent to review some issues raised by Valerie Fraser,[2] who states that from the 1930s to the 1960s, Latin America exhibited an unmatched ingenuity and creative modernist architectural production. This fact was supported by governments that saw in modernity a way of getting away from the colonial past, creating a future that would be modern and progressive. The world took notice, and for thirty years, it paid attention.

2 Valerie Fraser, *Building the New World: Studies in The Modern Architecture of Latin America 1930–1960*, 1–3.

According to Fraser, the climactic moment came when Brasilia was designed in 1956 and completed in 1960, as Brazil's federal capital. The new city was devised from scratch as the ultimate modernist urban planning endeavor. Its design brought both commendation and fierce criticism from Europe and the United States. In 1954, and before Brasilia's inauguration, a concomitant critical effort had been set in motion from Europe and the United States, disqualifying especially but not exclusively Brazilian architecture. Liernur sarcastically describes what the criticism consisted of, stating that "in 1954 … an unusual tribunal was raised at the prestigious headquarters of Architectural Review in which it proceeded to judge [the architecture of] Brazil objectively. The force of nature was transformed into anarchy of the jungle, the youth's impulse into childish whims, and the myth's mystery into overloaded sensuality. Ernesto Rogers and Max Bill safely lowered their hammer of custodians of the 'true' modernist legality, and since then, the accused has been thinned out of civilized circles."[3] After additional criticism from the West was voiced, as Fraser stated, the field of architecture on the continent went into obscurity and for decades only negligible inclusions of its history were internationally covered. However, the continent has an impressive amount of modern built architecture, from the 1920s up to today.

3 Liernur, *Escritos de Arquitectura del Siglo XX en América Latina*, 42. All translations from Spanish author's own unless otherwise stated.

Drawing attention to the commanding place of modern architecture in Latin America during this specific time, Peter Smithson (1923–2003), the British architect associated with the New Brutalism, recalled that "between 1939 and 1949 there was no new architecture in Europe; building ceased because of the war. To see a new building that had been built during those ten years, you had to go to Scandinavia or South America. The whole Brazilian thing occurred during the wartime period, but it was so far away."[4]

4 Catherine Spellman and Karl Unglaub, eds., *Peter Smithson: Conversation with Students–A Space for Our Generation* (New York: Princeton Architectural Press, 2004.), 16.

Between 1943 and 1955 the Museum of Modern Art was central in surveying the exceptional blooming of early modernism in Latin America, first focusing on Brazilian architecture with *Brazil Builds: New and Old, 1652–1942* (1943), and then with *Latin American Architecture since 1945* (1955), with Henry-Russel Hitchcock, which covered Argentina, Brazil, Chile, Colombia, Cuba, Mexico, Puerto Rico, Panama, Peru, Uruguay, and Venezuela. After these two important international showcases, the whole continent disappeared from the international history of architecture in modern times to timidly begin to resurface again at the onset of the twenty-first century.

A renewed international interest in architectural modernism in Latin America began to be brought to light in 2003 with the exhibition *Utopie et Cruauté: Villes et Paysages d'Amérique Latine* at CIVA, the Centre International pour la Ville, l'Architecture et le Paysage de Bruxelles. This show traveled to Miami and was accompanied by a catalog in English called *Utopia and Cruelty: Cities and Landscapes of Latin America* (New York: Princeton Architectural Press, 2005.) As recently as in 2015, this show was followed by the Museum of Modern Art exhibition titled *Latin America in Construction 1955–1980.* Commenting on the process of conceptualization of it in an article called "Latin American Architecture at MoMA," Carlos Eduardo Comas, one of the guest curators of the show, explained the vanishing of the continent from international architectural chronicles, alluding first to the critical expressions toward modern architecture in the sub-continent mentioned above, and then emphasizing that by the 1970s "Latin American architecture was totally irrelevant [from the perspective of the international dialogue], as can be read in Manfredo Tafuri and Francesco dal Co, *Architettura Contemporanea* … or Kenneth Frampton, *A Critical History of Modern Architecture* … The exception [to] the rule was Luis Barragán, who exhibited at MoMA in 1977 and won the Pritzker Prize in 1980."[5] An impressive gap that lasted for decades was created by the lack of international recording, analysis, and incorporation of the development of modernism in the region. The exception has been the somewhat recent work being done in academic circles, a fact

5 Carlos Eduardo Dias Comas, "Latin American Architecture at MOMA," arq urb, Issue 20 (September–December 2017); 158–159.

mentioned by Liernur when he remarked in 2014: "in recent decades of the historiography of modern architecture in Latin America ... for the most part, the studies on the subject have manifested themselves as the result of the increasing proliferation and expansion of scholarship on the subject, both within the region itself as well as in the United States, and to a much lesser extent, in Europe."[6]

6 Liernur, "Forewords," XII.

Despite this negligence, the modern movement kept on taking shape and developing in all areas of the region. In the subcontinent, the main demands for the new architecture were planned expansion due to population growth in city centers and industrial growth to facilitate these new urban needs. Valerie Fraser adds, "for modernizing governments, modern architecture seemed to bring together all the various essential components of construction: utility and strength with economy and modernity."[7] Modernity was a tool for nation-building and to put forth an image of "progress."

7 Fraser, *Building the New World: Studies in The Modern Architecture of Latin America 1930–1960*, 7.

For Latin Americans of the period, modern meant newness also in the sense of making use of new technologies and new materials. The internal urban migration brought a cheap and skilled construction workforce to the cities. This was a versatile labor pool adept in traditional wood and adobe technique that was effortlessly redeployed to that of reinforced cement, which became the backbone of Latin American modern architecture.

Fraser states that from the late 1920s and on, a generation of Latin American architects borrowed ideas from Russian and Italian architects, and more specifically from Adolf Loos, Walter Gropius, and above all, from Le Corbusier, who became the dominant influence throughout the continent. Le Corbusier's ideas evolved throughout the years, but the onset of capturing countless architects' imagination in the sub-continent was his early stance, based on the "five points" for the new architecture. These five points referred to supplanting supporting walls by a structural grid of concrete columns (pilotis), open-plan interiors, an outer skin free of ornamentation, generous horizontal sliding windows for air and light, and a flat roof that could be purposed as a roof garden. His views on urban planning were also widely considered. The interest was mutual, and Le Corbusier's relationship with the Latin American continent spanned many decades. He saw in the territories a fertile ground to apply his pioneering ideas on modern architecture and urbanism. He traveled to many countries (Argentina, Brazil, Colombia, Mexico, Uruguay, Venezuela) giving lectures, proposing urban schemes, and elaborating projects. Architects were very enthusiastic about his ideas, and those of other contemporaries, but at the same time,

they adopted and developed them on their own terms. Fraser adds that the various manifestations of modernist architecture from the 1930s to the 1960s in Latin American ultimately constitute what she calls "alternative modernisms."[8] She adds, "with government backing, Latin American architects experimented with ways of adapting the European theories to contemporary Latin American reality, and each country came up with its own solutions, combining the modern and the national in different ways."[9]

8 Fraser, *Building the New World: Studies in The Modern Architecture of Latin America 1930–1960*, 15.

9 Fraser, *Building the New World: Studies in The Modern Architecture of Latin America 1930–1960*, 15.

Figure 5: Emilio Duhart on the Caracol staircase of the CEPAL Building, circa 1966.

MODERNISM IN CHILE

The illumination of the complete mapping of modernism in Chile is a significant task and not central to the aim of this book. However, the following section will present a selection of relevant information to provide a general view of the academic, architectural, and cultural background that Emilio Duhart was to confront in terms of the scene that was at play at that moment in time.

A CONSEQUENTIAL POINT OF CONTACT – MODERN LITERATURE AND ARCHITECTURE

History is woven through the intertwining of assemblages of collective alliances, sometimes propelled by individual initiatives and innovative ideas that manage to unleash crucial cultural developments. In the 1920s and 1930s, the modern architectural movement in Chile contained interesting lineages in the worlds of literature and the visual arts, specifically through two fundamental literary figures of the modern movement, Vicente Huidobro and Juan Emar. They both contributed with their uncontested zeal to the exposure and promulgation of their vanguardist views in Chile in all areas of culture, including architecture.

Born of a wealthy family, Vicente Huidobro (1893–1948) was a Chilean poet and a pivotal figure of the early avant-garde literary movement in Latin America and the Spanish-speaking world. In addition to being a radically innovative poet, he was also a novelist, playwright, scriptwriter, politician, and polemicist. In the late 1910s and the 1920s, he spent time in Paris and Madrid, leaving a recognized legacy as a creative force and theorist of modernism in literature. When returning to Chile in 1925, he was welcomed by modern poets such as Pablo de Rokha, Rosamel del Valle, and Pablo Neruda.

In Paris, he became acquainted with numerous preeminent literary and visual arts figures such as Guillaume Apollinaire, Louis Aragon, André Breton, Blaise Cendrars, Jean Cocteau, Paul Éluard, Max Ernst, Juan Gris, Joan Miró, Amedeo Modigliani, Francis Picabia, Pablo Picasso, Pierre Reverdy, Tristan Tzara, and more. In Madrid, he met with Robert and Sonya

Delaunay, his long-time collaborator Rafael Cansinos-Assens, and many other important figures. His ideas left in Spain a long-lasting imprint on contemporary literary circles.

Huidobro also created and participated in countless critical cultural magazines in Chile, Spain, and France. Among them is his contribution to the publication on modernity *L'Esprit Nouveau* founded in 1920 by Le Corbusier and painter Amédée Ozenfant and edited by poet Paul Dermée. The periodical was active until 1925, by which time 28 issues were printed. It contained essays on experimental aesthetics, painting, sculpture, architecture, literature, music, film, theater, furniture, and more: in sum, articles about the new aesthetic of modern life, written by prominent personalities of the European avant-garde. The editors defined it as "the first magazine in the world devoted to the aesthetics of our time, in all its manifestations."[10] Le Corbusier wrote essays in every issue declaring his primordial ideas about architecture and urbanism and his vision of a modern constructed environment. Six of these articles were later part of his transcendental book *Vers une Architecture*, published in French in 1923 and English in 1927.

10 *L'Esprit Nouveau: Revue Internationale D'Esthétique* n° 1, III. http://arti.sba.uniroma3.it/esprit/viewer/web/viewer.

Huidobro's contribution to *L'Esprit Nouveau* magazine consisted of four articles published in issues 1, 7, 15, and 18. In issue number 1, he writes about contemporary Spanish-language literature in general; in number 18, about the current literature in Spain; and in issues number 7 and 15, he elaborated on his ideas about modern aesthetic. Around 1916 and 1918 he had coined the new aesthetic "creationism". Theorizing around it, Huidobro expressed, *"la vérité extérieure qui existe a priori est méprisable au point de vue de l'art. Il cherche seulement la vérité intérieure, celle à laquelle le créateur donne forme et vie et qui n'existerait pas sans lui...ainsi, il y a deux vérités; la vérité de la vie et la verité de l'art* ("from the point of view of art, the external truth that exists a priori is negligible. [Creationism] only seeks the inner truth, the one to which the creator gives form and life and which *without him* would not exist... in this way, there are two truths; the truth of life and the truth of art.")[11] Thus he argued for the artist's ability to create something entirely new, born of the imagination instead of mimicking the natural world. During that time, Huidobro had turned into a vital figure of a modern international network that united the avant-guards of Chile, Spain, France, and Europe. In appreciation of Huidobro's work, Le Corbusier remarked: "Mon Cher Huidobro [does] nothing descriptive, nothing anecdotal. He makes a poem like nature makes a tree,"[12] a commentary that represents a testament to how much Le Corbusier appreciated his writings.

11 *L'Esprit Nouveau: Revue Internationale D'Esthétique* n° 1, III.

12 Fundación Vicente Huidobro, "El oxígeno invisible, Huidobro visto por otros", *Altazor Revista Electrónica de Literatura*, nº1, Época/Año 3, (August 2021).

A contemporary of Huidobro, Juan Emar, was the son of a powerful lawyer, politician and diplomat who lived off and on between Chile and Paris. Emar, née Álvaro Yáñez Bianchi (1893–1964), was an avant-garde novelist largely ignored during his lifetime by the literary world in Chile for the audacity and novelty of his writings. His work began resurfacing after his death during the 1970s and currently he is thought of as one of the pioneering fiction writers in Latin America. His moniker derived from the French expression *"j'en ai marre"* (I am fed up; phonetically in French "Jean Emar," which in translation into Spanish resulted in Juan Emar.) In one of his prolonged stays in the French capital between 1919 and 1923, Emar assisted at the Académie de la Grande Chaumière, a modern art school free of academic rules, and also at the same time traveled around Europe. In Paris he was adamant about participating in encounters with intellectuals and artists in cafes and studios around Montparnasse. This way he met Vicente Huidobro and his Parisian entourage.

Vicente Huidobro and Juan Emar were united by a friendship that lasted a lifetime, by their firsthand knowledge of the avant-garde scene in Paris and by their common beliefs about the new directions culture had to take. Once returning to Chile they both independently began rattling the cultural sphere with their forward-looking ideas. Their actions and influences opened the doors to the new territories that modernity was unveiling.

Once in Santiago in 1923, Emar joined an important newspaper called *La Nación,* owned by his father. There, Emar created the "Art Notes," a periodical column he wrote between 1923 and 1925, and when he returned to France in 1925, they were followed by the "Notes from Paris" in 1926, and "La Nación in Paris" in 1927. In his writings he explained the new modern ideas about the arts to the Chilean public, including painting, literature, music, architecture, and cinema. He advocated for a new aesthetic at a time when the Chilean conservative culture was hegemonic and completely against innovation. His efforts bore fruit through his affiliation with young artists bent on an aesthetic more in keeping with the times. Around 1929 the overall art scene had morphed, allowing a space for the avant-garde to be developed. However, he paid a high price for his revolutionary pursuits. Given his unrelenting critical stance toward the conservative Chilean artistic milieu, especially towards art criticism, Emar's own literary work was left with no diffusion nor appreciation during his lifetime.

Among the many topics Emar wrote about, there were occasional articles about modern architecture. In the first essay written by him about the subject in 1924, he refers to Le Corbusier and his recently published book *Vers une Architecture*, introducing to the Chilean public the basic ideas about the new architecture that was being elaborated by the French master of modernity. In the article Emar highlights the need to adopt Le Corbusier's new concepts to guide the architectural conception, such as the economy of means through a pure, rational aesthetic devoid of all gratuitous ornamentation, where beauty arises from the order and balance of different volumes and alluding to the scientific approach of the engineer.[13] In "Art Notes," "Notes from Paris," and "La Nación in Paris," he also reproduced some articles written by Le Corbusier and Amédée Ozenfant that had originally been printed in *L'Esprit Nouveau*. Additionally, he also addressed on a few occasions modern urban planning, referencing the new problems of the sprawling cities such as Santiago.

13 Juan Emar, "Notas de Arte. Ideas sueltas sobre arquitectura", *Diario La Nación*, June 18th, 1924.

Juan Emar and Vicente Huidobro, despite their appreciation of the modern movement in all areas of culture, were both particularly absorbed by the visual arts, and were both behind two exhibitions deemed pioneering in the history of modern art in Chile. In 1923 Juan Emar supported a show of young Chilean avant-garde artists among which was a group that had recently relocated to Santiago and whom he had met in Paris: the Montparnasse Group.[14] In the presentation were also included a series of calligrams by Vicente Huidobro and some works by European artists such as Juan Gris, Léger, Lipchitz, Marcoussis, and Picasso. The exhibition, called the *June Salon of 1925*, had been sponsored by the *La Nación* newspaper and Emar wrote several reviews in the paper to explain the meaning of their work to the larger public.

14 The Montparnasse members were Manuel and Julio Ortiz de Zárate, Luis Vargas Rosas, Henriette Petit, and José Perotti.

From early on, Vicente Huidobro, as a restless creator, was also interested in various artistic manifestations beyond the literary world. We can see it in his calligrams published as part of his book of poems *Songs at Night* in Chile in 1913, in his designs of "clothes poems" with Sonia Delaunay, and in his collaboration with Edgar Varèse for a piece of music where he provided the texts. Like Juan Emar, Huidobro was motivated in influencing the art scene to make a space for the avant-garde. In December of 1933 Huidobro organized an important exhibition of visual artists he discovered in Santiago and whom he supported and admired: the Decembristas. The group was composed of María Valencia, Gabriela Rivadeneria, Jaime Dvor[15] (José Dvoredsky) and Waldo Parraguez. In their work they explored collage techniques, incorporating unusual materials and colors, and three-

15 A pseudonym used by José Dvoredsky, 1914–2007, a Chilean architect of Russian-Jewish origin who did relevant work in Chile. He emigrated to the United States in the early 70s, where he died.

dimensional objects in the pictorial plane. Not surprisingly, this show took place on the second floor of the first properly modern building made in Chile, the Oberpaur, which had been inaugurated in 1930 and to which we will allude later in this book.

This encounter between Huidobro and the Decembristas is relevant to both the visual arts and modern architecture in Chile. It is one of the fruits of Huidobro's efforts in advancing the avant-garde beyond literature. Two of the group's initial members were studying architecture: José Dvoredsky and Waldo Parraguez. Along with them, a group of students, including Enrique Gebhard, Ventura Galván, and Juan Borchers, evolved into rebellious figures within the academic architectural environment. Starting in 1929, they became crucial references in the fight for changes within the academic field of the School of Architecture of the University of Chile, fighting for an architectural education more in line with the new century.[16] As part of their efforts to install a new contemporary perspective, in 1935, Parraguez and his classmate Enrique Gebhart created an architecture magazine that would become a catalyst for modern thought in the discipline. This magazine will be referred to later in this book when this undertaking intersects with Emilio Duhart's life.

Vicente Huidobro's and Juan Emar's vision of a modern world in Chile paved the way for generations of visual artists and architects. They realigned the cultural field and developed the understructure from which the avant-garde set its roots, expanding the cultural sphere to include modernism in all the creative areas, and impacting the course of history for decades to come.

GENERATIONAL ALLIANCE WITHIN THE ARCHITECTURE STUDENT BODY

In the academic world of the 1920s and 1930s, history began shifting towards the advent of new possibilities for the new epoch. The process was slow and controversial and was initiated by the new generations.

At its origins the Faculty of Architecture at the Pontifical Catholic University of Chile, in which Emilio Duhart studied, was a subordinate division of the department of engineering. To achieve its independence, the faculty was founded in 1920. It provided an academic education based on the Beaux-Arts to train architects who fundamentally served the privileged class that sought European architectural styles. In the early 1930s, and for more than

16 It is essential to highlight that in 1932, at the University of Chile, a Reform Commission was created made up of professors, students, and alumni (among the students who participated were Octavio Tinoco Chacón, Alfredo Molina Lavín, Miguel Gana Molina, and Juan Borchers Fernández). This attempt at consensus failed because it did not satisfy the students' demands. Despite this, in 1933, a reform was carried out, which, far from calming spirits, motivated a growing rebellion exercised by a group of students determined to incorporate a curriculum that would more broadly integrate the most radical ideas of the modern movement. The disagreements between the students and the university directives increased, especially between June and August 1933, ending in harsh sanctions against the prominent leaders of the movement (suspensions of classes and/or exams, in some cases for periods of more than an academic year). Juan Borchers, Alfredo Molina, and Francisco Aedo Carrasco were the most drastically penalized students. Among those who received minor sanctions were Enrique Gebhard, Santiago Aguirre del Canto, Miguel Gana Molina, Federico Chester Murazo, Leopoldo Luisetti Martini, Raúl Véliz Montoya, and Carlos Villanueva Mayo.

Figure 6: Above, left; Sergio Larraín G-M and Jorge Arteaga, architects. Oberpaur Building, 1929, Santiago.

Figure 8: Left; Juan Martínez Gutiérrez, architect. University of Chile Law School, Santiago, 1934–1935.

Figure 7: Above; Roberto Dávila, architect. Cap Ducal Restaurant, 1936, Viña del Mar, Chile, photograph by Roberto Dávila, 1936.

a decade, the student body began to rebel against the parameters imposed by the school. They began putting pressure on the reformation of the architectural pedagogy, demanding modernism.

By the late 1920s, a group of architects had already introduced early modernism into the Chilean architectural landscape. These architects were part of a bourgeoisie that had the means to travel. Sergio Larraín García-Moreno and Jorge Arteaga built the first modern building in Santiago, the Edificio Oberpaur in 1929 (fig. 6); and Roberto Dávila, who worked for Le Corbusier and Peter Behrens, designed another exemplary early modern structure, the Cap Ducal restaurant in Viña del Mar in 1936 (fig. 7). In addition, works such as the Faculty of Law of the University of Chile (fig. 8), built between 1934 and 1938 by the architect Juan Martínez Gutiérrez; the Defense of the Race Building by Jorge Aguirre Silva and Gabriel Rodríguez, constructed between 1939 and 1941; and the Community Outreach Center Hipódromo Chile, designed by architects Enrique Gebhard and Jorge Aguirre Silva in 1940, are examples that stand out. These are part of a pioneering modern construction in the country; all works relatively contemporary to Duhart's student days. During this time, an intermediate generation of architects–who used to simultaneously design colonial, classical, modern, and other styles of architecture–represented an initial phase in the transition towards modernism, with projects that reflected a complex evolution towards the most purist version of the modern movement to which Duhart adhered.

In the early 1930s, some of this first generation of modernists were part of a half dozen prominent students who joined the University as assistants, causing a break in the balance of the institution's status quo when spreading curiosity amidst their students about the modern movement. Among these new assistants is the already mentioned Sergio Larraín García-Moreno, a professor at the university who would be key for Duhart and the student body during their training period and later become his partner and friend. These new assistants brought modernist concerns they had learned about through travels, magazines, books, and jobs abroad. They were aware of the Viennese Secession, Constructivism, German Expressionism, and the Bauhaus.[17]

17 Alfredo, Junemann Gazmuri, *Jorge Aguirre Silva: Un Arquitecto del Movimiento Moderno en Chile* (Santiago: Ediciones ARQ, 1996), 17.

The teaching of architecture at the school Duhart attended had been changing progressively since the 1930s, marking a more noticeable shift towards modernity around 1949, when the reform of architectural education began to take effect. However, long before the academic reforms, in workshops and graduate thesis work, students had already started to express their interest regarding modern aesthetics. Sergio Larraín García-Moreno and Jorge Aguirre Silva were instrumental in driving these changes.

The multiple interpretations of modernity of the first wave of modern architects were in many cases aesthetically driven. The generation that followed revolted against this lack of professional definition and began to fight for a more coherent exercise of the practice, incorporating a more consistent rational modernism where styles were not the focus. The Bauhaus' predicaments planted strong roots among Duhart's generation of architects, and in the two most important universities where architecture was taught: the Pontifical Catholic University of Chile and the University of Chile.

Moreover, the social disparities that existed in Santiago at that time could not be ignored. The mass displacement of a rural population to the cities and the ensuing homeless misery that lasted for decades motivated the young aspiring architects to demand to be taught a new type of architecture for all people, concurring that modernism was the answer. As in the rest of Latin America, they were very attentive to Le Corbusier's ideas, both in architecture and urban planning; however, the Bauhaus in Chile caused a particularly profound impact resulting in a generation of architects determined to put social housing and urban planning into practice.

The investigation of David Maulen de Los Reyes, a Chilean scholar dedicated to the research of the Bauhaus in Latin America, elaborates on the deep-rooted influences of the Bauhaus in the country. He affirms that both faculties of the leading universities of architecture in Santiago developed their educational reform plans (1945 at the University of Chile and 1949 at the Pontifical Catholic University) following two points of view: each distinct but both derivative of the Bauhaus School. He asserts that "on the one hand, there were the ideas of Josef Albers and Walter Gropius, adopted by the [Pontifical] Catholic University."[18] Josef Albers lived in Chile in the early 1950s with his wife Annie Albers and taught at the Faculty of Architecture at the Pontifical Catholic University, and according to Maulen, his teachings were centered around the idea that architecture is the most artistic of the sciences and the most scientific of the arts, emphasizing a scientific method approach to the field. Maulen continues: "on the other side was Hannes Meyer, the second director of the Bauhaus, who rejected any elitist model. [Meyer] claimed, 'the needs of the people [had priority] over the needs of luxury.' The University of Chile followed this trend … where the figure of the artist-architect is changed by that of a multidisciplinary technician at the

18 Ulrike Prinz, "La Herencia de la Bauhaus en América Latina", Deutschland.de, accessed 09/15/20, https://www.deutschland.de/es/tras-las-huellas-de-la-bauhaus-en-america-latina.

service of society's needs,"[19] emphasizing a socially conscious approach to the profession. Tibor Weiner, a former Bauhaus member taught at the Faculty of Architecture at this university (1939–1948). One of his main contributions was his collaboration in the preparation of the 1946 reform of the Faculty of Architecture of the University of Chile. Furthermore, he carried out various architectural projects both in Santiago and in the provinces.

19 Prinz, "La Herencia de la Bauhaus en América Latina."

The second generation of modern architects, to which Duhart belonged, made modernity their standard practice and lexicon. Duhart, who was fluent in Spanish, French, and English, was of an inquisitive nature. According to his collaborators, he was always very well-informed about architecture.[20] With his multiple travels, he was a facilitating agent in cross-pollinating the field of architecture with his knowledge and close contact with the founders of modernity.

20 Cristián Izquiero, "Interview with Architect Cristián de Groote," in "Traducciones: Intención/Palabra/Representación–Produccion del Anteproyecto para Naciones Unidas," in Taller VII de Investigación, Professor Fernando Pérez Oyarzun, 2005.

Initially, in 1929, when the first modern building was raised, there was considerable resistance to the modern movement. However, from the early 1950s an exponential acceptance of its practice resulted in an important increase in construction based on those concepts. Professionally, Duhart's most active years, during which he created the bulk of his projects in Chile, spanned from 1940 to 1970. Through his career, one can trace an essential portion of the outbreak of modernism in the continental far south.

This book will follow Emilio Duhart's footsteps, from his birthplace to childhood and adolescence in France, and his architecture studies in Chile. Subsequently, it will describe his time at Harvard's Graduate School of Design and the United States, and his initial career in Chile, to finish on his return from Paris in 1952 after having worked for Le Corbusier. Finally, the last chapter presents a comprehensive critical review of his work. The book constitutes a multi-perspective undertaking that aims to unveil the evolution of the architect's ideas, his recurring precepts and the territories in the field he covered, permitting both their influences and Duhart's particularities to shine through. This deep look into the universe of this architect will allow us to delineate his role more clearly in the establishment of modernism and his contribution to the history of architecture in his native country.

EMILIO DUHART – CULTURAL POSITIONING

Emilio Duhart's early years contain some intriguing factors, such as his being born in an extremely remote area in the south of Chile, at a time when that territory was still in the process of being colonized. What happened in his surroundings that made him interested in architecture, and how did his early life contribute to him becoming one of the most important modern architects of Latin America? These interrogations led to a more extensive look into his youth. All the literature that has dealt in depth with Duhart's career makes only cursory references to his formative years, beginning around the time he left Chile to study architecture at Harvard in 1941. However, a detailed scrutiny of his early life exposes an array of information that is critical to understand how, subsequently, he developed as an architect.

Looking more deeply into the architect's younger days reveals his character as an independent-minded person elaborating on what was, at the time, an innovative vision about architecture. Furthermore, even though he did not have a formal training in modernism at the architecture school in Chile, as a student he declared a firm determination to pursue that path before having gone to study with Gropius or having worked with Le Corbusier. Additionally, it is paramount to know he was initially interested in urbanism. This predilection surfaced in his degree project of 1941, and he revisited urbanism time and again throughout his career. This interest explains, in part, his early competence in being multi-scalar, a common attribute to contemporary architects but a rare characteristic at a time in the late 1930s in Chile when urbanism was an incipient discipline. During his career, he was involved in sizeable urban planning, as is the case, for example, with the urban planning design of the university city of Concepción, a project he was dedicated to for ten years. This grand-scale view of the territory is best expressed by him when describing his CEPAL Building the following way: "The building fully engages in the surrounding geographical space and the sky of Santiago … The perimeter and terraces [of the building] finish off the complex with the value of a fifth façade, highly visible from the neighboring hills and the planes of the nearby airport."[1] The fifth façade, as he calls it, is the bird's eye view of the structure, the imaginary aerial perspective which he could foresee as a new experience of the compound, a sort of mind-flying contact. The building roof was meticulously thought over, as an additional

1 AUCA, "Edificio de las Naciones Unidas en Vitacura," Arquitectura, Urbanismo, Construccion, Arte, AUCA 3, 1966, 31.

exterior plane that was intentionally designed. It had a rainwater gathering system, an auditorium, and an observation deck, explicitly devised to be experienced and looked down on from the surrounding hilltops and aircraft. The fifth facade is an amplified perspective of the basic architectural plan, the two-dimensional representation that registers the design ideas looked at from above.

Although common to today's architectural training, Duhart displayed a heightened sensitivity to the topographic fields and a keen insight of climatic conditions of the locality in consideration, seeing in them the necessary elements from which to depart on a creative architectural journey. In this regard, the architect Alberto Montealegre, who worked for him for about a decade, remarked that most of Duhart's planimetry indicated the position of the surrounding hills of the projects with a sign specially conceived by him.[2] His responses to the climate were expressed through an explicit architectural acknowledgment of those conditions. He provided coverage for rain and sun as a ubiquitous feature in his work, especially in the form of roofed open-air corridors, tree alignments, collection of rainwater, and more. Additionally, hc was interested in the life of the people, their culture, and the preservation and care of nature. In this respect, he was a visionary, an aspect of his legacy that has not yet been sufficiently explored and analyzed.

2 Phone conversation with Alberto Montealegre on July 3, 2020.

Because of the nation's insular quality and the authoritative preponderance of the capital, natives of Santiago tend to see the territory as centered only within the limits of the metropolis, a distinct and domineering view of its inhabitants towards the provinces. This characteristic was held by many architects, including those who had the privilege of travel. However, Duhart, who was profoundly connected to a remote area in the south of the country and who had lived in France and the Basque country, had a much more expansive inner geographical space as compared to his contemporaries. In one of the drawings for the San Quintin Fishing Base (also called Taitao Fishing Base,) a personal detail can be observed when he adds the text "the same latitude as Bordeaux -47º."[3] Alberto Montealegre Klenner, one of his last professional partners, commented on some of the particularities of his way of thinking when he said, "one tends to have a restrained imaginary habitable space [and] in the case of Emilio the limits were wider … He had a more geographical than urban vision … the cognitive map of people from Santiago has indisputable limits, and in Emilio, they were broader."[4] Montealegre added, "being a foreigner also helped him; he made projects throughout the country."[5]

3 Annotation found in *Drawing for Fishing Base: Geographical and Topographical Plan 2* – Emilio Duhart. Bordeaux in France was the closest big French city to the French Basque territories and in the 1930s an important port of exit towards Latin America.

4 Evelyn Meynard, "Interview with Alberto Montealegre Klenner," recorded interview, Santiago, December 27, 2019.

5 Meynard, "Interview with Alberto Montealegre Klenner."

Figure 9: Emilio Duhart and President Eduardo Frei Montalva in 1966.

Being born in Chile, raised in Paris, and returning to his native country as a teenager, in addition to being of French-Basque descent had many consequences for the architect. However, crucially, his descent meant a strong relationship with the French-Basque community in the south of Chile and its territory and the French community in Santiago. For the latter group, he designed an array of buildings, among which the most prominent are the Lycée Alliance Française de Saint Exupéry, in Santiago; the Lycée Charles De Gaulle, in Concepción; and the French Embassy, the French Cultural Institute (unrealized), and the Club House Sport Français, all in Santiago.

It becomes apparent after delving deeper into the life of the young Duhart that in those early years, one can find the substratum from which Duhart would undertake his initial exploration of the architectural occupation. In the following sections Duhart's journey will be reconstructed through his personal account and expanded with the multiple historical and geographical explanations of the locations that his life touched.

RESIDUES OF SCATTERED LOCALITIES

Duhart's biographical itinerary was stirred by migration, displacements, and travels, events that deeply affected his architectural journey. The singular nature of his life is essential to highlight since it is a defining aspect that would bring about his unique response to the world with which he interacted. That is relevant because his output meant transformations in the physical world he shared with his fellow nationals and will remain, for the most part, in the urban landscape for a long time, affecting, with their presence, the architectural lexicon of the locale.

The relocation, transfers, and repositioning of individuals, groups, and populations to new destinations, temporary or permanent, have been intrinsic to humankind. These movements have always carried transformations into the constructed environment of the landing-places. As expressed by Jilly Traganou, "the whole world history of material production could be rewritten by taking into account encounters among different groups, rather than essences of cultures, as they occurred due to trading, colonization, missionary expeditions, and other processes that brought groups in contact with each other."[6] Furthermore, as asserted by Akcan, "architects, architectural ideas, images, information, and technologies have been moving around the world for centuries, and this movement – this neither smooth nor egalitarian translation – has become an ordinary experience during modern times."[7] They engender hybrids which are "sources [that] can be traced back to different places."[8] In contemporary times, these blended manifestations have been occurring to the point where "there is hardly anything more common than an architectural hybrid."[9]

Under this light, Duhart's work is the product of an amalgamation of cultures, which situates him at an interconnecting point of multiple provenances. In the architectural domain, he can also be defined as a societal actor that redistributed intellectual elaborations of converging information inscribed within his selfhood. Duhart's role as a cultural agent is remarkable since architecture can be considered a visual language and as Akcan defines it, it is, therefore, a highly transmittable vocabulary. She declares

6 Jilly Traganou, "From Nation-Bound Histories to Global Narratives of Architecture" in *Global Design History* (London and New Yprk: Routledge, 2011), 167.

7 Akcan, *Architecture in Translation: Germany, Turkey & the Modern House*, 21.

8 Akcan, *Architecture in Translation: Germany, Turkey & the Modern House*, 22.

9 Akcan, *Architecture in Translation: Germany, Turkey & the Modern House*, 22.

> "Although a linguistic text needs to be converted for reception in another language, no such conversion is required for visual culture. The visual original does not need to be transformed in order to circulate across geographical space... If we disregard, for one moment, the connoted or culturally coded nature of images, we would have to conclude that the smooth transportability of visual culture from one place to another, in comparison to the linguistic, has facilitated its flow on a global scale and has thus accelerated the hybridization of different populations around the world."[10]

10 Akcan, *Architecture in Translation: Germany, Turkey & the Modern House*, 7.

The processes outlined above are pervasive in the architectural realm and in particular, in modernism in Latin America and in Chile. Duhart's life is a perfect illustration in this regard.

The circumstances of Duhart's upbringing were unique and peculiar. Three periods of his early life led to the understanding of the depth of the three cultural underpinnings that these periods represent, and which subsequently shaped his positioning in the domain of architecture. Paradoxically, from his remote birthplace in the south of Chile, Duhart's life brought him first to Paris, where he grew up, back to Chile, and finally to the centers where architectural modernity was thriving. The reconstruction of this chain of events will reveal the personal experiences that molded Duhart's sense of self, intending to understand how his early personal path was echoed in his architectural work.

ARAUCANÍA AND THE FRENCH BASQUE COLONY 1917-1920

Emilio Duhart Harosteguy was born in 1917 in Temuco, Chile, an intriguing fact which represents a singular convergence of distinctive factors. Both parents were of French Basque descent and were part of a large group of settlers, which formed a cohesive colony in an area vehemently defended by an indigenous population, the Mapuche. This population resisted colonization for over two hundred years; however, by the time of Emilio Duhart's birth, they had become somewhat subdued.

His maternal grandmother had a house in Temuco, the central city in the broader area of the Araucanía and his mother decided to be near her to give birth to her child, the third of four children (one sister and two brothers). The parental house was located in Cañete, a small village situated in what is even today a very remote area, some 110 miles to the northeast. This locality is near the coastal mountain chain of Nahuelbuta in deep Mapuche territory.

Figure 10: Conguillio National Park, Araucanía, Chile, 2018.

His father had inherited numerous successful businesses in this region and traveled back and forth from France to Chile. During one of his extended stays in Chile, he married Ana Marta Harosteguy Elissage, also of French Basque descent, and started a family. When Emilio Duhart Harosteguy was two and a half, the family moved to Paris to achieve the dream of every French Basque member of the colony to educate their offspring in France.

The history of the French-Basque immigrants in the South of Chile and the Duhart family, in particular, is a very unusual one. They lived a confined life in partial physical and cultural isolation. How did that happen? What were the particularities of this social group from which Emilio Duhart Harosteguy came from? To understand what was at play during the time of Duhart's birth, we need to bring to light some historical events occurring in the South of Chile and in the French Basque country during the nineteenth century.

The influx of the French Basque population in Chile, prompted by an intense political and economic crisis in the Old Continent[11] began in the last third of the nineteenth century and continued until the start of the Second World War.[12] They were attracted to the southern part of the country, concentrating mostly in the Concepción and Arauco regions. The landscape and its climate reminded the newcomers of the homeland they had left behind (fig. 10).

11 Patricio Legarraga, *Los Vascos de Francia en Chile* (Santiago: Patricio Legarraga Raddatz, 2006), 10.

12 Legarraga, *Los Vascos de Francia en Chile*, 10.

The greenery of the plains and foothills with their abundant and exuberant native rainforest, flora, and fauna, mostly untouched by civilization, and the proximity of the Nahuelbuta Mountain chain, reminded them of the lower Pyrénées.

The French-Basque migration began half a century after the Chilean declaration of independence in 1810, at a time when the country did not yet have a linguistic or ethnic unity, nor territorial continuity,[13] and long stretches of the territory to the South were still unexplored. The Kingdom of Chile, as the territories were called during colonial times, endured a continuous war sustained by the Mapuche indigenous people against the Spanish invasion (fig. 11). The Bío-Bío River marked the frontier to the South (430 miles to the south of Santiago), where the Mapuche territories started and extended some 400 miles further South. It was at this frontier that the Mapuche people fiercely combated the Spanish colonizers, an ongoing war that manifested their determined rejection of the conqueror and resulted in a failed subjugation.

13 Armando Cartes Montory, *Bío Bío: Bibliografía Historica Regional* (Santiago: Coeditors: Ediciones de la Dirección de Bibliotecas, Archivos y Museos; Centro de Investigaciones Diego Barros Arana; Editorial Universidad de Concepción, 2014), 29.

The Mapuche people organized their territories into distinct regions that extended from the ocean to the Andes Mountains, separated by natural features such as plains, rivers, and mountains.[14] This ethnic group spoke a common language called Mapudungun and was a semi-nomadic population that migrated from west to east during the winter and east to west during the summer. This cultural fact meant an existential threat because they had a deep-rooted relationship to the land where the population pursued its livelihood following what the land could provide them each season and continuously migrated from the coast to the mountain and vice versa. This movement ran in the opposite direction of the interest of the country of Chile, which wanted territorial unity running north to south. Additionally, the colonizers wanted to own the indigenous population's land, threatening the Mapuche world as their ancestry had created it.

14 Cartes Montory, *Bío Bío: Bibliografía Histórica Regional*, 42.

The Arauco province situated to the south of the frontier, the borderline which pushed colonization in a consistent line of occupation, was established in 1852. It was part of a semi-autonomous region where villages functioned more like enclaves that kept a precarious existence due to the recurring indigenous uprisings, resulting in a limited foreign population.[15] This province includes five communes, among which is Cañete. In the late nineteenth and early twentieth century, it is in the city and commune of Cañete where significant economic activities in the region developed.[16]

15 Cartes Montory, *Bío Bío: Bibliografía Histórica Regional*, 44.

16 Cartes Montory, *Bío Bío: Bibliografía Histórica Regional*, 83.

Figure 11: Mapuche women, early twentieth century, drawing on paper, pencil and Indian ink by José Pérez de Arce, 1984.

Cañete was utterly destroyed by the Mapuche in 1598 and was re-founded in 1868 during the process called the occupation of Araucanía,[17] when the state began to impose its jurisdiction, stimulating and facilitating the allocation of European immigrants to the region. It is thus that the frontier society and the occupation of the Araucanía by foreign colonies constitute a singular phenomenon in the history of the nascent nation of Chile. Among the foreigners arriving in this distant area of the country, there was a significant group of French Basque immigrants who resided there in large numbers. Along with German, English, Swiss, and Belgian settlers, they left an essential imprint in the architecture, economy, and society of the villages and cities of the Mapuche territories.[18]

One must go back more than a century to imagine the firm determination of these Basque immigrants to repatriate in such a distant, isolated, and inaccessible area in the world. The trip from Bordeaux in Southern France, the port of exit most of them used to South America, was long and perilous, and their new destiny was extremely far off, making it very difficult and expensive to travel back to their motherland. Hence, they built tight-knit communities with their compatriots, creating robust support systems among which everybody knew each other well. Most of them were farmers, who dedicated themselves to agriculture. In their country of origin, they owned small lots of land, but in Chile, they could afford large expanses of farming fields. Most of the immigrants were male and young, and once they prospered, they traveled back to the French Basque country to find a spouse and return to their new homeland to build a family. However, they would always dream of going back to their native land and particularly of educating their offspring in France,[19] to keep their cultural legacy.

17 Cartes Montory, *Bío Bío: Bibliografía Histórica Regional*, 86.

18 Cartes Montory, *Bío Bío: Bibliografía Histórica Regional*, 87-88.

19 Legarraga, *Los Vascos de Francia en Chile*, 10.

In the last three-quarters of the nineteenth century, promoted by these new immigrants, the Arauco region began an early industrial, agricultural, and economic development, at first with the build-up of wheat plantations for export, bringing economic stability to the region and most significantly ending the Chilean territorial discontinuity.[20] Further along in time, these immigrants developed a series of businesses in different areas excelling in agriculture, commerce, banking, and industries such as leather and footwear, flour milling, and more.

20 Cartes Montory, *Bío Bío: Bibliografía Histórica Regional,* 96-97.

The most financially successful returned to France, where they were called "Americanos" and enjoyed the admirations of their fellow countrymen and women. When re-establishing themselves in their motherland, they applied the newly acquired experience and knowledge in their fields of expertise, infusing their native place with novel ways of doing business in commerce, management, banking practices, agriculture, and some of them even pursued positions in their local governments. They were central in stimulating the local economy of the Pays Basque at the beginning of the twentieth century.[21]

21 Legarraga, *Los Vascos de Francia en Chile,* 140.

One of the most prominent families involved in the economic progress of the Arauco Province is the Duhart family, originators of Ustaritz, France, in the department of the Pyrénées Atlantiques, in the commune of Bayonne. It is believed that almost all the French-Basque commerce in the Arauco Province derived from Duhart Hermanos (Duhart Brothers), a commercial house that started in the city of Lota and had numerous branches throughout the Araucanía, selling an array of local and imported goods. It was a thriving enterprise developed first by Duhart's grandfather, Pierre Duhart Labrouche, one of the most successful businessmen of the era, in which many French-Basque employees learned and later developed their own business in the region. Pierre Duhart had arrived in Araucanía in 1852 and returned to Ustaritz in 1902, where he died in 1905. In 1860 he associated with his two brothers, Baptiste and Charles Duhart Labrouche, and established the Duhart Hermanos headquarters in Cañete in 1878. Over decades, Duhart Hermanos diversified into a cluster of businesses such as mills, alcohol distilleries, extensive farms, power plants, breeding and cattle, export, financial, and capital investment businesses.

Prior to the First World War, Duhart's father, Émile Pierre Duhart Ainciondo, oversaw the family businesses with his brother Hubert Duhart Ainciondo. Émile Pierre Duhart Ainciondo spent most of his time in Paris, and the businesses in Chile were led by his brother Hubert. However, with the advent of the war, Duhart's father had to travel back to Chile many times for extended stays. Around the time of the economic crisis of 1929, Duhart's uncle, Hubert Duhart, made some substantial investment in coal mines in Coronel, Chile, with disastrous consequences, and Duhart's father had to hastily return to Chile to save the family businesses.[22]

22 Legarraga, *Los Vascos de Francia en Chile,* 147.

In Chile, Émile Duhart Hartosteguy's family lived in a poorly populated area sharing their lives mostly among compatriots of French Basque descent. The interaction with the existing Chilean culture was diluted by the characteristics of the Araucanía, with a low-density population and the presence of an indigenous people with little interest in interacting with foreigners.

Nevertheless, the relationship to the landscape and the sense of place ran deep in both sides of Duhart's family. Their Basque descent, their language, and traditions were the uniting thread to their existence. Additionally, the experience of living in such a remote place in the world at a time when traveling was difficult and rare, and survival laborious and burdensome, presumably gave the colony a profound awareness of belonging to an out of the ordinary experience and place.

Émile Duhart Harosteguy was born in this extraordinary place but left the South of Chile to go to Paris with his family when very young. However, he is part of the story of this particular group of people, who belonged to both places, the French-Basque country, and the Araucanía, an area where his family had left a substantial imprint, and which would be re-visited by him much later in his life. This territory would be explored by Duhart as a teenager, and young adult, and will represent the foundational ground for his deep interest in nature, history, and geography.

GROWING UP IN THE METROPOLIS – PARIS 1920-1935

Arriving in the French capital in 1920 at three years old, Émile Duhart and his family lived in the Neuilly-Sur Seine neighborhood located at the center of the city, and adjacent to the Parc de Bagatelle, the Bois de Boulogne, and the Seine River. The Arc de Triomphe, the Eiffel Tower, and the Musée du Louvre were all at a reasonable walking distance. In the same area, in the Boulevard Victor Hugo, Duhart attended primary and secondary school at the École Sainte Croix de Neuilly, a traditional Catholic school.

He grew up in the city between 1920 and 1935, the years between the two world wars, commonly defined as "les années folles" ("the crazy years".) In 1921 the French economy was booming, and Paris was the center of fashion, music halls, and movie theaters in addition to displaying an exuberant nightlife of "faire la fête." Most importantly, Paris was consolidating itself as the capital of modern art, music, literature, and cinema, and a series of art movements were flourishing: Dadaism, Surrealism, Cubism, and Futurism.

The city's population was expanding with the arrival of immigrants from all over Europe, escaping conflicts in their countries of origin (Italians, Czechs, Slovaks, Polish, Russian, Spaniards, Armenians, French from the islands of the Caribbean, and the colonies in Africa). Additionally, commerce was burgeoning in the grand department stores such as Belle Époque, Bon Marché, Galeries Lafayette, BHV, Printemps, and La Samaritaine. The livelihood of this modern city was enhanced by the development of new ways of urban mobility, with tramways, buses, and the growing presence of private automobiles and taxicabs.

However, it is in the City of Lights' architecture and urban planning that we may find compelling sources of visual, experiential, and aesthetic considerations that would have significant value in the architectural career of Emilio Duhart. As Cristián Berrríos noted in his book *Emilio Duhart: Elaboración de un Espacio Urbano - Ciudad Universitaria de Concepción,* Paris constituted for him a lesson in urbanism. The young Duhart lived in the middle of "an organized urban structure"[23] devised by Baron Haussmann in the middle of the nineteenth century.

23 Cristián Berrios, *Emilio Duhart: Elaboración de un Espacio Urbano* (Santiago LOM Ediciones, 2019), 33.

Haussmann's effort did not stop at the embellishment of the city. The remodeling of the urban space had multiple fields of novel developments such as the construction of public infrastructure, the organization of public transportation, building hospitals, schools, sewers and water supplies facilities, gas installations, and allowing the local government to intervene into private properties, which collectively created a more centralized urbanism.[24] The inner working of the metropolis was organized as a whole in ways that had never been done before, facilitating the citizenry with more efficient use of its urban resources.

24 Florence Bourillon, "Changer la Ville, la Question Urbaine au Milieu du 19° Siècle," *Vingtième Siècle, Revue d'Histoire* N° 64, Numéro Spécial: Villes en Crises? (Oct.–Dec. 1999), 18-22.

At the time of its conception, these transformations of the city's fabric were the consequence of a significant effort to apply analytical criteria and novel concepts of city planning. Furthermore, as stated by Colin Jones, "Paris rebuilt, boulevardised and mythologised became over that period the archetypal city of modernity [...]"[25] This modern urban conception, in its outlook and its functioning, once unconsciously absorbed, must have shaped the young Duhart's understanding of the metropolitan urban structure in ways that would have profound implications for the future architect and urban planner. Émile Duhart grew up in the most relevant metropolis of this epoch, a hub of international cultural exchanges. Despite his young age, he must have absorbed

25 Colin Jones, "Theodore Vacquer and the Archaeology of Modernity in Haussmann's Paris," Transactions of the Royal Historical Society, Sixth Series, Vol. 17 (2007), 159.

some of the zeitgeist which would later represent a radical reference in his future professional life.

When growing up Duhart did not express any particular interest in architecture, but he was competent in drawing and was passionate about airplanes and navigation. In an interview in 1993–1994, Émile Duhart recounted a visit to his class by students of architecture at the École des Beaux-Arts. Even though the visit date is unknown, one could infer that these talks happened when Duhart was near ending secondary school, between 1931 and 1933. He described them as having an amusing and marginal semblance with their velvet berets and substantial multicolored ties, sarcastically calling them "artists." Nevertheless, Duhart expressed great admiration for their "column, capital, and cornice"[26] drawings, qualifying them as extraordinary and describing the different mediums they utilized, such as Chinese ink, charcoal, and watercolor, with presumably sensual pleasure. Duhart had a drawing class at school, which he much enjoyed, admitting that he had great admiration for those skills and recounted that at that age, he used to draw with a particular proficiency. Duhart also asserted that architecture per se did not impress him, appearing to him as being "divorced from the living world."[27]

26 Fernando Pérez Oyarzun and Pilar Urrejola, "Series of interviews with Emilio Duhart," audio interview, Part 1 of 8, Émilio Duhart Archive Pontifical Catholic University of Chile, Santiago Chile, 1993-1994.

27 Pérez Oyarzun and Urrejola, "Series of interviews with Emilio Duhart," audio interview, Part 1 of 8.

During the 1920s, aviation had become increasingly ubiquitous, with the establishment of the first commercial airline service in the world between Paris and London in 1919, the first transatlantic flight between New York and Le Bourget in 1927, and the founding of Air France as the national airline in 1933. Luxury commercial navigation was equally novel, and the most notorious example was the Normandie Ocean liner representing a new type of luxury and France's symbol of national pride. Duhart undoubtedly would have been aware of these technological advancements, and, to his young mind, they must have represented a world of wonder. Back then, his keen interest in ships and aviation led him to independently study naval construction and making models. Presumably this was a sign of a budding interest in architecture. Further along, drawings and making models would become central to his professional life, and these early exercises must have represented a training ground to apply spatial awareness and the representation of ideas: the forethought converging into a physical rendering. Additionally, one can also speculate that given the intensity with which Duhart pursued this interest, he was showing a particular penchant for what was new, original, progressive, and innovative, a fact that is worth remembering when unearthing his later choices and career decisions.

One can also infer a nascent interest in the working of things, a curiosity for the technological aspect of an object, and above all an antipathy towards ornamentation when he commented, "in France, at the end of secondary school, the teaching of l'École des Beaux-Arts already seemed to me to be at odds with the life of the 20th century and I was more interested in the naval or aeronautical architecture to which I would have devoted myself if I had remained in Paris. The beauty of a fighter plane or a cruise ship that did not include anything superfluous impressed me more than the decorative gratuitousness of the architecture of that time,"[28] an interesting observation where Duhart concedes the prevalence of functionalism over embellishment, anticipating an important precept of the modern movement at a moment when he was not even considering the field of architecture.

28 Emilio Duhart, "Tesis de Grado 1940," *Revista ARQ* Nº 23, Santiago de Chile, 1993, 8 -11.

Duhart returned to Chile in 1935, when he was a seventeen-year-old teenager and had completed secondary school. France and the French language surrounded him during his decisive formative years. In 1934, the surge of fascism in Italy and Germany, and the impact of the Russian Communist International, gave agency to the French extreme left and right resulting in uprisings in Paris. However, the agitated political climate in the French capital was not the main reason why the Duhart family had to swiftly move back to Chile. The economic crisis of 1929 had greatly destabilized the family businesses in Chile and Duhart's father needed to re-settle there to attempt to rescue them.

Duhart had been to Chile only once when he was eight years old, joining his father on a short business trip. This fact attests to the short time he was in his birthplace during his childhood. While in France, the family's French-Basque affiliation was never forgotten and every summer they spent time in Ustaritz in the French-Basque country.

COLLIDING WORLDS – DEFINING YEARS 1935-1936

At seventeen, Duhart was a young French national on his way to an unknown destination. After finishing his secondary school in the spring of 1935, Émile Duhart spent the summer in Europe and then traveled to Chile in the Reina del Pacífico, built in 1930, one of the largest and fastest motor liners at the time. In 1993 Duhart recalled that among the stops the cruise ship made in the Caribbean, Havana was for him his first encounter with Latin America, a comment that demonstrates how little direct contact with the subcontinent he had during his early life.

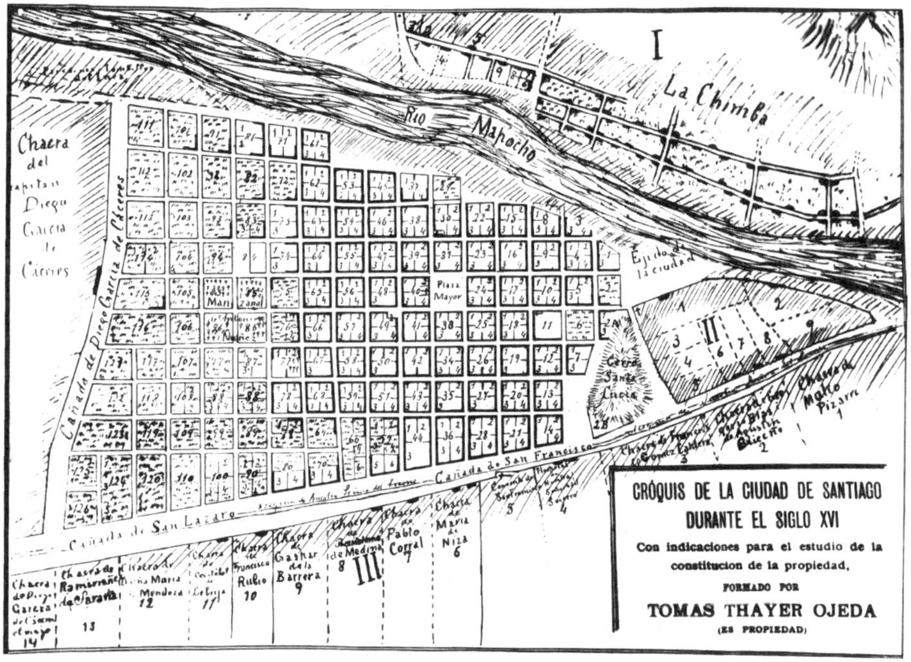

Figure 12: Sketch of the city of Santiago during the sixteenth century, with indications for the study of the constitution of property formed by Tomás Thayer Ojeda, Santiago: s.n., photograph, 1905.

Figure 13: Santiago de Chile. View of Alameda, photograph, 1930. Public domain.

The years 1935 and 1936 were a defining time for the young Émile and were marked by three significant events: moving to a new country, a critical family loss, and deciding which career to pursue. Of this important period in his life, Duhart later commented that "the move to Chile [...] was a profound mutation that provoked [. . .] a necessary essential reflection to situate myself regarding the place of my birth in the south, its nature, and its people. I lived this process with youthful enthusiasm and sympathy while not devoid of nostalgia for Europe."[29] This relocation meant to him a profound effort to comprehend his new circumstance.

29 Duhart, "Tesis de Grado 1940," 8 -11.

Once in Chile, Duhart felt a bit lost in his new surroundings. He could not foresee his future and spent his time trying to understand the Chilean way of life. He had lived in Paris, a cosmopolitan city that was home to him. In contrast, he deemed Santiago as a mixture of poverty and dignity, slightly torn down and dusty, far off from the center, and isolated, which made him feel disjointed.

The city of Santiago represented a type of urban space he had never confronted before. Founded in 1541 by Pedro de Valdivia, the capital was designed around a plaza surrounded by a church and the most important municipal buildings. It constituted an urban plot devised by the conquistador; a template utilized in all cities throughout Latin America (fig. 12). In Santiago, this foundational grid expanded over the centuries. By the time Duhart arrived in Santiago, a civic center had sprung up adjacent to the colonial core with numerous large buildings inspired not by Spanish but by European neoclassical architecture (fig. 13). The most crucial avenue running from east to west, the Alameda, contained large family houses on both sides called "palacios," also inspired by European styles. These were the areas inhabited by the powerful elite, a clear sign that architecture at the time was at the service of the wealthy class. This was a neighborhood familiar to Duhart, as it was in the vicinity of his early student accommodation.

While the center of the capital had an organized layout, since the turn of the twentieth century, the peripheries had grown in a chaotic way. Architecture and urban planning did not participate in its development. The exponential growth of the population due to rural migration almost doubled between 1900 and 1930. While the population of Paris was almost 3 million when Duhart left the city, the total population in Chile was approximately 4 million, and 2.4 million were illiterate. Santiago's inhabitant count in 1935 was approaching 1 million people, of which a third lived in extreme poverty in part because the depression of 1929 had devastated the economy of the country.

The more impoverished areas were overcrowded and mired in their misery. The underprivileged were underserved: Santiago's center had cobblestone streets, whereas the peripheral areas did not, and the technological advances of the era (transportation, electricity, and the like) were only present in the well-to-do areas.

This environment must have represented a dramatic contrast to the one in which Duhart had been raised. The city of Santiago had an organized core, but the rest was left to its own devices, with no infrastructure and development support. Additionally, the clear distribution of the city by class, with the wealthy strata showing a fearless appropriation of some European conceits, must have been a curious realization for the young Duhart. Very quickly he noticed that the most prominent architecture referenced a lot of the styles of the Parisian buildings, observing that the designs had no real connection to the place, a fact that baffled him.

Most probably, the divergent reality in Chile must have represented a challenging realization for the young Duhart. However, notwithstanding the dissimilitude between both contexts (Paris and Santiago,) Duhart appreciated the place and its people. He thought this was a conservative society, living in the nineteenth century, but concurrently, he felt there was an authenticity that he highly enjoyed. Aside from noting a distinct sense of humor in the Chilean character, he was particularly taken by what he defined as the great human quality, thoughtful attention, and kindness of its people, and by the fact that there were more human contact and direct relationships among them.

To overcome his sense of estrangement and to apprehend his new reality, Duhart pursued two distinct paths. On the one hand, he dedicated himself to the study of the history and geography of Chile, an interest to which he remained devoted with increasing passion over the years. On the other hand, he explored the landscape which he inspected through a variety of wanderings and drifts. When spending time at his family estate in Cañete he loved to ride horses, making comprehensive excursions around the territory of the Araucanía region, which he qualified as extraordinarily beautiful. Additionally, he did extensive mountain climbing, meandering through the Andes Mountain range, and making some difficult ascents. He was trying to gain control of his new existence intellectually and corporeally through immersion into a new physical and cultural reality. In a way, Duhart was conducting a field survey, approaching the new environment as a space or territory, like an architect would do in the first phase of the architectural design process, observing, researching, analyzing, and gathering information.

When around the family properties in the South at the end of 1935 and the beginning of 1936, Duhart showed interest in technological matters and expressed keen interest in the mining industry. Additionally, his father had a mill, and Émile made friends with the technicians who worked there with wood and steel. In one instance, while talking with his father's partner in a coal mining business, about prospective careers he could pursue, the partner suggested for Émile to study mine engineering. His father consented and Émile left the South, went to Santiago, and started studying engineering at the University of Chile, an effort that lasted just a few months. He discovered this was not his vocation, while technical quality and excellence in fabrication remained preeminent preoccupations for the future architect.

This was happening at the beginning of the school year in March 1936, when his dear brother and friend, Alfredo, died: it was a family tragedy that left Duhart in disarray. For this reason, he described that year as a failure. However, it is during that same period that he foresaw his way in life when he started being interested in architecture. He recounts, "and there I made up my mind and saw my way. But I saw it, not so much for architecture in the traditional sense of the word, but for planning. There was a small group that were pioneers [who] studied urban planning and regional development a little on their own. But it was very incipient. That aspect of the studies interested me enormously. And so, it was that I chose to enter architecture."[30]

30 Pérez Oyarzun and Urrejola, "Series of interviews with Emilio Duhart," audio interview, Part 1 of 8.

This was the decisive moment when Duhart opted to study architecture. For reasons not specified, he registered in architecture at the Pontifical Catholic University, the competing higher education institution. It is essential to point out that in the first instance, it was not architecture per se that appealed to him, but rather the specific field of urban planning and regional development. This inclination might have been triggered by society's lack of attendance to the social disparities he witnessed around Santiago when he settled there, seeing in urbanism a way of ameliorating some of its problems.

Although no allusion was found in Duhart's testimonies to certain events that were occurring at the school of architecture of the University of Chile during the second half of the 1930s in relation to urban planning, it is important to pay attention to them. The motivation to look at this more carefully is found in the above allusion that the architect made to a group of young pioneers that he met at the University of Chile while studying engineering and who were independently studying urban planning and regional development.

These events refer to a crucial precedent that marked the architectural community between 1935 and 1936, the controversial publication of a short-lived magazine that caused a commotion in the architecture environment. It was *ARQquitectura*, edited by Enrique Gebhard and Waldo Parraguéz, two young architecture students who were at the genesis of the reform movement of the University of Chile of 1946. Of the six published issues of *ARQuitectura*, four of them managed to rattle the foundations of the dominant Beaux-Arts architectural thought of the moment.

According to Horacio Torrent, in its first four issues, the publication appealed to urban planning as an organizer of collective life. It referred to the four basic functions of urbanism as developed by the CIAM: dwelling, work, recreation, and transportation. They also addressed urban problems in Santiago, proposing a functional city, low-income housing, and the need to integrate various disciplines to come up with proper solutions.

In their program, the editors linked architecture, the city, urban planning, and social programs to the transformation of the country's living conditions. Discussions about the new notions published created a division between those for and against the editors' convictions. What is particularly significant is that they selected their sources in correlation to the local contextuality.[31] They disseminated up-to-date writings and theories and reproduced texts by intellectuals central to modernism. These included texts by Gropius, Van Doesburg, Giedion, and Le Corbusier, and most of the texts were those presented at the CIAM of 1929 and 1930.[32]

The controversy that derived from *ARQuitectura* magazine was occurring while Duhart began his studies in engineering at the University of Chile. There is no account from Duhart on this issue, but he undoubtedly must have known about the magazines, its authors, and presumably had read the publications. As the timing coincides, perhaps these arguments were present within the University of Chile when he was studying there, or even he might have known of Gebhard and Parraguéz during his short passage by the faculty of engineering. Those discussions might have been at the source of his decision to turn to architecture, although there is no proof of it.

The choice of studying architecture was a defining juncture in Duhart's career path, and his primary interest in urbanism revealed a larger scope of interest and vision of action. It was an interest in physically organizing the life of communities and not solely designing structures. In 1935, after discovering this pivotal interest, Duhart dropped his engineering studies and transferred to the architecture faculty of the Pontifical Catholic University of Chile.

31 Horacio Torrent, "Otras Direcciones de la Vanguardia: La Revista ARQuitectura en Chile 1935-1936," in *Entre Puntos Cardinales: Debates sobre una Nueva Arquitectura* (1920-1950), ed. Ana María Rigotti and Silvia Pampinella (Rosario, Argentina: Prohistoria Ediciones, 2012), 243.

32 Texts published included: Walter Gropius, "Sociological Premises for the Minimum Dwelling of Urban Industrial Populations" (CIAM 1929); Walter Gropius, "Houses, Walk-Ups or High-Rise Apartment Blocks?" (CIAM 1930); Walter Gropius, "Functional Architecture" (CIAM 1930); letter exchanges between Moisei Ginzburg and Le Corbusier about the city and green areas; Le Corbusier, "The Division of the Land of the Cities" (CIAM 1930); Le Corbusier, "Primitive Art and the modern House (Cahiers d'Arts 1930); the partial reproduction of the text and images of Le Corbusier's the Ville Radieuse, published in 1935; Sigfried Giedion on the organization of the CiAM, and the extract of the statutes with the graphics and organization charts; Sigfried Giedion, "Le Corbusier and Contemporary Architecture"; Theo Van Doesburg "The Fundamental Spirit of Contemporary Architecture."

LAYERED IDENTITIES

At seventeen, in 1935, when Duhart went back to the country where he was born, all the elements of a multiplicity of cultural connections were perfectly set. His journey was completing full-circle a life trajectory that had begun in the south of Chile and had brought him back to the same place. By then, his inherited family identity and his French identity were already deeply ingrained within him. However, still relatively young, he was to add yet another space of belonging to his various affiliations, deepening his association with his birthplace. Developing his Chilean selfhood completed the trio of identities with which he confronted his adult life. The riches of belongings that constitute the basic characteristic of Duhart's early life is a defining aspect that would be later endowed in his thoughts and work.

As expressed by Jilly Traganou in relation to contemporary architecture and "also as a way of reconsidering architecture's history … immigration alters ethnic demographics of most regions throughout the globe, and cases of multiple national affiliations are proliferating, the association of people's identity with place and origin is becoming complicated."[33] Although the author is focusing on contemporary times, we recognize in Duhart's background an origin of the phenomenon alluded above and one that today has become so ubiquitous.

33 Traganou, "From Nation-Bound Histories to Global Narratives of Architecture", 166.

The layered complexities of Duhart's early years, revealed through the young architect's origins and upbringing, would converge in the foundational construction of his sense of self which would later interact with his professional journey. In this regard, he was challenged from very early on. Akin to geological stratum, each layer of his identity–his family's French-Basque lineage, the family's history in southern Chile, and his upbringing in Paris–contains divergent and significant residues of his life. These layered identities originating from disparate localities created the platform from which Duhart would orient himself to operate as an architect and urban planner in the professional sphere.

Like a receiving vessel, a young person apprehends what by chance or destiny is inherently given to them through culture, language, and place. These influxes constitute the foundation and the filter from which the individual will observe, reflect, and then act in the world. As a consequence of migrations, when the self has had manifold cultural absorptions, the mind is rewarded with multiple perspectives and acquires an acute ability to have numerous focal points of view. As opposed to having a cultural background that is inherited and stable, the psyche is also challenged with continually having to recontextualize its position in the world and having to fight against a sense of estrangement and artificiality: deciphering, re-interpreting, and analyzing, by comparison, become second nature to the migratory human mind. Arjun Appadurai explains this unique way of being in the world, which he calls trans-locality, when he states, "… people live, as it were, in layered places, which in themselves have a variety of attachment, engagement, and, if you like, reality … The work of the imagination allows people to inhabit either multiple localities or a kind of single and complex sense of locality, in which many different empirical spaces co-exist."[34]

34 Arjun Appadurai, "The Right to Participate in the Work of the Imagination," in *TransUrbanism*, ed. Arjen Mulder (Rotterdam: V2_ Publishing/NAI Publishers, 2002), 43.

Emilio Duhart's identity was forged between the three places, three languages, and three circumstances of his early life. These identities were the French-Basque identity of his descendants, the French identity, acquired in Paris where he grew up until he was a teenager, and the Chilean identity where he first studied architecture and exercised his profession. Later, these three identities merged inside of him into two opposite poles of tension, with which he defined the nature of his architecture, drawing from one or the other in each case. On the one hand, these two poles could be defined as his cosmopolitan nature and, on the other, his regional nature. In architectural terms, ultimately those two poles translated various degrees of mixture of modernism and regionalism.

The cosmopolitan nature within Duhart was first acquired in Paris during childhood and further developed when studying with Walter Gropius, working with Le Corbusier, and with his constant traveling. His cosmopolitan being is also expressed through his profound knowledge and awareness of architectural culture, his ability to speak fluently in French and English, mediums that facilitated his access to information from the centers of modernism, and the distinguished interpersonal relationships he forged later in life. Duhart's regional nature originated in the sense of remoteness imprinted in the Duhart family of the French-Basque territories in addition to the Araucanía region in Chile. He profoundly knew both paradigms by being deeply immersed in them early in his life, which gave him an entrenched sense of what both archetypical worlds really meant. His Chilean identity would be elaborated threading those opposing forces, providing him with the advantage of knowing the world through the elasticity of a more expansive perspective.

BETWEEN TWO POLES – MODERNISM AND REGIONALISM

After having mapped Duhart's early bibliographical path, the present section will uncover his trajectory as a student of architecture. From early on Duhart manifested an interest in modernism. However, his initial encounter with the field was a period of an independent personal search where the formal education at the university did not provide him with the knowledge in the areas that interested him the most. At the time, getting acquainted with modernism was a process of self-discovery, inquiry, and questioning, attributes that reveal a character of serious commitment and pursuit of his own vision.

A RESOLUTE MODERNISM

When Émile Duhart started studying in 1936, the School of Architecture of the Pontifical Catholic University in Santiago imparted a rigorously classical education. To him, the school instilled a nineteenth-century vision of the field through a program that was the perfect reflection of Santiago's prudish and conservative society. It clearly followed the Beaux-Arts tradition that permeated most of the architecture schools in the world. According to Duhart, "L'École des Beaux-Arts was a kind of beacon flooding and projecting its lights [, and] the true international architecture was l'École des Beaux-Arts. There you can talk about international architecture. With all the defects that it entails."[35] In this regard he noted: "However, the architecture pedagogy in these early years was very academic, closely following the methods of l'École des Beaux-Arts, with its eclecticism and its demanding discipline in traditional architectural drawing. Although I stuck to these demands for two years, I felt a contradiction between the passive application of the historical styles of European education and a young nation like Chile with the characteristics of its space and time,"[36] indicating a personal stance where architecture had to have a close relationship to the locale and its present historical period. For him, architecture could not be imitated but had to be generated from the place itself, a realization that was at the base of his attempt to articulate a regional language.

35 Pérez Oyarzun and Urrejola, "Series of interviews with Emilio Duhart," audio interview, Part 1 of 8.

36 Duhart, "Tesis de Grado 1940," 8 -11.

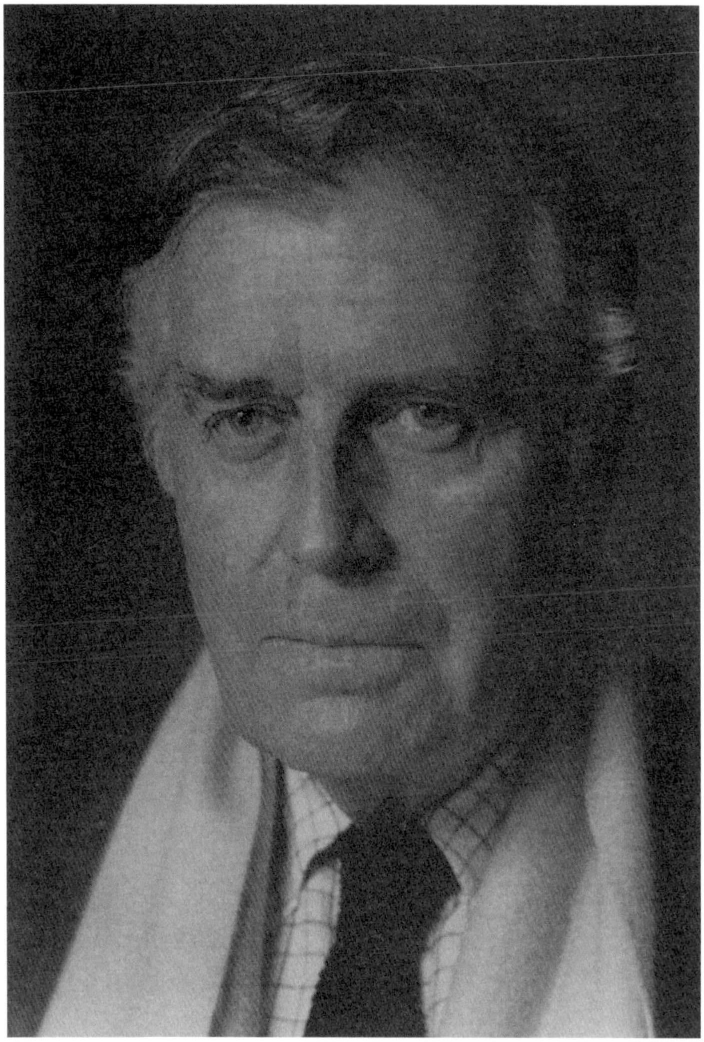

Figure 14: Emilio Duhart Harosteguy, photograph, c. 1970.

Explaining the program at the school, he said that "you started with styles ... studies, proportions, washed drawings all excellent and demanding. It was in that respect very good. It must be said that painting and drawing were practiced a lot and there were good teachers."[37] Recalling the type of project students got involved with, Duhart mentioned "big projects were done in style: a cenotaph for 10,000 dead policemen … in the Greek Doric style; or a rise inside a park in the skirts of the Andes Mountain range, in the Ionic style, with stairs, terraces, pergolas ... There was freedom and everyone chose their own thing [within the constraints of the Beaux-Art cannon]."[38] He remarked that the majority of the students followed the program without opposition, indicating in him a much more inquisitive spirit than most of his classmates. However, he was never an opponent of what he termed "the ancient School."[39]

37 Pérez Oyarzun and Urrejola, "Series of interviews with Emilio Duhart," audio interview, Part 1 of 8.

38 Pérez Oyarzun and Urrejola, "Series of interviews with Emilio Duhart," audio interview, Part 1 of 8.

39 Pérez Oyarzun and Urrejola, "Series of interviews with Emilio Duhart," audio interview, Part 1 of 8.

In the late 1930s, some architects, professors, and students were interested in the neocolonial architectural style. It was an orientation that Chilean historian Max Aguirre describes as a secondary development that tried to fulfill the role of mitigating the arrival and acceptance of modern architecture in the country.[40] It attempted to keep alive a sense of style revisiting the colonial architecture derived from the Spanish colonists. Duhart was profoundly repelled by this approach. In that regard, he commented, "I think they distort, excuse me, dear historians, they distort the truth a little. All that neo-ranchism or 'neo-patronal houses' did not have much."[41] However, he still respected the existing vernacular architecture when he wrote, "at the same time I was shocked that the few examples of colonial architecture in Santiago were demolished, which were testimony to a culture, perhaps poor, but coherent and of its own. All this induced in me and some colleagues the search for a more authentic expression of the Chilean reality."[42]

40 Evelyn Meynard, "Interview with Max Aguirre," recorded interview, Santiago, January 16, 2020.

41 Pérez Oyarzun and Urrejola, "Series of interviews with Emilio Duhart," audio interview, Part 1 of 8.

42 Duhart, "Tesis de Grado 1940," 8.

From very early on, Duhart felt a strong opposition to pursuing architecture with either the Beaux-Arts or the neocolonial approach. In architecture he did not seem to tolerate looking back towards the past and had a natural penchant towards the forward-looking, in this sense echoing the same attitude as the modern movement at the time. Nevertheless, simultaneously, he saw virtue in the type of architectural education imparted by his school and could not envision any other possibility. According to him, "it was a natural way … Santiago needed a transitional phase to go from the early nineteenth century to modernity."[43]

43 Pérez Oyarzun and Urrejola, "Series of interviews with Emilio Duhart," audio interview, Part 1 of 8.

Around 1937-1938, a profound cultural change within the student body began to take shape, and the school's program came under scrutiny by the students. Duhart and his peers had independently developed a nascent awareness of modernity and a committed inquiry about it was emerging. These manifestations of curiosity gradually grew until they became firm demands for pivoting towards teaching modern architecture, an inclination that the higher ranks of the school resisted for quite some time. Commenting on those years Duhart wrote in 1993: "At that time, this yearning had motivated some valuable tests of modern architecture, incipient although little understood and valued by the environment."[44] This interest was mirrored by similar manifestations within the students in the School of Architecture in the University of Chile which Duhart esteemed very valuable as a parallel story. Both developments did not converge completely but had mutual resonance.

44 Duhart, "Tesis de Grado 1940," 8.

One of the teachers who promoted this interest in modernity was Sergio Larraín García-Moreno. According to Duhart, Larraín displayed a graceful skepticism towards the way architecture was taught and had a restless position towards architectural modernism. Larraín was a cultured man, who had traveled through Europe in the late 1920s, and was aware of the developments in early modernism. According to Duhart, Larraín took it as a challenge to infuse curiosity about contemporary architectural ideas, facilitating an opening towards novel possibilities. At that time, in Sergio Larraín's workshop, there were already spontaneously conceived modern-leaning projects done by the students.

Concurrently, Duhart had become exasperated with the kind of architecture aligned toward European architectural styles that the school was still promoting and became completely repulsed by it. To him confronting architecture under those tenets was a falsehood and a facsimile that did not interest him anymore:

> In Chile during my studies as an architect, the lack of coherence and truth of public or private buildings that imitated the models of 19thcentury Parisian architecture, but with stuccoed facades imitating non-existent stones caught my attention. The brick structure with reinforced concrete coatings was covered with an epidermal makeup. The falsity of that prevailing architecture in Santiago was obvious and produced an instinctive rejection, reinforced by the fact that I had lived in France. The architecture was imitated in Chile, outside its historical and geographical context.[45]

45 Duhart, "Tesis de Grado 1940," 8.

Having grown up in Paris, Duhart possessed an insider knowledge of the city, which helped him have a critical eye toward what he was seeing in Santiago as an architectural expression that did not belong to the place.

This revelation developed in him the conviction that architecture had to be an endemic statement of the locality and not a mere application of styles as a decorative feature: architecture had to relate to the environment, its history, and geography.

As stated by Duhart, since the students at the school frequently practiced drawing and painting, it was through those classes that they first became aware of the modern movement in the arts. Art magazines and publications gave them their initial visual access to modernity and they became interested in participating in its development. Duhart also recounts that of all his readings, Le Corbusier's *When the Cathedrals Were White* had the most significant impression on him, at a time when Duhart did not know his work.[46] The impact of this book is not surprising as it expounds Le Corbusier's theories about urban planning, a subject of critical interest to the architect.

46 Duhart, "Tesis de Grado 1940," 8.

Although the school's architectural program had presented two paths to go forward, Beaux-Arts or Neo-Colonial architecture, Emilio Duhart, while still a student, chose another alternative which he was determined to pursue on his own: modernism. From around 1938 on, he singularly committed himself to modern architecture, a determination he began expressing through his student work, most notably through his degree project, the Fishing Base of San Quintin. This decision made him feel profoundly motivated and his professors did not hamper his determination. A resolved and defined focus was set in his mind, providing him with a clear perspective from which to address his future in his chosen field.

EXPLORATORY TRAVELS – FIELD SURVEYS

Between 1939 and 1940, Emilio Duhart undertook two crucial trips, each at opposite sides of the spectrum and expressions of his competing inclinations: one to New York City and one to an isolated area in the far south in Chile. Both occurred in territories outside the norm for him, considering he had grown up in a European city. The New York trip was an exploration into the preeminent modern metropolis, with its skyscrapers and new architecture. This undertaking was the expression of the cosmopolitan young adult with the opportunity to explore one of the centers of innovative architecture at the time. The trip to the extreme south of Chile was an exploration into a territory with minimum human intervention, where the artificial had not yet arrived. In this second choice we can find the expression of how Duhart's

Figure 15: Left; Detail of the Futurama diorama, by Richard Garrison. Public domain.

Figure 16: Right; The Finnish Pavilion at the 1939 New York World's Fair designed by Alvar Aalto. Public domain.

regional side had begun to exercise pressure within him to the point he had to create the circumstances to reflect and elaborate around the tensions created by both identities, a seemingly intricate dilemma.

Duhart traveled to New York with a group of fellow classmates, a trip organized by his school to visit the New York World's Fair of 1939. In later recollections, he only mentions two pavilions: the "Futurama" exhibition by Norman Geddes (fig. 15), and the Finnish Pavilion by Alvar Aalto (fig. 16).

The New York World's Fair was one of the most notorious international exhibitions of the twentieth century in the United States. At the center of the site held in Flushing Meadows in Queens, stood the symbols of the fair, the Trylon, a 700-foot obelisk, and the Perisphere, a 200-foot globe. The theme of the fair was "Building the World of Tomorrow," highlighting the hopes of a technological future exhibiting forward-looking views of the world. It included almost sixty nations, thirty-three US states, and over a thousand exhibitors, among them some of the largest corporations in the United States. The fair attracted forty-five million visitors.

Alongside exhibitors such as the American Telephone and Telegraph Company, the Borden Company, and the Westinghouse Company, there was General Motors with its extravagant presentation titled "Futurama," designed by industrial designer Norman Bel Geddes.[47] As described by

47 "New York World's Fair 1939 and 1940 Incorporated Records," The New York Public Library, Manuscripts and Archives Division, accessed 04/01/20. http://archives.nypl.org/mss/2233.

Adnan Morshed, "Bel Geddes hypothesized the future as a one-acre animated model of an American utopia as it might appear in the year 1960 to citizens traveling in an airplane, a transportation technology that, in the late 1930s, still fascinated a whole generation of Americans."[48]

The model was composed of 500,000 houses, more than a million trees, and 50,000 vehicle models of which 10,000 were in motion in highways and bridges. Conceptually, Geddes devised a city grid, "fusing an array of ideological contents and practical projections, Futurama aspired to be the culmination of early twentieth-century planning visions."[49] The public was carried over the 35,738 square-foot scenery seated and mobilized by a conveyor belt suspended over it, imitating an airplane flight experience. Norman Geddes had been a stage designer, a background mentioned as influential for his outstanding abilities as a salesperson. The spectacular mise-en-scène was enhanced with lighting and sound, mesmerizing the spectators, and drawing an average of 28,000 people per day.

As for the Finnish Pavilion designed by Alvar Aalto at the New York World's Fair of 1939, it was a single sinuous space, three stories high which Sigfried Giedion described in the following way:

> This was, without doubt, the most daring piece of architecture in the New York World Fair of 1939; an inclined wooden screen three stories high embraces the interior space in a freely drawn curve. The screen consists of three sections, each cantilevered over the other: at the same time, the whole structure leans forward, intensifying thereby the impression of continuous movement. A series of vertical ribs and the rhythm of their changing shadows animate the surface of the huge screen.[50]

Conceptually, the architecture integrated the undulating interior with an exhibition of photographs, objects, and industrial products, representing traditional and contemporary Finnish culture evoking the Nordic Forest and its natural formations. In the catalogue of the exhibition *Alvar Aalto: Through the Eyes of Shigeru Ban,* Ban wrote: "The Pavilion was a highly successful demonstration of a new, regionally tuned, humanistic architecture, whilst simultaneously acting as a presentation of Finnish culture."[51]

Comparing the two exhibitions, which Duhart calls attention to in his recollections, it is interesting to note that they allude to opposite spheres: the mechanistic, technological, and metropolitan future in the case of Geddes' Pavilion, and the natural, biological, and regional future in the case of Aalto's Pavilion.

48 Adnan Morshed, "The Master Builder as Superman: Norman Bel Gedde's Futurama," University of Minnesota Press, (2015), 3, https://www.jstor.org/stable/10.5749/j.ctt1287nsj.7.

49 Morshed, "The Master Builder as Superman: Norman Bel Gedde's Futurama," 5.

50 Sigfried Giedion, "Alvar Aalto," *The Architectural Review* (Archive: 1896-2005), Vol. 107, Iss. 638 (Feb 1, 1950): 79.

51 Shigeru Ban, "Finnish Pavilion, New York World's Fair," in *Alvar Aalto Through the Eyes of Shigeru Ban,* ed. Juhani Pallasmaa and Tomoko Sato (London: Black Dog Publishing in association with Barbican Art Gallery, 2007), 146.

The trip lasted about a month and a half and Duhart observed that it was a very instructive and cultivating experience. He commented that the New York World's Fair was slightly disappointing, especially because he expected more of the French and the British pavilions. However, it is at this fair that he discovered Nordic architecture and specifically that of Alvar Aalto: "The architects discovered the Finnish pavilion by Aalto. We had our antennas tuned in. We did not have a sophisticated, in-depth culture. It was much more spontaneous, sensitive, but not for that reason less discriminating [...]."[52] Alto's blending of modernism with the curvilinear arrangements of the pavilion that echoed natural patterns, in addition to the wooden materiality of the interior, must have genuinely resonated in the architect's mind and might have opened the door to thinking about possible avenues for regional modern architecture in a local way.

52 Pérez Oyarzun and Urrejola, "Series of interviews with Emilio Duhart," audio interview, Part 1 of 8.

In contrast, he responded unequivocally to the Futurama show. He said: "In addition, there was a General Motors Pavilion, which touched me a lot because of its presumptions and almost evil qualities. There you saw the current world for the first time, the current moment imagined and loved by that huge beast of General Motors. There were highways, the world of the automobile, but with twenty years of anticipation. It was there and I remember that it touched me, I did not commend it, but it touched me."[53] He was fascinated and distressed at the same time, expressing a profound suspicion that the power of technology and large corporations could generate unforeseen aftereffects.

53 Pérez Oyarzun and Urrejola, "Series of interviews with Emilio Duhart," audio interview, Part 1 of 8.

In 1939, Duhart was twenty-two years old and had a determined penchant towards modernism. However, beyond that, he had already developed more nuanced ideas about it and was exhibiting a preference towards the natural in conjunction with the forward-looking.

At the end of his studies and looking for a pristine natural environment that would inspire his degree project, Duhart embarked on a three-month-long trip to the southern latitudes in Chile: an extremely inaccessible region called Aysén located around 1,120 miles from Santiago. The trip was lengthy and arduous. Arriving there, he encountered an unexplored region of contrasting landscapes and climates, populated by scattered and isolated settlers who led a precarious and hard life. No inland route existed at the time, and the trip was made by horse and small boats, improvising the journey as it progressed.

It is important to examine further the attributes of the location at the time, to comprehend the courage and uniqueness of Duhart's expedition choice.

Although the third-largest area in the country (41,890 square miles), the Aysén region is even today Chile's most sparsely populated province with approximately 91,500 inhabitants. The area features cool summers and cold winters with a relatively narrow annual temperature range and few temperature extremes. It also presents abundant precipitation throughout the year (158 inches), high humidity, and strong winds. The characteristics of the landscape are its archipelago formation with the presence of lakes, channels, and fjords in addition to several glaciers, among which is the Southern Patagonian Ice Field, the third largest in the world. Because of the oceanic climate, the vegetation is composed of a very dense and low forest mass, some cold-season grasses, abundant ferns, and lichens. Before 1980, when a highway was completed, the region was still only accessible by boat, plane, or extremely rudimentary roads. The Aysén Region was the last area to be annexed to the Chilean territories. During colonial times, the indigenous population was scarce, substantially declining in the eighteenth century. The area was mostly visited by fishermen, lumberjacks, and hunters from the adjacent regions to the north. For this reason, the territory earned a reputation for its desolation. During the nineteenth century, the indigenous population was further diminished, and settlers from southern Chile and Europe began sporadically replacing them.

This locality in the times of Duhart's excursion was lonely, little known, and far-off, revealing in him an exceptionally determined character, in search of a utopic blank slate from which to depart on an intellectual reconnaissance. He was looking for a theme and a program that would motivate him to think about his future thesis project: "I looked for a theme and a program that would encourage me to reflect deeply on a clear and basic foundation to test the intuitions that emanated from my personal experience … I looked for a virgin and almost unexplored environment."[54]

54 Duhart, "Tesis de Grado 1940," 9.

Once back in Santiago, Duhart started to work on his thesis project, which he presented six months later with unanticipated outcomes. It was over the course of two years when still remarkably young (twenty-one to twenty-two years of age) that Duhart produced several projects that were well ahead of their time. Through these visionary projects, Duhart delineated a framework for the integration of modernism with the specific circumstances of Chile. Such a framework, expressed through these models, can still serve today as exercises to reflect upon the architectural task.

Travel to Aysén

Watercolors

E. DUHART. H.

CONSEQUENTIAL EXERCISES

The output of an architect's work mirrors the stage of thought about the discipline in which the person is in, and it is undoubtedly the case with the thesis project and the first house commission that Duhart designed. Both projects are suffused with his most profound thoughts about the field. They are laboratories for the young architect, testing his ideas and turning them into realities. For this reason, and their value per se, they are of keen interest in analyzing, and they represent manifesto-like templates of considerable significance.

AN AUTONOMOUS FISHING BASE IN THE BAY OF SAN QUINTÍN

Until this moment in time, the aspiring architect had had no formal education in modernism. In his first project, presented in 1941, Duhart displays the mind of an independent thinker, melding his reflections on architecture and urbanism in this incipient proposal. The motivations at the origins of Duhart's degree project are manifold, and they represent the fundamental concepts that molded the structural foundation from which his career departed. Many of these ideas would be present in countless projects he would realize throughout his trajectory.

Some of the catalysts of the project have already been explained. For instance, Duhart's dislike for the traditional type of education imparted at the university, with its eclecticism and gratuitous promotion of stylistic imitation of French architecture, based in the Beaux-Arts. He was also profoundly troubled by the lack of coherence and as he expressed it, "truth" of the public and private buildings in Santiago, which imitated the Parisian architectural landscape. This rejection was justified since he had lived in France, and he could see with transparent clarity from where those approaches were emanating. For him, architecture out of its historical and geographical context made no sense, a concept he consistently applied, and which became a central feature in his future work.

Additionally, he was acutely inspired by Chilean nature. On a variety of occasions, Duhart acknowledged his enthusiasm for the beautiful native scenery of the unexploited forests of the south. In particular, he much admired the araucaria forest of the mountain range of Nahuelbuta, near Cañete. During the 1930s and 1940s, Duhart witnessed in consternation the burning of numerous native forests practiced by colonists who wanted to use the land for agriculture, a method widely adopted throughout the south. On this subject, Duhart concluded, "this impact was very much in my mind when I discovered in the human-nature relationship the potential importance of the architect's task in considering this relationship as a living and evolutionary reality,"[55] manifesting a profound preoccupation for the care of the environment in addition to seeing this human-nature binary of pivotal importance in the practice of the profession.

55 Duhart, "Tesis de Grado 1940," 8.

Most notably, Duhart had noticed a critical lack of knowledge in the variety and richness of the country's different regions and an absence of response to those qualities in the architectural field, an observation that attested to his broader geographical inner space alluded to at the beginning of the book. He was interested in a search for a more authentic expression of the Chilean reality, and his degree project aimed to address these issues.

With reference to the Chilean social reality of the late 1930s and early 1940s, as a future architect, Duhart was troubled by the numerous problems of the lower social strata and, in particular, of the Chilean extreme urban and rural poverty of the times. That made him think of the need to establish a new type of architecture that would respond to such realities. Moreover, most importantly, he hypothesized that "regional and urban planning seemed … to acquire a relevance that was not perceived then and seemed inextricably linked to architecture as a foundation that could legitimize it."[56] This remark confirms once more that urbanism was central to his concerns. He had been captivated by this discipline before beginning his formal studies. Concerning this project, it is also critical to bring to the fore Duhart's reading *When the Cathedrals Were White*, which he mentioned as an essential book for him. In it, Le Corbusier states that to respond to contemporary human needs on every level, the architect must grasp the new conditions of the era, including knowledge of technical progress. Hence, to understand those circumstances, the architect must study them from every perspective. Additionally, Le Corbusier declared that the architect must be in "attentive contact with the world of industry, labor, materials, and organization...and here the architect is like the engineer; a severe form of thinking is demanded of him."[57] As we will see, the degree project involved extensive studies, in addition to integrating technological advances and industrial production into its design.

56 Duhart, "Tesis de Grado 1940," 8.

57 Le Corbusier, *When the Cathedrals Were White* (New York: McGraw-Hill Book Company, 1964), 206.

Finally, he also considered the trip to New York and his first encounter with the architecture of Alvar Aalto as elements that were in his mind when he was initiating his degree project. That is not a minor detail in the architect's scrutiny given that in his conception of modernity, he was paying attention to the use of wood and organic forms in Aalto's Pavilion. Hence Duhart was decoupling the typical construction materials used in modernism (cement, steel, and glass) from the functionalist approach to architecture, opening a space of freedom in modern architectural conceit.

In his thesis proposal, Duhart blended the conditions given by nature, technological advances of the times, and a modernist approach to architecture with volumes devoid of ornament and a detailed separation and articulation of functions, in an all-encompassing urban setting. The Fishing Base project conceived an autonomous urban enclave for a cooperative community of fishermen in the Bay of San Quintín, which included all the essential elements for self-subsistence including an industrial facility for the processing of seafood in a secluded and unaltered environment. The community settlement was designed to accommodate a population of three thousand people including the fishermen and their families and was to be built with materials encountered in the area, mainly a rich array of wood and slate. In addition, the program assumed expansion with an eventual growth of the community and the further development of its fishing industry.

According to Duhart, through the project, he wanted to answer the following question:

> Considering a rudimentary reality [the San Quintín Bay] and in a synthesis between an enduring nature, the habits of a prospective population, and the requirements of the cultural and technical progress of the modern era, is it possible to create a community that could be at the same time clearly contemporary?[58]

58 Duhart, "Tesis de Grado 1940," 9.

This inquiry is fundamental, since it represents the constitutional questioning that the young architect was asking himself and needed to resolve to build a solid conceptual platform. He was asking whether it was possible to articulate modernism with the local. He responded to that fundamental question by elaborating a utopian but real solution.

During his trip to the Aysén Region, Duhart found the site he was searching for in the Taitao peninsula and more precisely in the virginal Bay of Quintín, an area that significantly impacted him. Around this location, he had

Figure 17: Left; Chile. Armada. Ba. San Quintín (cartographic material) by the Chilean Navy, map library, 1952.

Figure 18: Above; South subsidiary summit of Mount San Valentín. Lago General Carrera, Chile, Patagonia, South America, 2020.

observed that a small group of "local fishermen pushed their boats across the Isthmus of Ofqui and then the Rio Negro that flows near the continental snowdrift that reflected in the bay of San Quintin south of San Rafael."[59] In-situ he collected as much geographic and historical data as he could and began writing a detailed program, including an analysis of everything that he had been able to discover.

59 Duhart, "Tesis de Grado 1940," 8.

The prospective architect had determined that the best location for the port and fishing base within the large San Quintín Bay was the Angamos Point on the south coast, within a smaller inner bay called Aldunate, duly oriented to the north and protected to the south by the high hills (fig. 17). Duhart added that another factor for the location choice was "the spectacle offered by the great Andes Mountains to the east of the Bay of San Quintín, [which] is undoubtedly one of the most astonishing that can be contemplated; Mount San Valentin is seen over its 2.5-mile height, extending to the south by steep mountain chains, crowning the snowdrifts of San Rafael and San Quintín … reflected in the calm waters of the bay"[60] (fig. 18). In this spot the coasts are high and clean and the width at the entrance to the Aldunate Strait is one and a half miles, large enough for safe navigation.

60 Duhart, "Tesis de Grado 1940," 11.

The proposal was above all an imaginary but feasible urban planning endeavor for which Duhart had to conduct extensive and comprehensive research with a careful study of a wide variety of factors, including topography, climate, light, tides, soil, material resources for construction, human resources and culture, hydrographic conditions, and so on. The research comprised meteorological conditions (average temperatures between 50 – 54 degrees Fahrenheit, with a maximum of 39 degrees Fahrenheit, during the cold season–winds from North and Southwest), tides with a maximum amplitude of seven feet, currents, water depth and levels, and the inclination of the solar rays in summer and winter times. He also studied the topographical conditions with detailed position and height of the hills, coastlines, and vegetation, observing in the dense forest the ideal quality and variety of wood. He noted in the western and north-western parts of the area the presence of a thick layer of topsoil and land which could lend itself very well once cleared to livestock and agriculture.

Furthermore, Duhart consulted the National Hydrography and Fishing Reports, concluding first that the fishing industry, duly organized, could be of critical importance for the country; second, that the southern part of the country is ideal for the fishing that would constitute the raw material for a canning industry; and third, that this industry could have secure markets inside and outside the country. He concluded that there was a need for a properly located fishing base for the purpose of centralizing and coordinating fishing in the region, and for commercial convenience, the canneries should be located on-site. The Bay of San Quintin was a location recommended by the reports for its size, having the best hydrographic conditions for its setting, and for being protected from winds and tidal waves to the south by a thirteen-mile-long peninsula.

Duhart asserted that one of the main objectives of his project was to seek an architectural expression which would be the result of the Chilean nature and territory, and to serve the activities of its people, who he named the "structure of the nation."[61] Duhart was particularly interested in the potential social and cultural engagement of architecture and in this regard, he affirmed: "I was also very motivated by the development of the social type. That was a virtue of the school [of Architecture of the Pontifical Catholic University] … a great motivation for socio-cultural responsibility … That motivation endured for many years, but at that time it was a reason for basic, fundamental concern, integrated with the architect."[62] In that regard, among Duhart's considerations was the character and traditions of the Chilean island fishermen for whom the fishing base would be designed, offering them the possibility of expanding their industrial production.

61 Duhart, "Tesis de Grado 1940," 9.

62 Pérez Oyarzun and Urrejola, "Series of interviews with Emilio Duhart," audio interview, Part 1 of 8.

Among the examinations conducted by the architect were some unusual ones related to ethnography and infrastructure. He observed that the fishermen utilized small boats that held four or five men for fishing excursions lasting two to three days. Duhart considered equipping them with a motor that would afford them with a larger radius of operation. The main fishing group would gather fish (red conger, sierra, silverside), and shellfish (mussels, sea urchins, razor clams, scallops. abalones, etc.) found in abundance in the surrounding shallow depths and clear water. The second group of fishermen, the whalers, with an annual normal hunting capacity of about 400 whales, made longer trips on larger vessels under the command of a skipper. The third group he devised was for sea lion hunting, a type of fishing very abundant in the region. This group would have medium size boats and would hunt in well-defined seasons. He considered an additional group, the seasonal fishermen, who would live only temporarily in the community, a population he envisioned would come from the northernmost islands and archipelagos. The stable population of fishermen would have the possibility to cultivate the land and have farms for their own consumption.

The urban planning was laid on the slope of a topography that converged on the waterfront facing Mount San Valentin, which was reflected on the archipelago's water. It was made up of a longitudinal development on the coastal edge with a nucleus of community services oriented towards the water from which emanated functional administrative, educational, health, recreational, industrial, and religious units in an organized layout that favored efficiency (pg. 90). The communal center articulates the residential area up the hill in a somewhat concentric free configuration adapted to the nature of the topography. The residential area had a very different logic to its arrangement than the rest of the urbanization, being governed by a more spontaneous and loose composition, with the units scattered on the hill outside an imaginary grid and connected by sinuous paths.

The urban formation was centered around a U-shaped common public zone from where all other structures emanated, to the north, south, and up the slope forming a defined pole of attraction for communal life. The main dock faced the communal plaza in three levels up the slope, where the church was the focal point at the top of the large plaza. Most important to the survival of the community and located to the north, Duhart devised a large fishing industrial area, for the canning, treatment, and preservation of the products. The factory compound was placed away from the housing quarters, protected from the winds, and with access routes to the rest of the fishing base. Slightly separated from the communal center to the south were a fishing school, a livestock breeding quarter, the sawmills, a dry dock, and further to the south a soccer field, in addition to the lighthouse, meteorological and radio stations, and the communications antenna.

The architecture was abstract, linear, and geometric, mostly composed of rectangular and L-shape structures deprived of ornament. Attesting to the comprehensive thought the architect put into the design of the urban enclave are a series of buildings that imagine the life of the community in a holistic way. The spiritual center is marked by the prominence of the ogival church at the top of the plaza, a structure that is reminiscent of an inverted boat (pg. 91, below). To the southern side of the church, and erected from the ground up, there was a minimalist tall and narrow bell tower crowned with a cross, the transcendental symbol. Large compound buildings to both sides of the central square were joined by a continuous covered U-shaped outdoor corridor which functioned as protection from the extreme rain conditions (pg. 92, below). For the same reason, the buildings surrounding the central plaza have either a mono-pitched roof, for the most prominent (the Guild House), or gable roofs. The application of mono-pitched roofs to two large buildings on the central plaza, one to the right and one to the left, were particularly original for the time and place.

A parish was located adjacent to the chapel, and to the north was the Guild House, a large four-floor building with an administration section, meeting rooms, a recreational center, and a hotel area for the seasonal population (pg. 93). On the south side of the plaza, there was the Marine House (pg. 94, below), the cooperatives, and a large barn. Further to the south on the coastal edge, there was the municipal market and storage facilities. Dispersed and radiating up the hill were several hundred single-family units, two primary schools, two living quarters for single workers. Near the back of the church the hospital and polyclinic were located. The housing area was distributed by types of fishermen, A, B, and C: permanent, seasonal singles, and families (pg. 95). Each family house would have an orientation to the sun, views, and independence.

The construction materials specified, wood and slate, reflected an intention to integrate the native surroundings with modern architecture, an effort that might have been inspired by the Finnish Pavilion by Alvar Aalto that the architect had recently witnessed. Duhart conducted exhaustive research on all the local wood, their characteristics, and their sizes. He considered them for their mechanical and acoustical qualities. He also thought of minute details for their use; for instance, that the source of energy for the community would be firewood and more specifically tepú wood, an endemic species very abundant in the region.

He also incorporated some of the native construction techniques complementing them with modern spatiality and functionality. The specified wooden construction of the ogival church is a reticular diamond-shaped carpentry structure, covered with a waterproofed tongue and grove wooden layer, and finished with larch shingles. The main construction system for the buildings was specified as braced framed with internal triangulation wooden formations, fire-hardened wooden structural pillars, and as exterior finish, horizontal wood-paneling. For the family units, a log construction was used with triangular groove perforations to stack them horizontally, one on top of the other. Slate, found in abundance on the nearby shores and riverbeds, was widely suggested for floor and foundation applications throughout the compound. On the communal buildings Duhart commented that "the treatment of the buildings, proportion, light and shadow, cladding, accentuates the general rhythm of the whole, with a contrasting pause on the façade of the Guild House."[63] The materials naturally synchronized with the surrounding landscape. On this subject Duhart elaborated:

> The cloudy atmosphere excludes the chosen colors typical of the hard sky countries. There is here a kind of mimicry with the environment. The buildings will have their natural wood impregnated with oil, only the windows [will be] painted white, the roofs [will be finished with] natural larch tiles, [and] will be silvered by the rain. In bad weather, the colors will be those of the environment, a range of gray, ash green and brown, but with the appearance of the sun, everything changes; strong blue skies, multiple greens of the rain forest are everywhere present.[64]

Related to his thesis presentation exam Duhart commented:

> The project consisted of twenty-five renderings drawn with ink, in black and white, with very few touches of color and framed on boards. Additionally, I presented a monochromatic model and color drawings with watercolor. It was a big hit that caused shock and resonance. I say this not as a matter of personal merit, but because of the circumstances. The students were enthusiastic about the project. The exam was passed with Sergio Larraín, Alberto Cruz Eyzaguirre, Alfredo Johnson.[65]

In the ten years prior to Emilio Duhart's thesis presentation, there had been a handful of thesis projects at the university that had caused a significant

63 Emilio Duhart, Annotations in drawing "Urban Study–Compositional Study," San Quintín Fishing Base, 1941. Emilio Duhart Archive in Archivo de Originales. Centro de Información y Documentación Sergio Larraín García-Moreno. Facultad de Arquitectura, Diseño y Estudios Urbanos. Pontificia. Universidad Católica de Chile.

64 Duhart, Annotations in drawing "Urban Study – Compositional Study," San Quintín Fishing Base, 1941.

65 Pérez Oyarzun and Urrejola, "Series of interviews with Emilio Duhart," audio interview, Part 1 of 8.

degree of interest. To name just a few, in 1932, Roberto Matta[66] presented a project named "The Congress of Religions" that he located in an unknown place in Antarctica. In 1935, Jorge Aguirre created "The Speed Palace" an automobile show located in a "Mechanical City," reflecting on the concepts of time and speed in a utopian and futuristic urban space. In 1934, Armando Celis revealed an "Interplanetary Communication Station" to establish contact with extraterrestrial beings.[67] These projects were the testimony of a student body forging an incipient approach towards modernity. Although all possessed modernist inclinations, around the time of Duhart's presentation the proposals were moving away from utopian visions and getting more in contact with reality (1941 – Graciela Marcos Mora's "A School Colony"; 1941 – Alberto Piwonka "A Modern Art Museum"; 1941 – Mario Perez de Arce "Hotel in Ranco Lake.")[68] However, Duhart's project was the only one to obtain maximum distinction and elicited profuse praise, commanding much attention. Though his project was not to be realized, it was rigorously based on real facts and emerged from real data and a specific environment and people.

The Fishing Base of San Quintín project was a declaration of intentions, views, objectives, and motives that would organize and govern Duhart's future practice, aspects that at the origin emerged from his formative years and his encounter with his birthplace. As he stated, he had considered the human/nature interplay as a binary system which he defined as a "living evolutionary relationship,"[69] a supporting structure from which life could come forth. Duhart had discovered that in this relationship lies one of the cruxes of the architect's task.

The project arose from the study of the surrounding nature, the habits of its people, and the innovative integration of the modern era's cultural and technical progress. The industrial quarter of the compound highlighted the nature of the port, reflecting the adaptation to the new technological requirements of modern life. The architectural and urban design emanated from a sympathetic fusion of the regional environment and the local culture with a firm modernist inclination. In its geometric liberties (the orthogonal building versus sinuous arrangements and paths of the residential areas) and in the use of materials (local wood and slate versus cement, glass, and steel,) Duhart is exercising a type of relaxed modernism which showcased the importance of his early encounter with the architecture of Alvar Aalto. When embarking on the creation of his degree project, Duhart was simultaneously building for himself the groundwork that would constitute the conceptual frame of reference he would invoke in his future work.

66 Roberto Matta Echaurren was the famous Chilean modern painter and preeminent figure of twentieth century abstract expressionism and surrealist art.

67 Alfredo Jüneman Gazmuri, *Jorge Aguirre Silva: Un Arquitecto del Movimiento Moderno en Chile* (Santiago: Ediciones ARQ, 1963), 23-25, 34.

68 Carolina Castillo Buttinghausen, "Base Pesquera en San Quintin," in "Emilio Duhart, Seminario de Investigación Fernando Pérez Oyarzun," Pontificia Universidad Católica de Chile, 2005, Chapter 1.

69 Duhart, "Tesis de Grado 1940," 8.

Following pages: Emilio Duhart, San Quintín Fishing Base, 1941.

Thesis Project
San Quintín Fishing Base

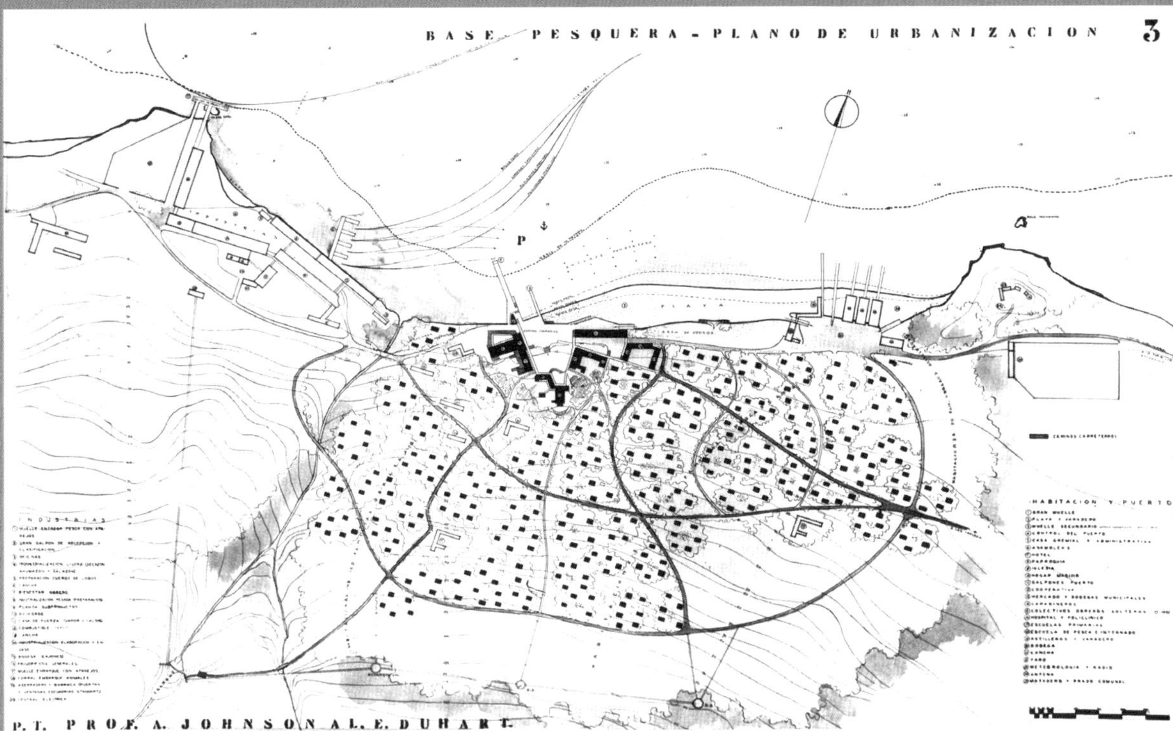

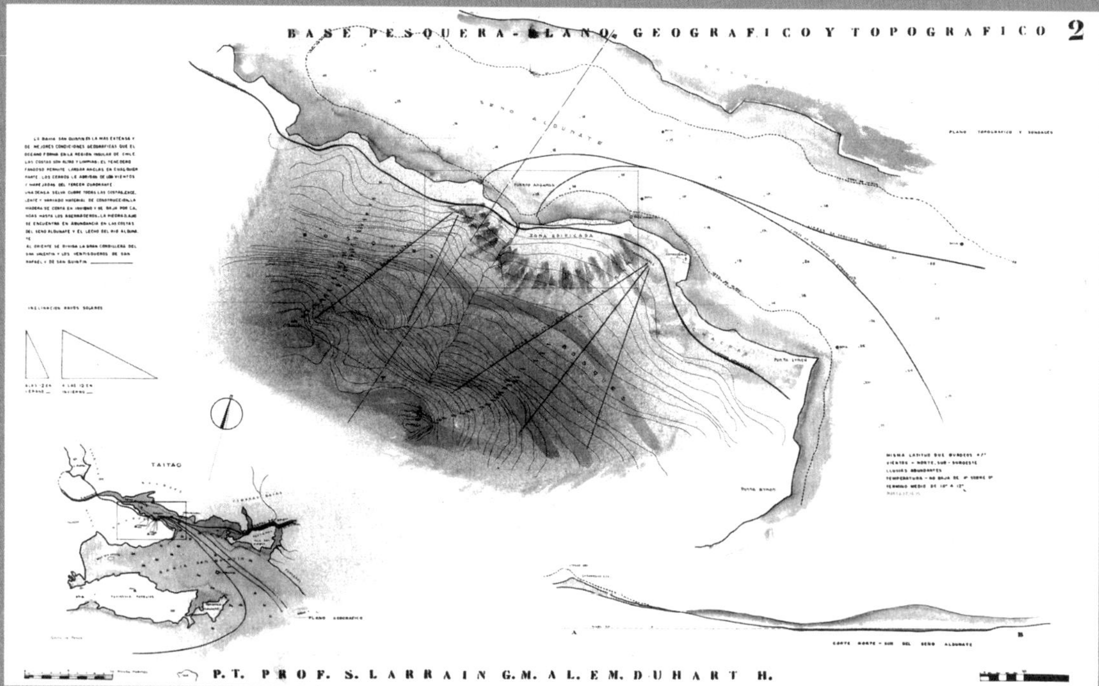
BASE PESQUERA - PLANO GEOGRAFICO Y TOPOGRAFICO 2
TAITAO
P.T. PROF. S. LARRAIN G.M. AL. E.M. DUHART H.

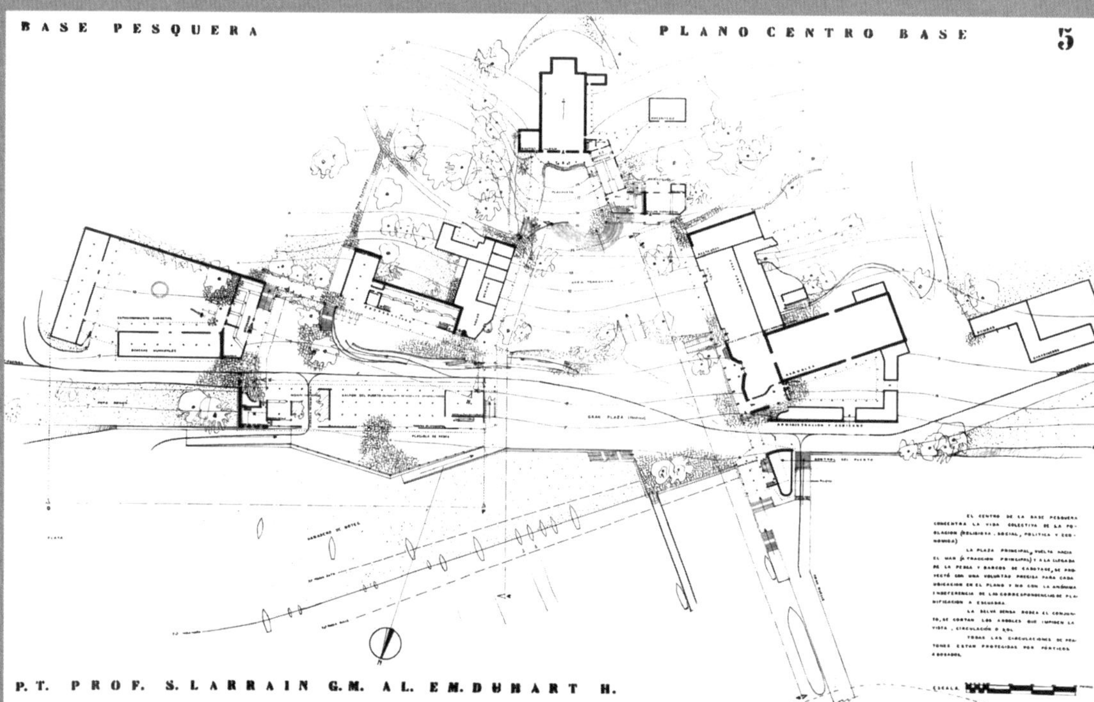
BASE PESQUERA
PLANO CENTRO BASE
5
P.T. PROF. S. LARRAIN G.M. AL. E.M. DUHART H.

BASE PESQUERA-PERSPECTIVAS PLAZAS
14
6.
7.
8.
9.
P. T. PROF. S. LARRAIN G.M. AL. EM. DUHARTH.

BASE PESQUERA-PERSPECTIVAS IGLESIA
17
10.
11.
12.
13.
P. T. PROF. S. LARRAIN G.M. AL. EM. DUHARTH.

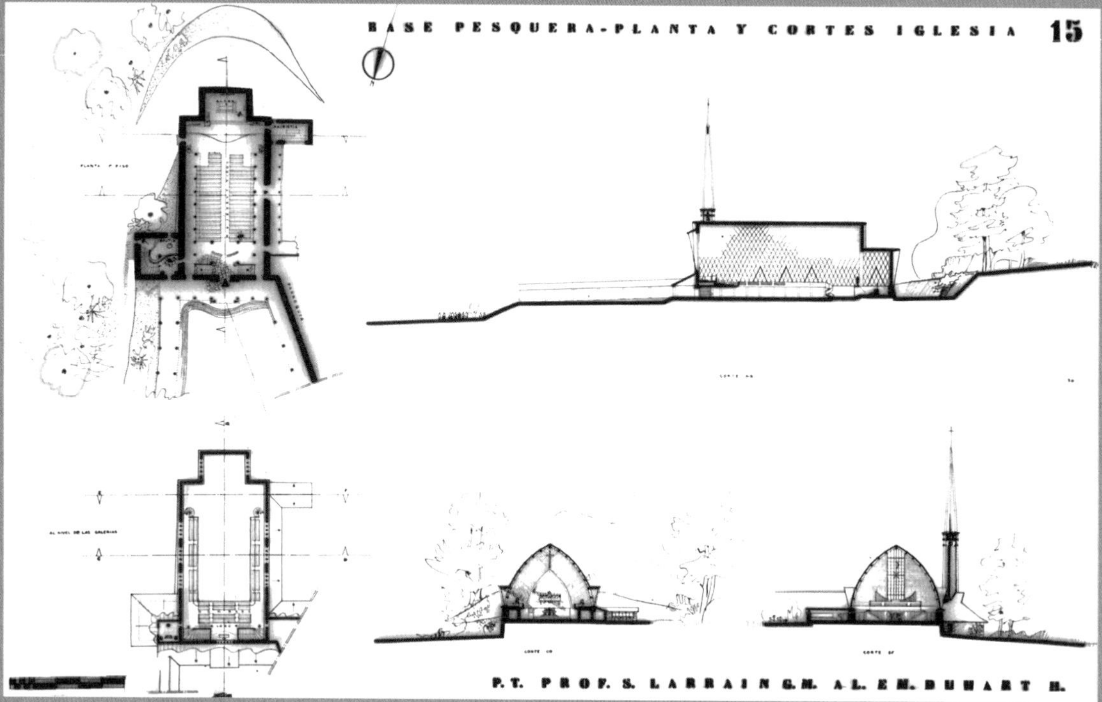
BASE PESQUERA-PLANTA Y CORTES IGLESIA 15
P.T. PROF. S. LARRAIN G.M. AL. EM. DUHART H.

BASE PESQUERA - PERSPECTIVA GENERAL DEL CENTRO 7
PROYECTO DE TITULO PROF. S. LARRAIN G.M. AL. EM. DUHART H.

BASE PESQUERA-PERSPECTIVAS CASA GREMIAL
12
1.
3.
4.
2.
5.
PROYECTO DE TITULO-PROF. S. LARRAIN G.M. AL. EM. DUHART H.

BASE PESQUERA-ELEVACIONES CASA GREMIAL
11
P. T. PROF. S. LARRAIN G.M. AL. EM. DUHART H.

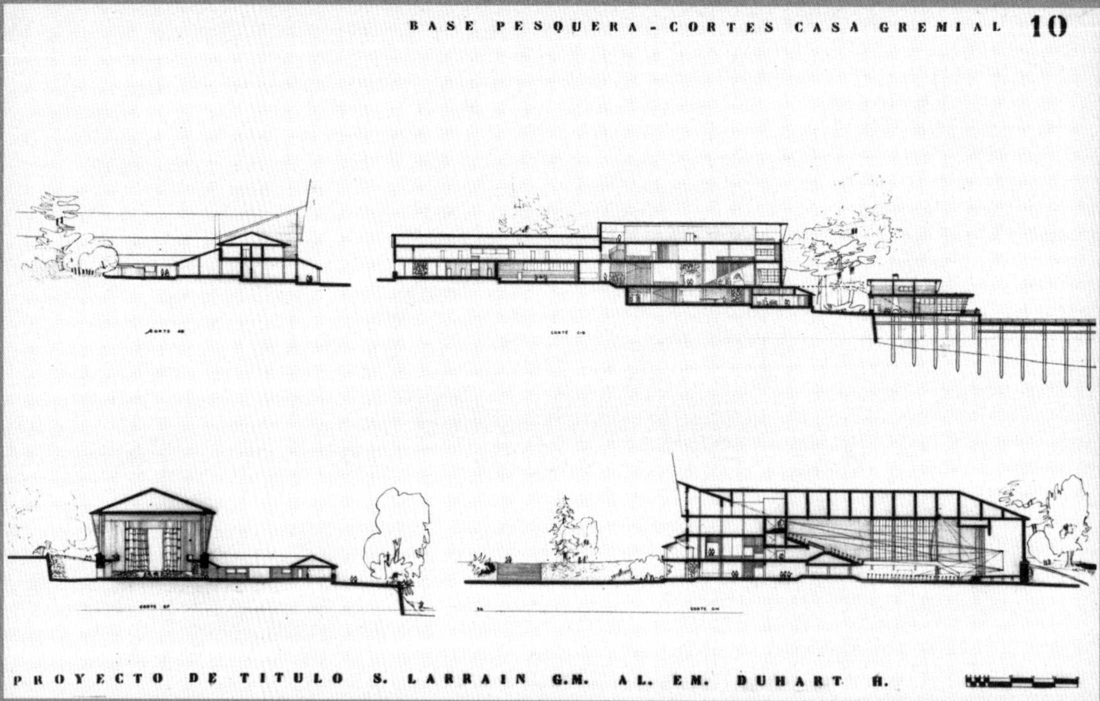
BASE PESQUERA - CORTES CASA GREMIAL 10
PROYECTO DE TITULO S. LARRAIN G.M. AL. EM. DUHART H.

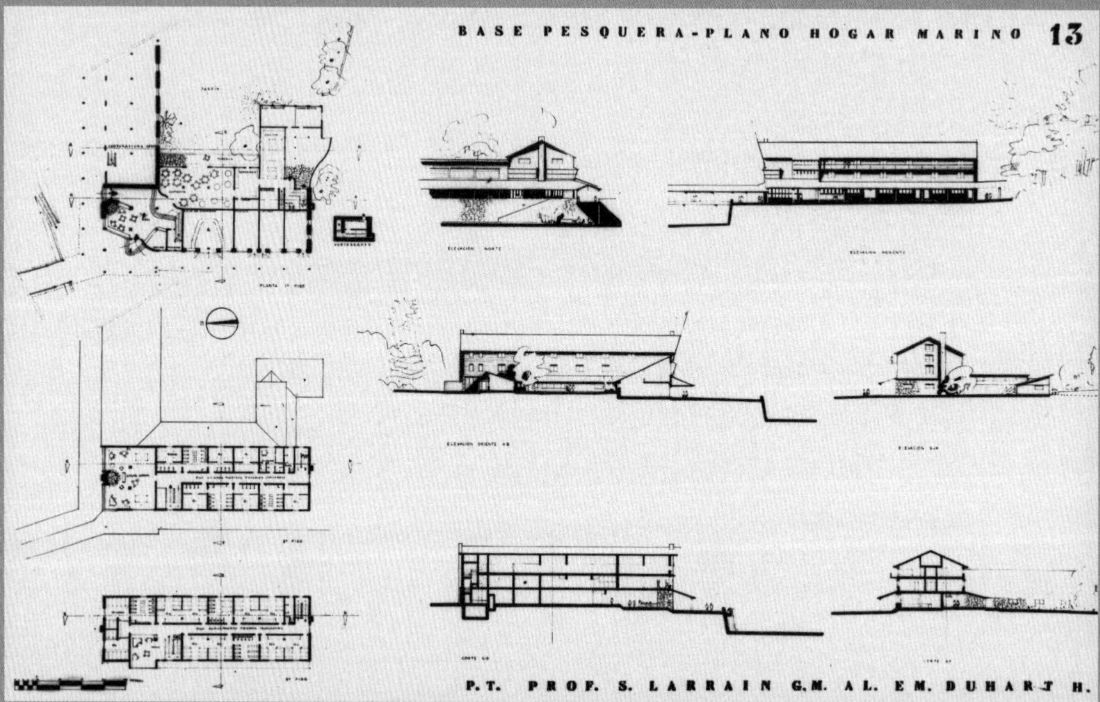
BASE PESQUERA - PLANO HOGAR MARINO 13
P.T. PROF. S. LARRAIN G.M. AL. EM. DUHART H.

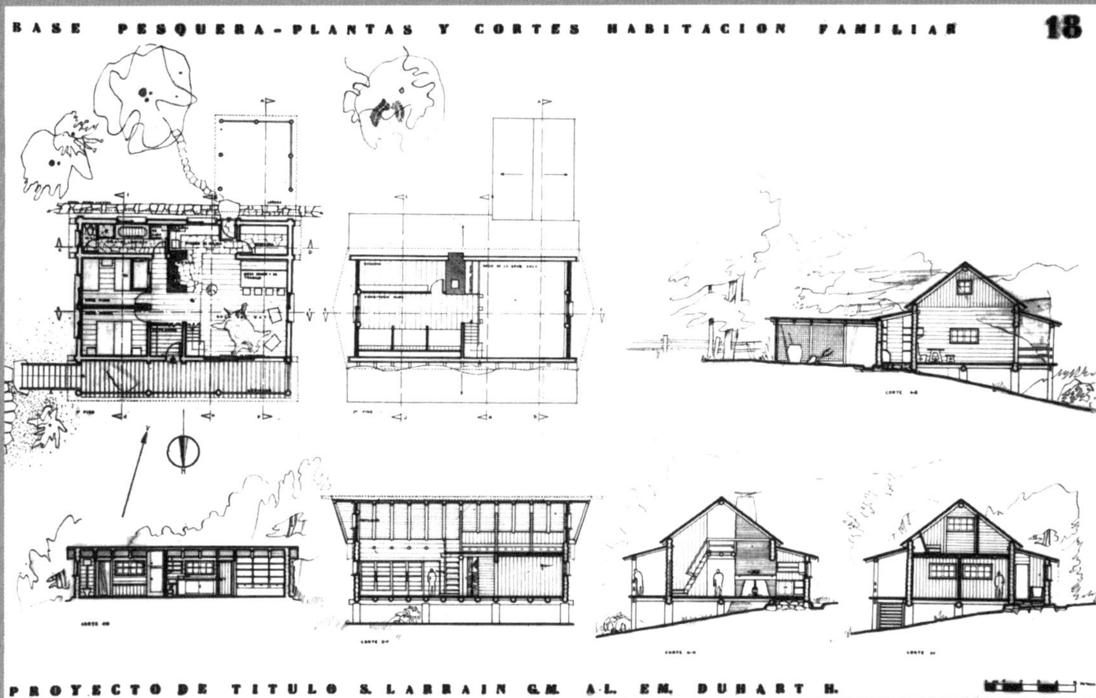
BASE PESQUERA-PLANTAS Y CORTES HABITACION FAMILIAR
18
PROYECTO DE TITULO S. LARRAIN G.M. A.L. EM. DUHART H.

BASE PESQUERA-ELEVACION HABITACION FAMILIAR
19
P.T. PROF. S. LARRAIN G.M. AL. EM. DUHART H.

FIRST PROFESSIONAL COMMISSION – THE LABBÉ HOUSE

In 1941, Duhart graduated with honors, got married to Raquel Echeverría Baeza, and began working at the Reconstruction and Relief Corporation, a government organization. The state had begun an effort to bring forth the first schemes to publicly introduce modern architecture more formally. In 1939, a powerful earthquake had caused around 28,000 deaths in the south, and the Reconstruction and Relief Corporation was created to bring solutions and rebuild the devastated areas, in predominantly poor zones of the country. Most of the deaths related to the earthquake had occurred because the colonial adobe construction did not withstand the impact of the quake. Adobe construction could be found in urban and rural areas all along the country. As stated by Professor Simon Collier, in Santiago "remembering the colonial era … nearly all its houses were still one-story, of adobe construction, with barred windows …[and] secluded".[70] At the corporation, Duhart dedicated himself to the study of adobe, a natural material widely available along with the traditional knowledge for its production. He became profoundly interested in researching it, and in that sense, he remarked he was "looking for the roots of [his] own architecture, not necessarily Chilean because Chilean or French, English or Japanese … shows a kind of patriotism, or nationalism, which seems inappropriate to me. It would be rather [searching for] an authenticity, something typical of the country, but involving nature. We must not forget that from its source, architecture is a thing that emerges from the physical world."[71] He was referencing a correlation between architectural materials and the natural context of the location of the designed structure, a principle that he revisited on several occasions in different iterations.

70 Simon Collier, *Chile: The Making of a Republic 1830-1865, Politics and Ideas* (Cambridge: Cambridge University Press, 2003), 11.

71 Pérez Oyarzun and Urrejola, "Series of interviews with Emilio Duhart," audio interview, Part 2 of 8.

In that same year, he got his first architectural appointment, a weekend house on the outskirts of Santiago. Being immersed in the adobe investigation, he decided to use it as one of the construction materials. Of the residence, he said, "this house was important, […] it had a bit of an impact on the local scene, in a somewhat scandalous way, in the sense that adobe was used in a rich, super-rich house."[72] The controversy emerged because of the perceived dissonance of utilizing adobe since it was a material from low-income people's houses.

72 Pérez Oyarzun and Urrejola, "Series of interviews with Emilio Duhart," audio interview, Part 2 of 8.

A wealthy patron, Rosa Labbé, commissioned the design of the house. Labbé was a cosmopolitan woman who lived in France between 1924 and 1931. She was aware of the modern movement in architecture in Paris, and on the advice of her son, an architectural student at the Pontifical

Catholic University, she contacted Emilio Duhart after her son had seen the presentation of his degree project. The weekend house project was carried out in partnership between Duhart and his friend and colleague Héctor Valdés Phillipps, who in time would become one of the principals of the important architecture firm Bresciani, Valdés, Castillo y Huidobro (BVCH.)

The house was located on a 161-acre lot of land in La Dehesa in the vicinity of Santiago, a commune that today accommodates residents of high social strata but at that time was rural land. The house was approximately 2,800 square feet and had a dining room, a living room, a large terrace, four bedrooms, two bathrooms, a kitchen, a pantry, a service bedroom, and a bathroom (figs. 19-22). The house was to be occupied during weekends to get out of the city and be in contact with nature, a new lifestyle proposition at the time, and which Labbé had observed among acquaintances while in Paris.

Of the site, Duhart asserted that, "La Dehesa was an open field that had extraordinary charm. It was a 'dehesa' [grassland in English,] flat, with pastures and with a view of the wonderful mountain range, [and] for ecological reasons, I made the house on the hill, on the rock and not below [...] I had the vision of an architectural urban development that would maximally preserve the agricultural lands [...]. The 'anti-Dehesa' was a gesture of building [the house] on the hill."[73] The house was placed 165 feet up the incline and looking northeast to obtain the maximum view of the valley and the Andes mountains.

73 Pérez Oyarzun and Urrejola, "Series of interviews with Emilio Duhart," audio interview, Part 1 of 8.

Duhart and Valdés defined the Labbé House as a residence that fluctuated between modernity and tradition. They were attempting to weave the local and the universal, unconventionally making use of both and inverting the flow direction from the "identity-giving culture" toward the universal and not the other way around. The design placed prominence on the endemic typology of the Chilean country house, with the bedroom wing, the kitchen, and service areas being more intimate and traditional. In contrast, the living/dining room plus the main terrace are spatially very modern and innovative. The living/dining area has a mono-pitch roof with the higher side open to the terrace for optimal immersion into the scenery. The large sliding window area goes from floor to ceiling, looking like a sizable screen accentuated by the slanted roof which opens towards the outdoor terrace.

Following pages:
Figures 19 - 22: Original plans Casa Labbé. Emilio Duhart and Héctor Valdés. Emilio Duhart Fund.

The architects responded to the request of a weekend house, a cosmopolitan concept, to create a new type of experience to counterbalance city life. They proposed a modern and rational assignment of the spaces neatly distributed between private and public.

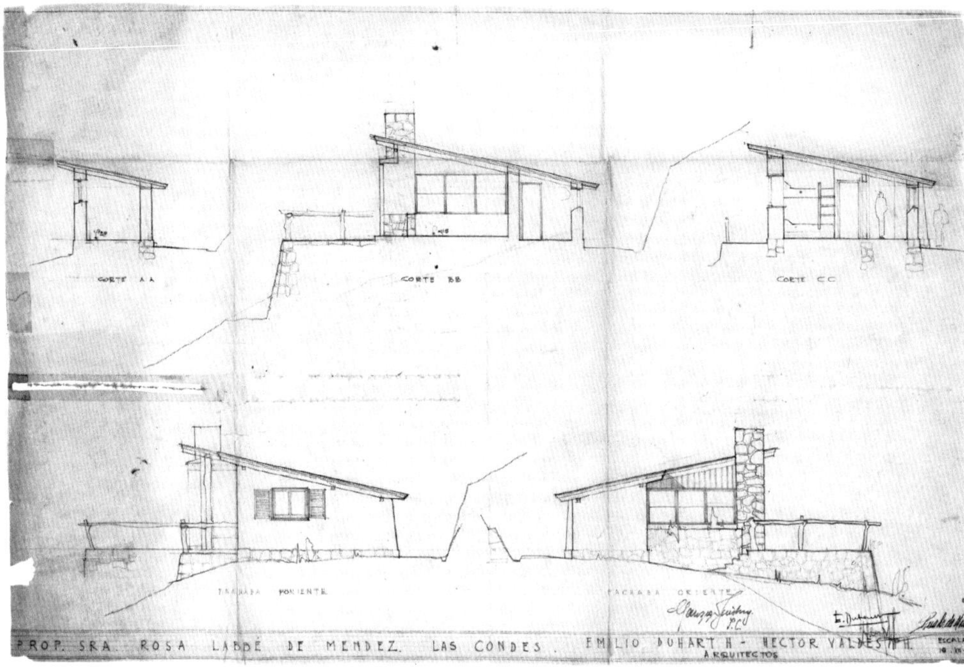
CORTE AA
CORTE BB
CORTE CC
FACHADA PONIENTE
FACHADA ORIENTE
PROP. SRA. ROSA LABBÉ DE MENDEZ. LAS CONDES. EMILIO DUHART H. - HECTOR VALDES
ARQUITECTOS

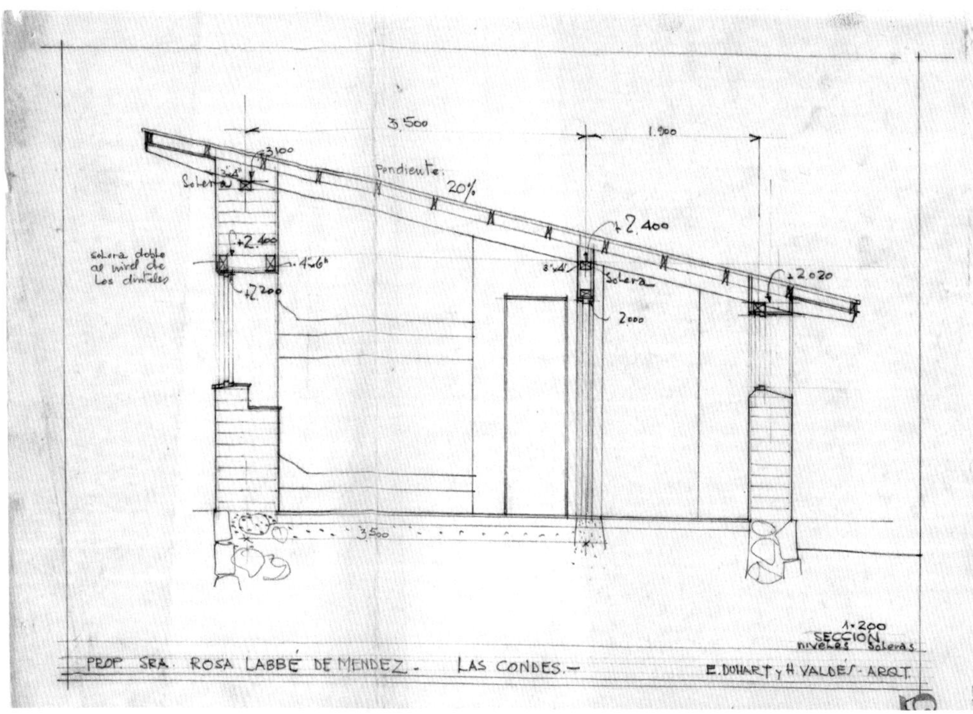
3.500
1.900
Pendiente 20%
+3100
Solera
+2.400
+2.400
4"x6"
+2.200
solera doble al nivel de los dinteles
Solera
+2.020
2.000
3.500
1:200
SECCION
niveles soleras
PROP. SRA. ROSA LABBÉ DE MENDEZ.- LAS CONDES.-
E. DUHART y H. VALDES - ARQT.

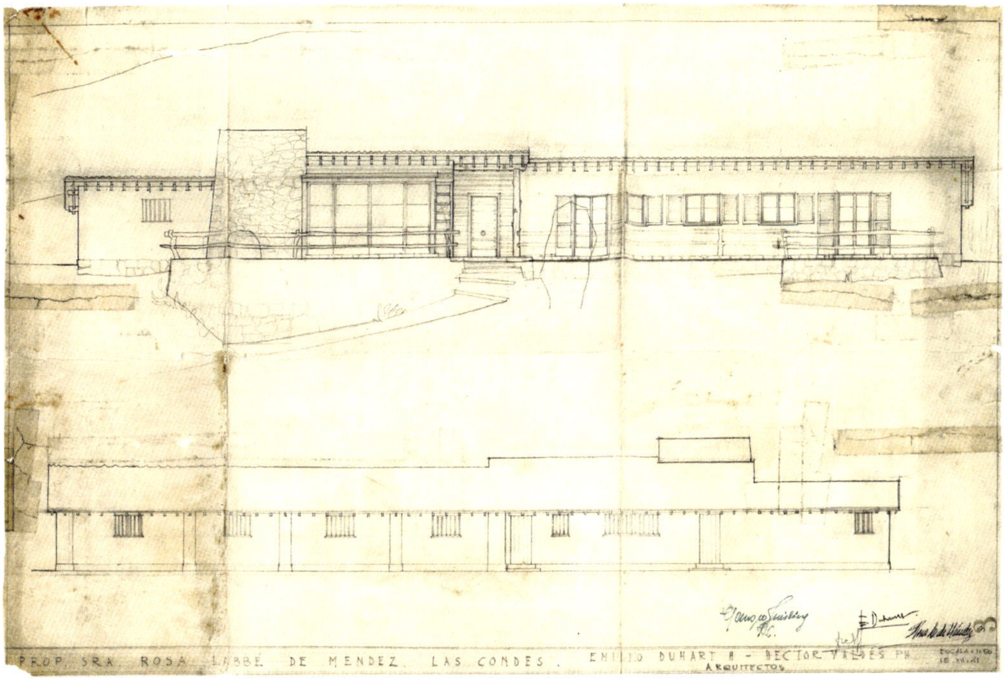
PROP SRA ROSA LABBÉ DE MENDEZ. LAS CONDES.
EMILIO DUHART H - HECTOR VALDES PH
ARQUITECTOS

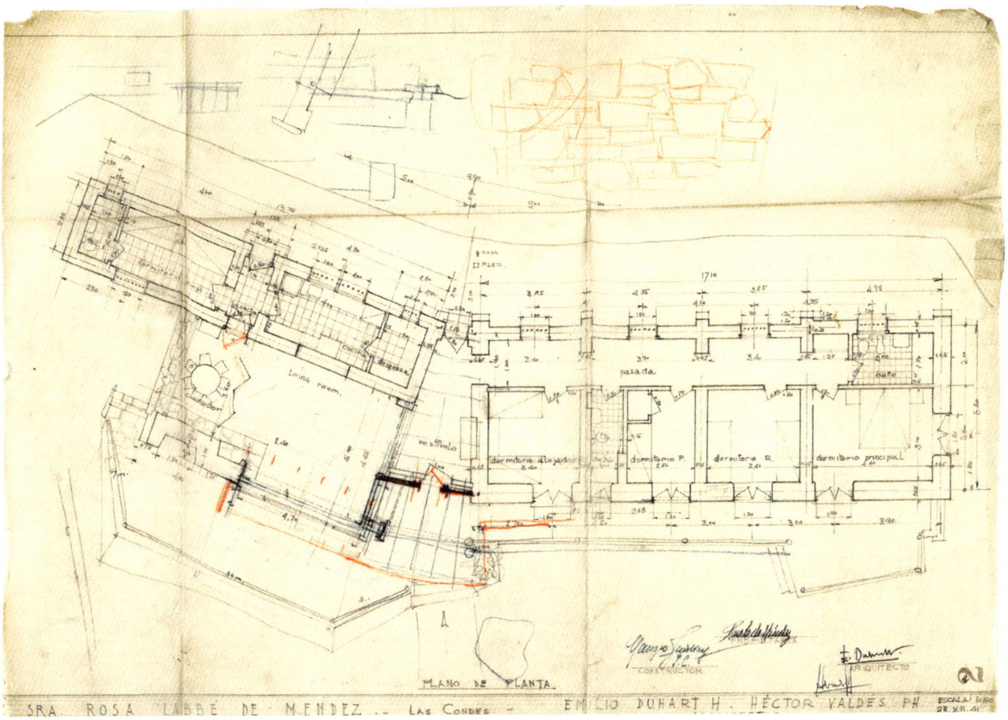
Living room
pasada
dormitorio principal
PLANO DE PLANTA
ARQUITECTO
SRA. ROSA LABBÉ DE MENDEZ .- LAS CONDES -
EMILIO DUHART H. HÉCTOR VALDÉS PH

The design had a functional distribution of its components, bedrooms to one side of the entry, and service and living to the other side. The orientation of the house was arranged for the maximal enjoyment of the landscape.

The house rested on a stereotomic stone base representing permanence in time, and adobe, wood, and clay tiles used for the volumes representing transience. The whole structure rested on a longitudinal platform made out of cut stone found in the area, of which the large chimney, access stair, and some of the outdoor floor coverings were also made. Set on the platform, three orthogonal volumes, one to one side and the other two on the other side, are displayed like an open fan, embracing the hill and with its opposite sides facing the landscape. The larger volume stands alone and was intended for the bedroom wing, and the two adjacent ones were for the dining and living rooms to the front, and the kitchen and service area to the back of the house. The juncture of both blocks constituted the entry hall. The portico leading to the main entrance of the house is a wooden roof structure supported by a column made of a rough tree trunk, a notable detail for its uniqueness as a gesture paying tribute to nature (fig. 23).

The allotment of materials was in close relationship to the function of the spaces: adobe for the intimate areas–bedrooms and service areas–wood for the public spaces, and stone for the base. Integrating the local modes of construction, the thick adobe structural walls of the private section with thinner separating compartments and small windows express the house's ability to embrace its inhabitants when retreating. In contrast, the house's public section was open to the outside, and was made out of wood to provide maximum height and durability, with an extra-large window made for contemplation of the outdoors (fig. 24).

Additionally, although designing a modern house, the architects integrated local ancient knowledge into the house. For example, they selected a local worker's recipe to paint the outer wall of the house in colonial red. It consisted of juice of prickly pear leaf mixed with colored soil. The compound resulted in a sticky, gluey consistency that allowed for preservation over time.[74]

74 Pérez Oyarzun and Urrejola, "Series of interviews with Emilio Duhart," audio interview, Part 1 of 8.

Given the geological characteristics of Chile, with its recurring and powerful earthquakes, this fundamental challenge for the design and construction of structures was detected from the beginning by the architect. In this sense, he paid particular attention to respond to this in different ways throughout his career. In his observations of the destruction that occurred during the 1939

Figure 23: Emilio Duhart and Héctor Valdés. Labbé House, 1941. Detail of roof and terrace.

Figure 24: Emilio Duhart and Héctor Valdés. Labbé House, 1941. View of living room and terrace.

earthquake, Duhart had concluded that the heavy ceilings led to much of the crumbling of the adobe buildings. In the Labbé house he wanted to address and solve this problem scientifically, simultaneously creating solutions utilizing adobe, a traditional material, that would result in a long-lasting house.[75]

75 Pérez Oyarzun and Urrejola, "Series of interviews with Emilio Duhart," audio interview, Part 1 of 8.

Technically, the design of the house concentrated on its anti-seismic stability with the additional challenge of using adobe and wood for the volumes. The whole structure acknowledged through its building technique the weakness of adobe and its susceptibility to earthquakes. However, it also expressed acceptance of such events through an interlaced construction method. The volumes of the private area of the residence—bedroom and service wings—were made of adobe, a heavier material with thicker perimeter and thinner transversal walls and with finishes in wood (floors, unions, doors, and windows). Because of the height and size of the area, the living-dining structure was designed in wood, a lighter material. The junctions between the adobe and the wood areas were devised in adaptive wooden arrangements to produce maximum elasticity in case of heavy movement. The light wooden roof was made with a twenty-degree slope to better distribute its weight to alleviate pressure on the lower parts and was finished with clay tiles. The overall structure with the heavy stable stone base, the thick and thinner adobe walls, and the wooden construction of the dining and living areas, the lightness of the roof, and the flexibility of the joints were all engineered to move in synchrony in case of an earthquake.

For the young architects using the local workforce was a smart way to compensate their presumed lack of building techniques. They created a new construction procedure with their help, thus making use of the local know-how and material culture. The local force represented a pool of knowledge in traditional modes of construction. Additionally, the materials were from nearby lumberyards and in that respect, Héctor Valdés commented that "at that time architecture was based on construction and fabrication ingenuity, because there was no large availability of materials. It was necessary to manage with what existed,"[76] attesting to the architects' audacity and inventiveness despite their youth and inexperience.

76 Alberto, Browne, "Casa Labbé: Un Modo de Pensar la Arquitectura," in Emilio Duhart, Seminario de Investigación Fernando Pérez Oyarzun, Volume 1, (Santiago: Pontificia Universidad Católica de Chile, 2005).

The nature-embracing structure was thought of as a "thing" that comes up from the surrounding physical world. The adobe, the stone, and the wood are all materials that, as a whole, functioned as mimetic elements to the specific natural environment. The materials were present in the surrounding region, resulting in a house in perfect visual symbiosis with its landscape.

Duhart and Valdés Phillips provided for the enjoyment of nature, expressed through the consideration of the human body. The design envisions subjects that look, contemplate, are engaged with the scenery, and are immersed in the outdoors. The large terrace with multiple possibilities of activities, and an outdoor chimney are there to welcome them. The parking space was set away from the house, forcing the residents to walk up a stretch, creating a transitional space between, first, city life, and then from technology (the car), and finally the natural retreat. The large chimney is a double exhaust one, for internal and external use. The surface of the terrace is as large as that of the living/dining area, an invitation to make extensive use of the outdoors, and presumably proposing lounging, dining, and with the presence of the fireplace an invitation to stay outside when temperatures were low. This fact, in addition to the size of the terrace and the outdoor chimney, pays tribute to the programmatic aspect of the project, the residence being a weekend house for getting out of the city to be in close contact with nature.

The Labbé House was a serious exercise in blending tradition and modernity. Adobe was at the center of the inquiry, a material which Duhart pursued further, both in Chile and during the period he lived in the United States in the early 1940s. Before going abroad, he had completed a countryside residence in adobe, the Larraín House (1942), a persistent effort to continue his application of the material. During that time, he was envisioning the use of adobe as a plan to develop a contemporary type of construction using it in an unorthodox manner.

Once in the United States, he continued this research in that pursuit. He met Vernon DeMars, the district architect for the Farm Security Administration (FSA) at the regional office in San Francisco, who had done extensive work in adobe. Duhart mentions this encounter as representing a critical exchange but does not mention any other details. DeMars was also renowned for the design of "dormitories, cabins, and community buildings for several thousand workers and their families in Vallejo, California, near the shipyards of San Francisco Bay"[77] which constituted one of the first prefabricated houses of the Second World War period. The FSA was a New Deal agency to combat rural poverty and was part of a series of programs enacted by President Roosevelt to bring relief to those affected by the Great Depression. This fact may indicate a common vision between De Mars and Duhart from which Duhart might have benefitted in some way, as both were interested in affordable housing for the lower classes.

77 Peter S. Reed, "Enlisting Modernism," in *World War II and the American Dream*, edited by Donald Albrecht (Massachussets: MIT Press, 1996), 9.

In 1945 when back in Chile, Duhart returned to work for the Reconstruction and Relief Corporation and to his immense disappointment the interest in his research was drying out. Duhart also learned that within the corporation, some officials and architects had a stigma around using adobe, as if getting into the mud and becoming dirty.[78] Furthermore, and against his expectations, he learned that people from small towns and rural areas and their representatives rejected the idea of using this material. They thought its selection meant they were looking down on them, assigning it a pejorative meaning. As expressed to Duhart, they thought that instead, new materials of construction would give them access to civilization and culture. For this reason, Duhart decided to submit his resignation to the Corporation and with a feeling of great disappointment and frustration abandoned his investigation on adobe, a material he had so intensely been invested in. He had been looking into a great many iterations of its application around the world. He was drawn to it for its accessibility, durability, and thermal insulation, knowing that the weakness of the material was its susceptibility to earthquakes. Caught between the negative opinions of both the upper and lower-classes, Duhart's aspiration to pursue adobe as a material to solve housing problems in Chile had been stopped short due to cultural constraints he could not control. The pursuit had come to a dead-end and Duhart never used adobe in a comprehensive way again.[79] This discontinued bifurcation remained as a suspended alternative, and one wonders about what would have happened if Duhart could have pursued this vein.

78 Pérez Oyarzun and Urrejola, "Series of interviews with Emilio Duhart," audio interview, Part 1 of 8.

79 Pérez Oyarzun and Urrejola, "Series of interviews with Emilio Duhart," audio interview, Part 1 of 8.

From a historical perspective, the Labbé House invites further interest. Reflecting on the importance of this house, Max Aguirre, a prominent Chilean modernist historian asserted, "that house is remarkable ... If one locates it in the year it was built [1941], it was decades ahead of the influential critical regionalism [of the 1980s] highlighted by Kenneth Frampton which coincided with the start of the Seminars of Latin American Architecture, where one of the most important concerns of the architects was to seek and recognize the identity of Latin American architecture … Ahead of its time [it] corresponded to the same independence of Scandinavian architects such as Alvar Aalto, making modern architecture without avoiding natural materials."[80] As insinuated by Aguirre, the kind of reflections that this house embodies pertains to the domain that Frampton was theorizing about during the 1980s. It may constitute, as Frampton put it, an "arrière-garde" that imparts an assertive resistance considering both an "identity-giving culture at the same time having discreet recourse to universal technique,"[81]

80 Evelyn Meynard, "Interview with Max Aguirre," recorded interview, Santiago, January 16, 2020.

81 Hal Foster, *The Anti-Aesthetic: Essays on Postmodern Culture* (Port Townsend, Washington: Bay Press, 1985), 20.

with the aim of intercepting with the universalization of the urban landscape throughout the world.

The Fishing Base of San Quintín and the Labbé House, both created in 1941, represent outstanding regional modern architectural models whose results still have resonance in our contemporary times for the way they make recourse of the existing "pattern languages" of the native surrounding. Describing a pattern language, Nikos Salingaros states that "[it] reflects different modes of life, customs, and behavior, and is appropriate to specific climates, geographies, cultures, and traditions,"[82] and applicable to these projects he adds that, "it is up to the designer/architect to extract specific non-universal patterns as needed, by examining the ways of life and tradition in a particular setting, and then to apply them to that situation."[83] Both projects make discreet use of the universal idiom of modernism allowing an architectural expression that integrates the endemic culture and the environment and by so doing they resist universalization. The projects showcase many levels of complexity in the use of endemic culture, materials and technology entwined with compositional principles guided by rationalism and functionalism. The resulting designs achieved are commendable illustrations in interlacing the modern with the local.

82 Nikos A. Salingaros, *A Theory of Architecture* (Kathmandu: Vajra Books, 2013), 220.

83 Salingaros, *A Theory of Architecture,* 220.

THE DEFINING DECADE – 1945-1952

In Duhart's life, the decade between 1942 and 1952 is framed at the beginning and at the end by close encounters with two of the most renowned figures in the creation of international modernism, Walter Gropius and Le Corbusier. This single fact is completely out of the ordinary and is remarkable in and of itself. Through travels, stays abroad, and multiple encounters with pivotal figures of architectural modernism, Duhart was able to build a robust network of relationships that further impacted and shaped his views about architecture and his work. His unique trajectory confirms that to assess architectural history, personal journeys, identities, and travels, channeled through the realized work of the architect, greatly impact the constructed environment. In this regard Jilly Traganou posits that, "thinking about contemporary architecture and also as a way of reconsidering architecture's history … .[There is a] need to perform a shift from the orthodox focus on the nation-state as a conflated political and cultural unit within which architecture emerges, to considering conditions of internal otherness, as well as architectural networks that operate beyond national borders, crystallized in an array of localities across the globe."[1] Traganou is referring to a phenomenon that has become pervasive in our contemporary times but in the case of the architect under study, in terms of displacements, his life turned out to be similar to that of many contemporary architects. During the decade between 1942 and 1952, Duhart navigated through the international world of modern architecture, collecting information from first-hand contact which he then spread over the built environment in the territory of Chile.

1 Traganou, "From Nation-Bound Histories to Global Narratives of Architecture", 166.

In 1942, Duhart went through a crucial threshold, embarking on a two-year trip to the United States. Before examining this period, it is essential to reassert what principles, ideas, and convictions he had elaborated before coming into close contact with international modernism.

As demonstrated in his degree project and the Labbé House, the architect had a vast capacity for reflection about what the profession could, would, and should mean. Derived from the cultural surrounding and the specific social conditions of the lower classes in Chile, he developed a sensitivity to social issues, reflecting on how the field could contribute to the betterment of human circumstances. He saw in urban planning a possibility for regional development where technological and economic development were issues of primal consideration.

Figure 25: Le Corbusier, photograph given and dedicated by the architect to Emilio Duhart, circa 1960.

Of particular interest is Duhart's understanding of the importance of the natural environment, understood as a region's climate, topography, traditions, and culture. He was confident that architecture had to have a deep-seated relationship with the environment, its geography, history, and people, making it necessary to study those existing conditions comprehensively. However, his vision of the local environment was broader. He saw nature and the human-made intrinsically intertwined and the human/nature relationship as the basis for the practice of the profession. He envisioned nature as a giving force and people as cultural transmitters of lessons learned from their natural surroundings, in a symbiotic kind of relationship. Accordingly, like an ethnographer, the architect had to observe those cultural lessons and derive from them how those practices and knowledge could be utilized, assisted, and enhanced.

Duhart considered architecture as a gathering of nature's goods which then were harmoniously deposited back on the topographic field, in structures of contemplation, positioning the buildings with the intention of inviting their inhabitants to look at and appreciate the natural landscape. To him, architecture entailed the elaboration of a regional language, attempting at this stage to express the modern language through native building techniques and materials. For him, technical quality and excellence in fabrication were fundamental in the making of structures, a fact that explains his heightened attention to the technique. In the case of the Chilean terrain, he needed to account for the violent seismic conditions of its geology.

At this early stage of his journey, he was convinced that his compositional language was modern with a firm rejection of imitative undertakings. He aligned to a type of modernism with an emphasis on the program, the prevalence of functionalism and rationalism, the rejection of gratuitous ornamentation and styles, with the inclusion of regional materials and modes of construction. The practice of architecture needed to be originated from its context and had to have an authentic and honest expression.

Finally, he also included the new circumstances of the modern era, with its technical and industrial advances, as representing additives to the urban planning program, especially for local communities. The provision of those well-thought-out additions could ensue a dignified subsistence conducive to sustainable growth. He understood communities' economic survival as being entrenched in the locality but with connectivity towards the metropolitan regions.

AT THE SOURCES OF MODERNISM I – THE UNITED STATES FIELD RECONNAISSANCE

The above outline is the conceptual foundation with which Duhart left for the United States in 1942. In a later interview, Duhart mentioned that his degree project had had resonance, and that the most notable outcome was being invited by the university to exhibit his project at its Honor Hall.[2] At the same time, in 1941, the Second Inter-American Congress of Municipalities, organized to stimulate commercial and cultural relations between the American Republics,[3] was taking place in Santiago. In these circumstances, three North American delegates witnessed the exhibition: Jacob Crane, the assistant coordinator of defense housing as the delegate of the American Committee for International Union of Local Authorities, Walter M. Brucher, in charge of the Federal Housing Administration in Washington, and Daniel W. Hoan from the Office of Civilian Defense. They liked the project so much that they requested an in-person presentation by the young student. According to Duhart, it was a long and thorough presentation after which Jacob Crane asked him if he desired to continue his studies in the United States, and if so, where. Duhart consented enthusiastically and responded that he would be interested in studying with Walter Gropius at Harvard University. After graduating, Duhart began working for the Reconstruction and Relief Corporation and months passed before he began receiving letters and application forms from the Graduate School of Design.[4] On being accepted to enter the master's degree program with two scholarships in 1942, he was to realize his aspiration to study with Walter Gropius.

THE WAR YEARS IN THE UNITED STATES

Emilio Duhart arrived in the United States in the midst of dramatic historical events that were shaping society in unprecedented and unusual ways. The Second World War was afoot in Europe, and with the German invasion of France in May 1940, the United States Army began a large-scale draft to support the Allies. By the end of the war in 1945, fourteen percent of the

2 José R. Camplá Lehmann, "Modernidad y Contextualidad Regional: El Caso de Emilio Duhart" (PhD diss., Universidad Politécnica de Madrid, 2012), 465.

3 *Victory, Official Weekly Bulletin of the Office for Emergency Management Index*, Library of Ohio State University, United States Government, Vol II, del 9 de julio de 1941 al 30 de diciembre de 1941, https://books.google.com/books?id=RLUDzBnsa8kC&pg=RA9-PA23&lpg=RA9PA23&dq=-jacob+crane+chile+in+1941&source=bl&ots=K-KZHEY6Yny&sig=AC-fU3U3sWiD64UETRhBg-vAKsqdOM1bFY4Q&hl=en&sa=X&ved=2ahUKEwiVz-JzMubpAhWmoHIEHYveD-FIQ6AEwAHoECAgQA-Q#v=onepage&q=jacob%20crane%20chile%20in%201941&f=false

4 Pérez Oyarzun and Urrejola, "Series of interviews with Emilio Duhart," audio interview, Part 1 of 8.

United States, roughly seventeen million people, served in the armed forces.[5] Triggered by the Japanese attack on Pearl Harbor on December 7, 1941, the Roosevelt administration started establishing a wartime economy, facilitating a series of events that forever changed the country's geopolitical and economic landscape. By spring 1942, the administration took control of the country's economy, implementing decisive measures to satisfy the national defense needs and the war efforts. Among the main actions taken were the closing down of the production of low-priority items, and the enforcement of strict constraints on the redistribution of materials and machinery including most notably those related to the building industry.

5 Donald Albrecht, "Introduction," in *World War II and the American Dream*, ed. Donald Albrecht (Cambridge, Massachusetts: MIT Press, 1995, XVII.

Guided by the requirements of the government, manufacturers refurbished, expanded, and built countless industrial installations. Paradoxically this effort engendered a revival of the economy, which had been substantially damaged during the Great Depression of the 30s. Industrial production increased from four percent before 1939 to fifteen percent from 1940 to 1944, generating the greatest economic boom in the history of the United States.[6] Nevertheless these were grim times. When men were overseas, women entered the workforce in large numbers, along with the African American population, and the result was a profound alteration in the landscape of American labor force. It was a period of sacrifice; yet despite their economic well-being at home, people in the United States did not spend their money, further reinforcing the country's prosperity in the postwar years.

6 Robert Friedel, "Scarcity and Promise," in *World War II and the American Dream*, ed. Donald Albrecht (Cambridge, Massachusetts: MIT Press, 1995), 74.

After 1940, with the military population growth inside and outside the country, the government initiated a massive building program to accommodate the country's largest military mobilization. Coming to a critical point by mid-1942 the reallocation and administration of resources by the government brought about severe shortages of materials. The only way to adapt to such a dire scenario was to search for material substitutions. The solutions arose progressively when the interest of divergent groups, academic, scientific, governmental, and manufacturers began coalescing to solve the perils of overusing traditional materials. Through creativity, design, methodology, and technological advances, they came together and devised a crucial array of innovative materials, most notably plywood, vinyl, acrylic, and new plastics, but also new construction components such as board made of wood pulp and ground newspaper bound with resin, and other alternatives for swift construction. By the spring of 1944, the end of the war was approaching, and discussions about the reconversion of the economy to normal times and deliberations about housing for the impending future, especially among architects, had become an imperative.

MASTER'S DEGREE AT THE GRADUATE SCHOOL OF DESIGN

During the late 1930s and early 1940s, the Graduate School of Design turned into a hub of modernism in the United States. To understand how this unfurled we need to delve into the series of events that made it possible. This will also aid in appreciating the outstanding circumstances in which Duhart would be involved when entering the school in the fall of 1942.

Over the course of the Great Depression, architects in the United States were under economic stress. This was a somber environment of mass unemployment, meager wages, and pessimistic prospects for the future. Teachers, students, and professionals began questioning the stylistic priority of the French Beaux-Arts theory system of education prevalent in all academic schools of architecture. On this subject, Jill Pearlman explains that "practitioners from all sides of the architectural spectrum joined forces to argue that the grand, anachronistic aspirations and theories of the French system had no place in [this] climate."[7] The practice of architecture and its pedagogy needed to be revised.

7 Jill Pearlman, *Inventing American Modernism: Joseph Hudnut, Walter Gropius and the Bauhaus Legacy at Harvard* (Charlottesville - University of Virginia Press), 2007, 51.

In 1935 at Harvard University, and in response to this new context, a new dean, Joseph Hudnut, was hired with a mission to renew and modernize its three schools: Architecture, City Planning, and Landscape Architecture. In 1936, Hudnut merged the three schools into a single entity, the Graduate School of Design (GSD), converting the former single schools into "departments," each with their own chair.[8] The three heads of the departments would work collaboratively under the leadership of the dean. He chose the name "design" to highlight the commonalities between architects, planners, and landscapers. The goal of the new dean was to turn GSD into the top school of modern design in the three fields under the precepts of a progressive educational philosophy, and to reduce the boundaries between architecture, planning, and landscaping.

8 Jill Pearlman, *Inventing American Modernism,* 59.

Joseph Hudnut remained chair of the Architectural Department until he hired Walter Gropius in 1937. Gropius had been appointed for having created, in Germany in 1919, a new type of pedagogy for designers and architects in the new technological world, advocating modes of expressive approaches in conformity with the new era. As the leader of the Bauhaus in Germany, Gropius's allure in Europe and in the United States was considerable. Not surprisingly, a year after his engagement at GSD, the school became the leading educational institution of architecture in the United States.[9] Furthermore, in the pre-war years, the growing interest in the United

9 Jill Pearlman, *Inventing American Modernism,* 104.

States for the resumption of new construction brought renewed enthusiasm in architecture. Additionally, the fact that most other institutions remained tied to the Beaux-Arts theories of education precipitated a concatenation of events, among them a substantial increase in enrollment at the GSD (forty percent more than pre-war years,)[10] and as Pearlman affirmed "within a few years Mies [van der Rohe] came to the Armour Institute in Chicago (1938), [Alvar] Aalto to MIT (1940), while Yale, Berkeley, and Oregon gradually reorganized their faculties after 1945. By the time Gropius had been teaching at Harvard for ten years, a modern pedagogical philosophy had supplanted the Beaux-Arts system in architecture schools throughout the United States."[11] The clear preeminence of the Graduate School of Design remained so until the early 1950s. During those years, a long list of distinguished architects, urban planners, teachers, and students from across the world had become affiliated with it, among which were Marcel Breuer, I. M. Pei, Paul Rudolph, Hugh Stubbins, Edward Larrabee Barnes, Philip Johnson, Henry N. Cobb, Ulrich Franzen, and members of the TAC (The Architects Collaborative). Pearlman affirmed, "the GDS was so successful in disseminating its brand of modern architecture and urbanism in an era of unprecedented building that it is no exaggeration to say that the school transformed the physical landscape worldwide."[12]

10 Jill Pearlman, *Inventing American Modernism,* 108.

11 Jill Pearlman, *Inventing American Modernism*, 108.

12 Jill Pearlman, *Inventing American Modernism*, 1.

WALTER GROPIUS AT THE GRADUATE SCHOOL OF DESIGN

Le Corbusier and Walter Gropius were considered the most important players in early modernism, the former as a creator and the latter as an architectural philosopher, educator, and "moral force,"[13] a fact that explains Gropius's success in the United States. Amongst the prevailing ideas that Gropius brought to GSD was that architects had the social responsibility to make good designs accessible to all people, a precept born out of a war environment in Europe, and which echoed further in the United States during the late Depression era. He believed that the conditions of a changing modern world demanded attention on the new functional and psychological needs, for which architects, urban planners, and landscape architects had to work collaboratively, sharing their skills with experts from other fields to achieve the best solutions. Gropius regarded urbanism as a crucial field of the new era, incorporating the central tenets that originated from the 1933 CIAM Athens Charter in which he had participated. The concept of the "'functional city,' with distinct residential, working, educational, and recreational districts set among alternating urban and rural zones,"[14] had been developed. At GSD under Gropius's leadership, housing became a central theme, and especially

13 Jill Pearlman, I*nventing American Modernism*, 110.

14 Jill Pearlman, *Inventing American Modernism*, 92.

Figura 26: Walter Gropius, photograph given by the architect to Emilio Duhart.

housing for lower-income workers, highlighting economy, flexibility, efficiency, and function as primary focuses. For densely populated areas he advocated for a ten-to-twelve story low-cost high-rise building set within greenery, and with apartments with enough air, sunlight, and privacy for everyone. Once in the United States he also developed an interest in single-family units, and the concept of flexibility led him to further elaborate extensively in prefabrication and mass-production of dwellings, thus he also encouraged his students to think in that vein.[15]

At the Graduate School of Design, contemporary ways of addressing the architectural project were being established. The students were incentivized to work in groups and confront the design problems in collaboration with a wide range of professionals from other fields (engineers, economists, developers, urban planners, public officials, manufacturers), making them aware of a spectrum of concerns in the decision-making process.[16] The assignments were in relation to real sites, restricted by practical constraints, and had to have extensive research as the basis of the design process.

As a pedagogical method, Gropius promoted the individual creativity of the students taking into consideration their particular frame of reference and providing guidance to elaborate solutions from the problems at hand as opposed to encouraging working on preconceived ideas. When considering any design problem, he aimed at instilling in his students the practice of integrating the elements of form, construction, economic efficiency, and materials, making them consider the issues on their own.[17]

As Fiona MacCarthy remarked, Gropius's way of teaching stood out "in allowing individual freedom of development rather than imposing a doctrinaire approach,"[18] enabling his students to evolve in their own individual paths, citing "Paul Rudolph, the radical exponent of neo-Brutalist concrete structures … [and] I.M. Pei, the architect of angularity, transparency, and mystery,"[19] as clear examples of contrasting figures who studied under his guidance. Of the hundreds of thesis works that Gropius witnessed during his fifteen years at GSD, he recognized I.M. Pei's project as the best student work produced at the school.[20] Pei designed a museum for Chinese Art in which he tested the limits of international modernism in the context of an Asian culture. In 1950, in an article in *Architecture d'Aujourd'hui*, Gropius wrote that Pei's work "clearly illustrates that an able designer can very well hold on to basic traditional features—which he has found are still alive—without sacrificing a progressive conception of design,"[21] attesting to his appreciation for the translation of the modern architectural language into non-western environments.

15 Jill Pearlman, *Inventing American Modernism,* 159-162.

16 Jill Pearlman, *Inventing American Modernism*, 106.

17 Jill Pearlman, *Inventing American Modernism,* 144.

18 Fiona MacCarthy, *Gropius: The Man who Built the Bauhaus* (Cambridge, Massachusetts: The Belknap Press of Harvard University Press, 2019), 407.

19 MacCarthy, *Gropius: The Man who Built the Bauhaus,* 407.

20 Ken Stewart, "Remembering Pei: Tracing the Architect's Legacy to the Harvard Graduate School of Design," Harvard University Graduate School of Design, accessed July 10, 2020, https://www.gsd.harvard.edu/2019/07/remembering-pei-tracing-the-architects-legacy-to-the-harvard-graduate-school-of-design/

21 Stewart, "Remembering Pei: Tracing the Architect's Legacy to the Harvard Graduate School of Design."

GROPIUS'S MASTER CLASS

Participating in the master's class was a privileged and an exceptional experience. It was given by Walter Gropius, assisted by Marcel Breuer, and followed in 1941 by Hugh Stubbins. Students came to GSD from both the United States and abroad and to be accepted they had to already have an architectural degree. To conclude the master's degree the students were required to complete four long-term projects, such as a school building, an apartment house, or a single-family unit. At the beginning of the first fall semester, to be selected for the master's class, students were given by Gropius a week-long sketch assignment which consisted of designing their own house. Of the thirty students on average accepted into the program, Gropius would select fifteen of them, a process that became increasingly more competitive as the school gained prestige. Classes took place on the second floor of Robinson Hall, in a studio that fit just about the same amount of drawing boards as students. Gropius visited the class twice a week, reviewing the work of each student at every session. Oncc an assignment was finished the students presented their work to a faculty jury and a large student audience. At the start of each new project period, Gropius would give long lectures about his architectural philosophy, collaboration, prefabrication, and low-cost housing. Discussions about different aspects of the design process among the students were also a common occurrence[22]

Gropius developed close relationships with his students, socializing with them during weekends, frequently at his own house, or at Breuer's house in Lincoln, Massachusetts.[23] There they discussed the Bauhaus and met the numerous former Bauhaus personalities that visited them (Joseph Albers, Herbert Bayer, Xanti Schawinsky, to name a few.)[24] The students were well-acquainted with other houses that Gropius and Breuer designed in the Boston area, and as Pearlman remarked these houses "shared a number of characteristics that students at the GSD brought to their own work.[25] The buildings all used similar materials – wood, fieldstone, and large areas of glass, the latter to allow the flow of space between indoors and out. The houses were in general light in weight, and they shared an emphasis on functionality and economy of means. They generally included terraces that extended living space to the outdoors, flat roofs, open space plans, and all were single-family houses built outside the city."[26] [27] Some of these design features would later appear in the subsequent students' work.

Within any school, people not only learn from the prevailing voices but also from the voices of dissent or divergence. Walter Gropius had a lot of weight

22 Pearlman, *Inventing American Modernism*, 106–108.

23 Pearlman, *Inventing American Modernism*, 181.

24 Pearlman, *Inventing American Modernism*, 105.

25 Some of the houses that Gropius and/or Breuer designed in the Boston area and beyond: Gropius House, Lincoln, Massachusetts, 1938; Breuer House Lincoln, Lincoln, Massachusetts, 1938; Frank House, Pittsburgh, Pennsylvania, 1940; Chamberlain Cottage, Chamberlain, Massachusetts, 1940; Robinson House, Williamstown, Massachusetts, 1947; Breuer House New Canaan, New Canaan, Connecticut, 1948; Wolfson House, Pleasant Valley, New York, 1949; Starkey House, Duluth, Minnesota, 1955.

26 Pearlman, *Inventing American Modernism*, 183-184.

27 Pearlman, *Inventing American Modernism,* 163

within GSD, but that did not imply that it was a monolithic culture. Among the personalities who over the years developed ideas opposed to or divergent from those of Gropius, one can most notably count Joseph Hudnut, the dean of GSD. Over time he distanced himself from Gropius, opposing the type of urbanism inspired by the 1933 CIAM, which Gropius promoted, and specifically against the high-rise buildings Gropius advocated for. As described by Pearlman, "Hudnut railed against the inhuman, sterile, institutional way of life imposed on the occupants of the tediously uniform high-rise projects set on islands sequestered from the heart of the city." Marcel Breuer, the assistant to Gropius until 1941, and thereafter an important professor at the school, was greatly appreciated by the students for inspiration, his artistic qualities, and his way of conceiving practical solutions. Breuer departed from Gropius for apparent general disagreements although they always maintained a close dialogue. The architect Bruno Zevi, a student at GSD at the time, with a group of students elaborated a manifesto called *An Opinion on Architecture,* expressing their dissatisfaction with GSD and echoing Martin Wagner's (an important professor in city planning) criticism of the school's formalist leanings, and preferences for originality instead of answering society's demands. Wagner had known Gropius for years and had collaborated with him in urban planning in Berlin. Upon joining Gropius at GSD he found him changed, alleging he had surrendered to American capitalism, and of departing from his initial principles of socially inclined modernism.[28] Likewise, the students' complaints expressed their discontent towards the school, which according to them, did not sufficiently echo society's needs and did not stress enough the precept of collaborative work.[29] The manifesto was followed by the first issue of *Task: A Magazine for the Younger Generation in Architecture*, initially published in 1941.

28 MacCarthy, *Gropius: The Man who Built the Bauhaus,* 405.

29 Pearlman, *Inventing American Modernism*, 180.

Around the time Duhart went to Harvard a polyphonic culture was underway, a fact that might have enhanced his experience and stimulated the mind of an independent thinker such as he was.

DUHART AT GSD

Duhart began his master's degree in architecture in 1942 in the midst of World War II, when enrollments at the school had declined, and young men were being called to serve the military. He was selected into Walter Gropius's master's degree class with a reduced group of students (seven according to Duhart), who in time would become well-known architects, including Ieoh Ming Pei (Chinese, 1917- 2019,) Philip Johnson (American, 1906-2005,)

Bruno Zevi (Italian, 1918-2000,) Eduardo Catalano (Argentinian, 1917-2010,) John Harkness (American, 1916-2016,) Robert McMillan (American, 1916-2001), and Jorge Arango (Colombian, 1917-2007).

Duhart recounted that upon arrival at Harvard he was greeted by Gropius. In that first interview, he was struck by Gropius's "richness, depth, great kindness, and human openness that explains much of his message."[30] He described Gropius as a matter-of-fact kind of person, who frequently addressed very serious matters, while at the same time being very calm and natural. Duhart also appreciated the type of enriching and constructive dialog that Gropius had with the students.[31] To Duhart, Gropius was a great philosopher of architecture, beyond even what could be understood through his writings. However, he agreed with the common opinion that as an architect Gropius was not at the same level as his thoughts.

30 Pérez Oyarzun and Urrejola, "Series of interviews with Emilio Duhart," audio interview, Part 1 of 8.

31 Pérez Oyarzun and Urrejola, "Series of interviews with Emilio Duhart," audio interview, Part 6 of 8.

Duhart was a serious student who wanted to take advantage of the school and, as he put it, his purpose was "to achieve results." While there, he made a special effort to stay up to date with the developments of contemporary architecture. According to him, there was at GSD a greater capacity of reflection and study than what he had experienced at the university in Chile, particularly praising its excellent library with documents from all over the world which he frequently consulted.

Of the many technical teachings at the school, Duhart rememorated for example "how to make a good terrace, how to do the details, the [window] flashing,[32] all the vocabulary that did not exist in Chile; things that had a metal window for example, so that they did not drip, the famous flashing. (laughs)."[33] He also highlighted how he had to learn a new way of presenting his proposals. In this regard, he commented that "quite the opposite of the spontaneous, picturesque, and nice things … that we used at the school [in Chile] … there [at Harvard, drawings] were, of impeccable rigor … the precise line drawing, was extraordinarily good, with quality of graphics, and of refinement in the renderings."[34] He remarked that, as opposed to assigning a disproportionate amount of importance to the free-hand drawing, the rigor of the GSD was, in a good way, almost shocking to him. He acknowledged that instead of spending hours at the drawing table, at Harvard the study prior to the conception, and the reflection on the project, were essential. As Duhart concluded, "the project must be projected,"[35] adding, that with an emphasis on drawing instead of working conceptually, the architect can lose the substance of the conceit by falling into the trap of liking its representation too much.

32 "Window flashing is a thin continuous piece of material that is installed to prevent water from getting into a structure from an angle or joint near windows. … It is typically used on roofs, around windows and doors, and around any opening for pipes or electrical lines. Window flashing can be exposed or concealed." https://www.certainteed.com/trim/window-flashing/

33 Pérez Oyarzun and Urrejola, "Series of interviews with Emilio Duhart," audio interview, Part 3 of 8.

34 Pérez Oyarzun and Urrejola, "Series of interviews with Emilio Duhart," audio interview, Part 2 of 8.

35 Pérez Oyarzun and Urrejola, "Series of interviews with Emilio Duhart," audio interview, Part 6 of 8.

By his own words, Duhart's passage through GSD substantially changed him. The contact with Gropius and all the Bauhaus people had a great impact on him. He developed a close relationship with Gropius, Breuer, Philip Johnson, I. M. Pei, and Jorge Arango. Philip Johnson was much older than the rest of the students and was the director of the Museum of Modern Art, having curated a series of important architectural exhibitions. About Johnson, Duhart remarked that he was a "character [and] without a doubt had some relevance within the school. He was more friends with Breuer than Gropius … deep down, with Gropius, there was a distance. There was like an annoying consciousness."[36] Furthermore, Duhart stated that the students had a lot of contact with Sigfried Giedion, the famed Swiss historian and critic of architecture. He also befriended Roberto Matta, the surrealist Chilean painter, with whom he often met in his trips to New York City, and added acquaintances there as well. He appreciated everything that New York represented, citing specifically his visits at the Museum of Modern Art as particularly enriching experiences.[37]

36 Pérez Oyarzun and Urrejola, "Series of interviews with Emilio Duhart," audio interview, Part 2 of 8.

37 Camplá Lehmann, "Modernidad y Contextualidad Regional: El Caso de Emilio Duhart," 468.

The school was much more strict, austere, and demanding than what Duhart had known until then. He appreciated gaining rigor and knowledge, but at the same time, he expressed that he lost his innocence and naivete, a fact that he qualified many years later as somewhat of a loss. Unfortunately, he did not elaborate on what that lost innocence and naivete could have represented to him. However, among the great benefits of his stay at Harvard were all the observations that he accumulated in terms of architectural pedagogy, which he would reference when back in Chile working as a professor at the Pontifical Catholic University in Santiago, a period that will be elaborated later in this book.

Duhart had great affection and respect for Gropius, but he could not abide by what was being projected around TAC a non-hierarchical architectural team association founded in 1946 with Gropius, Norman Fletcher, John Harkness, Sarah Harkness, Robert McMillan, Louis McMillen, and Benjamin Thompson. This organization was in its planning phase when Duhart was around Gropius between 1942 and 1944. Duhart thought Gropius wanted him to stay and work with the group, but he felt like a stranger among the other associates. John Harkness and Robert McMillan were classmates at GSD, but Duhart does not mention them as people with whom he developed close relationships, a fact that might explain a lack of affinity between them. The Collaborative put into practice Gropius's method of working as a team rather than on an individual basis. Duhart thought and confirmed much later with the evolution of the TAC undertaking that working in a non-hierarchical kind of structure had serious consequences. According to him, Gropius's postulates, which were of great generosity and idealism, had a serious cost, which was the loss of the backbone of the architectural creative process. Working in teams in such ways entailed reaching in unison a common denominator, an effort that, to Duhart, "fatally involved a loss of substance."[38] And he added, "despite the fact that what the TAC produced was good, in general much higher than the average production ... TAC did not live up to what Gropius was committing to,"[39] which made him realize that he could never embark on a similar scheme. However, Duhart, all along in his career, often worked in collaboration with other architects, a distinction that is worth making. Years later he commented that in his office he was the architect, and the others were collaborators, selecting like-minded associates, people who had a basic agreement regarding work philosophy and architectural beliefs, and with whom he could engage in fruitful dialogs.[40]

As indicated by Alberto Montealegre and Humberto Eliash,[41] with Duhart you could never address a work of architecture in terms of style or aesthetics. In a similar note, Pearlman indicated that Marcel Breuer "did not speak [to the students] about the aesthetic of architecture, almost as if this were a taboo subject, but rather he addressed the layout of plans, whether or not something could be built, and how the individual elements might all work together."[42] This remark, presumably indicates that at GSD this might have been a credo that Duhart made his own. On that same line of thought, Duhart expressed some resistance to the work of Mies van der Rohe because, as he expressed it, "he was a man of style. He was one of the first to stylize modern architecture, shall we say. He grabbed it and turned it into style, very consciously,"[43] hinting at a certain disdain for that way of understanding architecture. And commenting on Marcel Breuer at the school, he said "he was a great architect ... very different. [He] had an enormous influence; a little stylistic influence. I couldn't see things ... stylistically."[44]

Duhart's master's class projects were comprised first of a master plan for a new industrial city, a community in Wayland-Weston, Massachusetts;[45] second, the Wayland-Weston School of Dramatic Arts for 1,200 students (pgs. 122-124), which represented a further development of a specific area of the master plan mentioned above; and third, a church.[46] These three projects represented an interesting progression to working at multiple scales.

Alberto Montealegre, the author of the first monograph on Duhart, defines the church project as completely modern, in which "volumes are related in a dynamic balance where vertical and horizontal tensions are in contrast and

38 Pérez Oyarzun and Urrejola, "Series of interviews with Emilio Duhart," audio interview, Part 6 of 8.

39 Pérez Oyarzun and Urrejola, "Series of interviews with Emilio Duhart," audio interview, Part 6 of 8.

40 Pérez Oyarzun and Urrejola, "Series of interviews with Emilio Duhart," audio interview, Part 6 of 8.

41 Alberto Montealegre was an associate of Duhart and the author of the monography on his work *Emilio Duhart Arquitecto*; Humberto Eliash is an architect and important historian of modernity in Chile.

42 Pearlman, *Inventing American Modernism*, 111.

43 Pérez Oyarzun and Urrejola, "Series of interviews with Emilio Duhart," audio interview, Part 2 of 8.

44 Pérez Oyarzun and Urrejola, "Series of interviews with Emilio Duhart," audio interview, Part 2 of 8.

45 Pérez Oyarzun and Urrejola, "Series of interviews with Emilio Duhart," audio interview, Part 5 of 8.

46 Cristian Berríos, *Emilio Duhart: Elaboración de un Espacio Urbano. Ciudad Universitaria de Concepción* (Santiago: LOM Ediciones/ Universidad del Bío Bio, 2017), 49.

in which the only way to perceive the whole is by moving around it. It is a space-time conception."[47] He refers to the notion of modern architecture as an articulated organism which can be read by way of an experiential walk-through to reveal the architect's arrangement of the different spaces and how those spaces flow into one another.[48] In the same monograph mentioned above, there is a photograph of the model of the School of Dramatic Arts projected by Duhart, with no further information. However, Cristian Berríos briefly describes the project through analysis of this photograph with some interesting observations. He describes it in the following manner: "a square-plan building is identified, with an internal patio that separates the [larger] volume [into several structures] … [additionally, a ring-shaped formation] around the internal patio defines the perimeter of the building …. On the ground floor the perimeter is transparent. A load-bearing structure supporting the suspended volume appears in contrast to the solid surface of the upper levels. The ground floor generates a canopy around its entire contour, which defines an intermediate space between … the public and private [spheres, and] integrating the volume to the urban system."[49] This description is striking when comparing it to the CEPAL building of the 1960s. The square elevated volume, with internal patios and transparent first floor formation reappears years later and the above description of a conceit of 1942-1943 almost correctly describes it as well.

47 Alberto Montealegre Klenner, *Emilio Duhart Arquitecto* (Santiago: Ediciones ARQ, 1994), 42.

48 Phone conversation with Alberto Montealegre on July 3, 2020.

49 Berríos, *Emilio Duhart: Elaboración de un Espacio Urbano*, 49.

Duhart summarized his stay at GSD in the following way: "It was a crucial phase that allowed me to directly access the contribution of the pioneers of contemporary architecture, with the facilities and rigor of a university that … was a place of international exchange. In Gropius, I found a person of exceptional human quality: honest, generous, and deep. With him, I honed my architectural thinking and the interest in technical as well as formal refinement. The work emphasized large urban plans and housing problems."[50] Duhart was finally obtaining an education in modern architecture, and GSD was one of the epicenters of the world in architecture pedagogy, providing essential first-hand contact with crucial figures shaping architectural theory and practice.

50 Emilio Duhart, Speech for Reception of the National Prize of Architecture, of the College of Architecture of Chile, August 18, 1977.

Emilio Duhart, Theatre for a School of Dramatic Arts

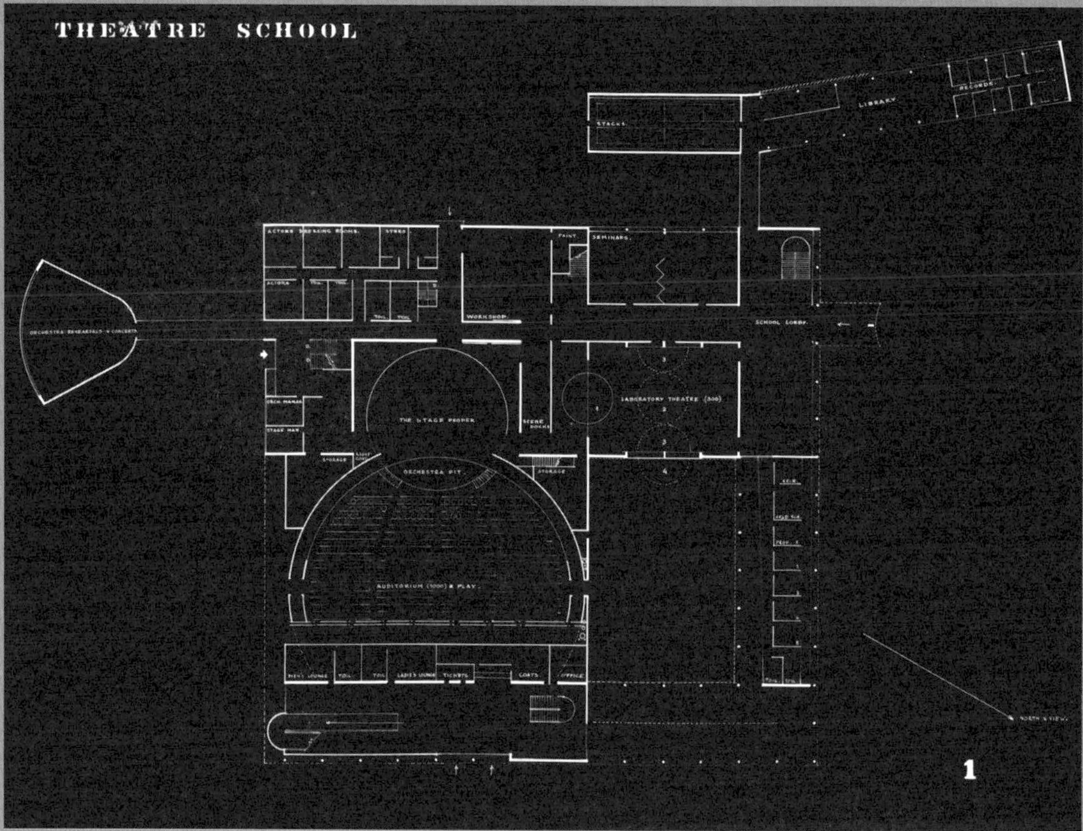

Emilio Duhart, Theatre for a School of Dramatic Arts, March-May 1943, photostats. School of Dance and Theatre, floor plans and elevations.

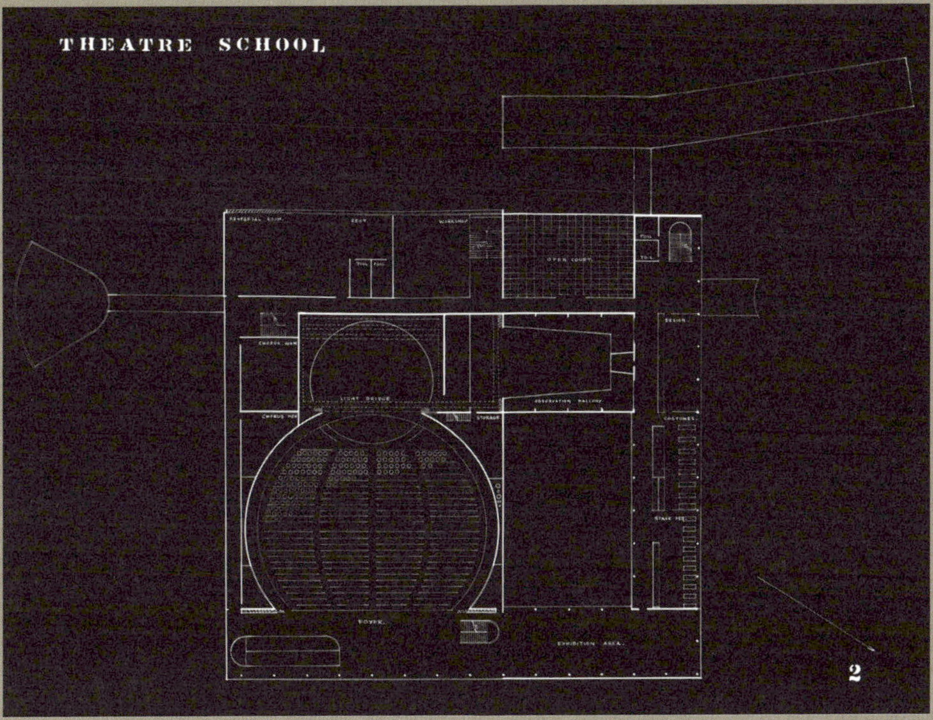
THEATRE SCHOOL
2

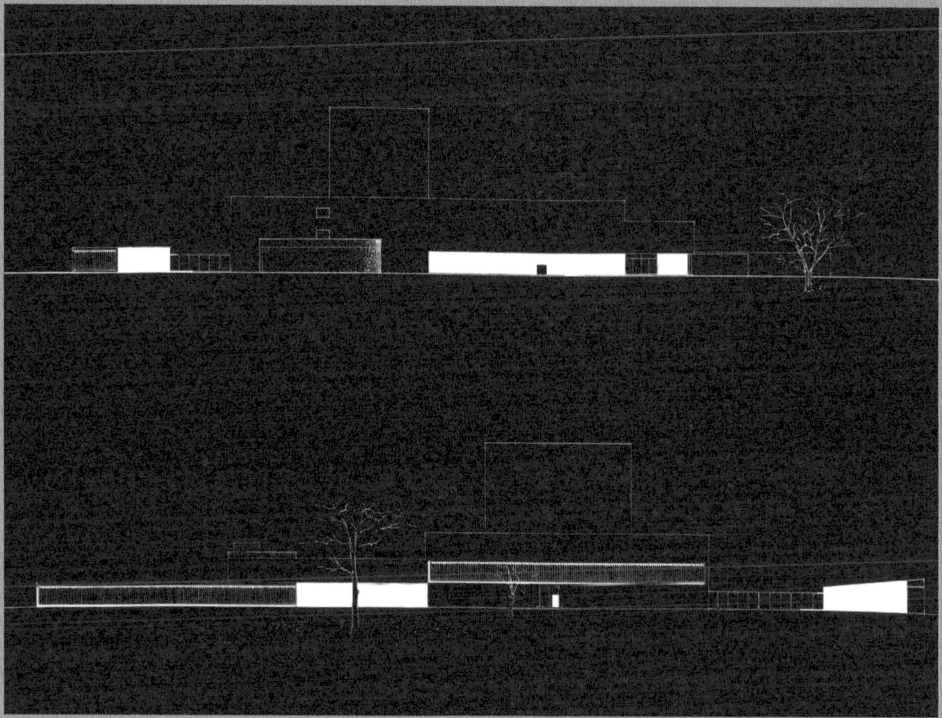

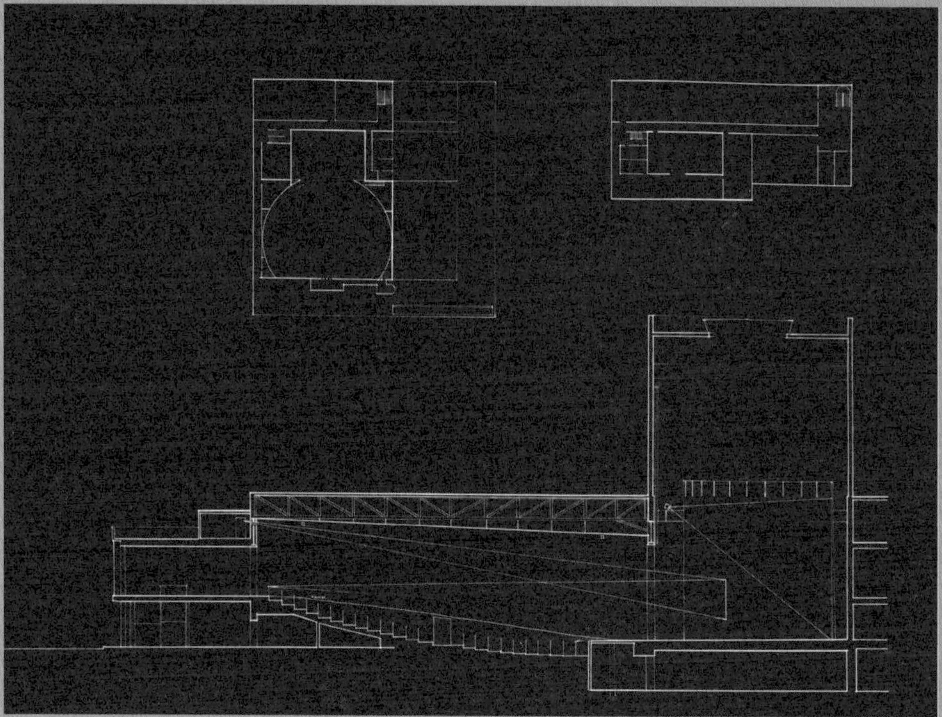

HARVARD UNIVERSITY
CAMBRIDGE
MASSACHUSETTS

GRADUATE SCHOOL OF DESIGN

DEPARTMENT OF ARCHITECTURE
WALTER GROPIUS — CHAIRMAN

October 15
1943

Mr. Emilio H. Duhart
1232 Fifth Avenue
San Francisco, California

Dear Duhart:

Thank you very much for your letter of October 4 telling me about your experiences in the west. I am very glad that you succeeded in getting work with Mr. Kump, to whom I ask you to give my best regards.

I hope very much that Mr. Kump will not forget the exhibition of his work for our School: I am looking forward to receiving his material.

I followed with great interest the results of the competition in which you won Second Prize. I was very much annoyed that the Forum brought my name in--which I think was entirely unnecessary. You and Pei have a very good scheme and I think it is even superior from a practical point of view to that which won First Prize, though the Saarinen scheme has certainly more publicity attractions and a type of flexibility which may be fertile for the future.

I cannot yet send you the new wording for our School pamphlet. It has only now been released by the Faculty and a final meeting will have to be held before it can be given to the printers. As soon as it is out I will be glad to send you a few copies.

Ati is in Black Mountain for the coming year and is exceedingly happy there. Mrs. Gropius joins me in wishing you both the very best for the future.

Sincerely yours,

Walter Gropius

Walter Gropius,
Professor of Architecture

WG/SR

Figure 27: Letter from Walter Gropius to Emilio Duhart, 15 October 1943.

PRE-FABRICATION STAGE IN THE UNITED STATES

As mentioned in previous sections, when Duhart left Chile to go to the United States, he worked for the Reconstruction and Relief Corporation, paying much attention to adobe as a low-cost material to presumably solve the housing problems of low-income people. In the late 1930s, this social problem was at a critical stage in the country due to the earthquake of 1939 and large-scale urban migration. Gropius's predicaments and interest in social issues, housing, and urban planning coincided with Duhart's concerns before getting to Harvard. As previously mentioned, while abroad, Duhart kept searching for solutions in the application of adobe in seismic terrains, a persistence aimed at providing a chcap and definitive answer to homelessness and overcrowding. Recalling the times after he presented his degree project, he noted, "I started to feel motivated to do something for the country in terms of architecture .... Furthermore, I was also very motivated by the development of the social type [of architecture]"[51] Seemingly, Harvard education's emphasis on the architect's social responsibility might have made Duhart feel a high affinity with the school's teachings.

51 Pérez Oyarzun and Urrejola, "Series of interviews with Emilio Duhart," audio interview, Part 7 of 8.

Moreover, the great attention to prefabrication at the school might have been an issue of keen interest to Duhart and in agreement with his interest in low-cost architecture. During his stay in the United States, Duhart participated in the Designs for Postwar Living Competition (1943), worked with Gropius and Konrad Wachsmann for their Packaged House System (1943), and for Ernest Kump in prefabricated housing for workers for the Kaiser Shipyards in California, among other educational projects (1944).

Duhart's interest in prefabrication was part of a broader phenomenon. Since the beginning of the twentieth century, in both Europe and the United States, the notion of prefabrication, with the idea of applying industrialization in architecture, motivated many architectural innovations. They were focusing on producing shelter to large sections of the population, and to applying industrialization based on the assembly line and mass production in times of economic hardship and war.

PREFABRICATION DURING WARTIMES

Prefabrication is a notion that had its origins in Europe, but during wartime it took a firm hold of the architects' imagination in the United States. The industrialization of construction has its most unambiguous origin in the Crystal Palace for the Great Exhibition of 1851 in London, a cast iron and plate glass structure, designed by Joseph Paxton. Moreover, in his book Histoire Mondiale de l'Architecture et l'Urbanisme Modernes, Michel Ragon cites an early 1915 catalog of the aviation and automobile industrialist Gabriel Voisin. In it, Voisin advertised "transportable houses, which are delivered by us on trucks, ready to be lived three days after the order."[52] Subsequently, Le Corbusier designed for him a series of prefabricated houses, including Domino in 1915, Monol in 1919, Citrohan in 1921.[53] As stated by Ragon, Walter Gropius was entertaining the idea of prefabrication since 1909. He was involved in the construction of prefabricated dwellings in the Haus am Horn in 1923, the Dessau-Törten Housing Estate in 1926, and a house in Weissenhof Siedlung in 1927, at the landmark modern urban residence settlement in Stuttgart, an exhibition complex of seventeen houses. In this latter example, Gropius presented a prefabricated single-family unit dry mounted with a light metal frame. In 1942, while at Harvard, Gropius and Konrad Wachsmann created the Packaged House System, a comprehensive prefabricated scheme for flexible housing.

52 Michel Ragon, *Histoire Mondiale de l'Architecture et de l'Urbanisme Modernes – Tome 2* (Paris: Casterman, 1972), 118-119.

53 Ragon, Histoire Mondiale de l'Architecture et de l'Urbanisme Modernes, 119.

In the United States, interest in prefabrication mounted exponentially. This was driven by, on the one hand, the national defense expansion of the war years and their newly created defense centers, and on the other hand by a massive migration inside the country. Approximately fifteen million people were drawn to those centers in search of well-paid work. To supply the military with low-cost and swift construction, in addition to housing for countless workers and their families transferred to new production centers and in need of shelter, prefabrication was the predominant answer. Among the most prevalent prefabricated, mobile, and easy-to-transport structures created at the time was the Quonset hut. The military used these as barracks, hospitals, and chapels. By 1946, an estimated 170,000 had been fabricated and lifted around the world. In relation to housing, whole new human enclaves were created near industrial complexes. The Farm Security Administration built thousands of minimum-standard single-family units in roughly forty-eight states. Notably, and as pointed out in the introduction to the book *World War II and the American Dream* by Donald Albrecht, "the surge in defense home building brought on by wartime migration gave impetus to America's long-standing interest in prefabricated housing. Architects, engineers, and manufacturers responded by inventing unusual residential schemes,"[54] adding that "in fact the war acted as

54 Albrecht, "Introduction," in *World War II and the American Dream*, XXIII.

a catalyst for both postwar suburban development and modern architecture, incorporating the avant-garde into the mainstream."[55]

55 Albrecht, "Introduction," in *World War II and the American Dream*, XXIII.

DESIGNS FOR POSTWAR LIVING COMPETITION

During his stay in the United States and while still at GSD, one of the notable moments for Duhart was the participation in 1943 with I.M. Pei in the Designs for Postwar Living Competition. Upon meeting as classmates, Duhart and Pei became close friends, and it was Pei who proposed to Duhart that they enter the competition as a team. They obtained second prize, gaining considerable attention and notoriety. Duhart gives us a hint of what this competition represented to them when he remarked, "since we were very up to date with the latest trends ... in that contest with Pei, we summarized almost all the pregnant ideas of the time, including prefabrication, which was a bit of the specialty that we had developed .... We got the second prize .... All the magazines wanted to know about our project. So, all of a sudden, we made ourselves known."[56]

56 Pérez Oyarzun and Urrejola, "Series of interviews with Emilio Duhart," audio interview, Part 1 of 8.

The competition was organized by *Arts & Architecture*, a pioneering West Coast magazine advocating for modern architecture in the United States that was becoming very prominent. In 1938, editor and owner John Entenza had acquired its former more conservative iteration called *Californian Arts & Architecture*. The most notorious and significant campaign of *Arts & Architecture* was the promotion and sponsorship of the Case Study House Program in 1945, the historically significant modern residential architecture commissions in which many well-known architects participated.[57] Case Study 8, the Eames House, became an icon of the mid-twentieth-century modern house. As the website of the Eames House states, "the design used prefabricated materials ordered from industrial and commercial catalogs."[58] The magazine published the project in May 1949.

57 Charles and Ray Eames, Craig Ellwood, Pierre Koenig, Richard Neutra, Eero Saarinen, Raphael Soriano, among others.

58 Eames Official Site Case Study House 8: The Eames House, https://www.eamesoffice.com/the-work/case-study-house-8/.

Under the leadership of Entenza the magazine was transformed, and he embarked on a series of essential measures to highlight and promote modern architecture. Among them, he enlisted as editorial associates noted modernist architects such as Harwell Hamilton Harris (October 1939), William Wurster (September 1940), Charles Eames (May 1942), Richard Neutra (February 1942), Eero Saarinen (December 1945), and Rafael Soriano (January 1947).[59] In 1942, Ray Eames was assigned to design the covers of the magazine to signal its clear modern leanings. In 1943, the magazine created the Designs for Postwar Living Competition, in which I.M Pei and Emilio Duhart participated.

59 Neil Jackson, *The Modern Steel House* (New York: Routledge, 2016), 43.

As mentioned previously, profound social, economic, and technological changes were underway. Entenza was predicting that the effects of the war with its technological advances could have consequences on the building industry. Besides, the imminent demand for new affordable housing for the return of veterans once the war ended, and the exponential growth of the population in California due to internal migrations, raised new concerns about the need for affordable and expeditious fabrication of new housing. Entenza particularly paid attention to prefabrication, a recurring theme of the magazine, about which "Entenza and [Charles] Eames reached the conclusion by early 1944 that the idea of the modern postwar house would best be served by taking advantage of the new science and technologies emerging from the industries in the war effort."[60]

60 Matthew W. Fisher, "Prefabrication and the Postwar House: the California Manifesto," Iowa State University, https://scholarworks.umass.edu/cgi/viewcontent.cgi?article=1014&context=wood

Announced in April 1943, the first Designs for Postwar Living Competition was devised as a probe of emerging technologies in the design of a modest house. Twenty-three building materials manufacturers sponsored it, and the jury members consisted of Charles Eames, Gregory Ain, Richard Neutra, John Leon Rex, and Sumner Spaulding. Among the 512 submissions, there were three awarded projects, and all three prize-holders incorporated prefabricated components in their designs. First place went to Eero Saarinen and Oliver Lundquist; second place went to I.M. Pei and Emilio Duhart; and third place to Raphael Soriano. From January of 1944 and in successive issues, the *Arts & Architecture* magazine published the winning schemes.

The I.M. Pei and Duhart project (figs. 28 & 29) was an approximately 1,819 square-feet technologically driven design of a prefabricated two-story orthogonal structure with a separate service unit annexed to the center, which consisted of a smaller two-floor rectangular addition with rounded corners. A connecting anchorage space between both acted as a discreet entry hall. The exterior of the building's main body was made out of an unspecified panel system hung on frames (figs. 30 & 31). On the first floor, the central body structure contained the living and dining areas, and on the second floor, the bedrooms. The attached semi-independent service unit, with its rounded corners made of prefabricated pressed steel panels, tectonically expressed the industrial and technological era. It contained on the first floor the kitchen and a powder room, and on the second floor, two bathrooms, and a mechanical room. The downstairs interior had an open plan configuration with the kitchen connected to the central space through expansive transparent windows (fig. 32). The guiding principle of the plan was a grid and the outer main structure's carcass consisted of an abstract rectangular and vertical lattice, subdivided in a fractional horizontal manner, according to the needs

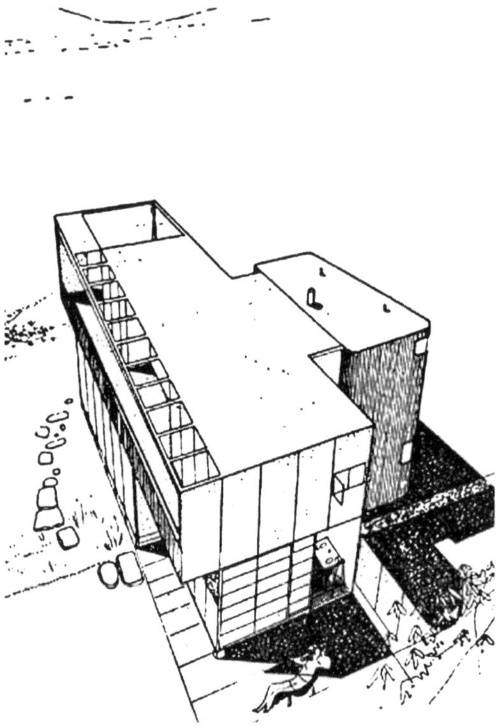

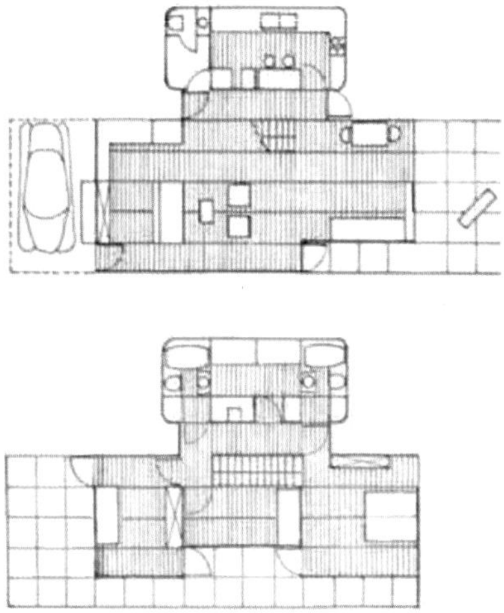

Figures 28 & 29: I. M. Pei and Emilio Duhart. Designs for Postwar Living Competition, perspective drawing and floor plans, 1943.

of the inner spaces (i.e., window, terraces,) or presumably, to give texture and variety to the exterior surface. The structure was a compact whole containing the terraces on the first and second floors, and the garage on the first floor.

As observed by Neil Jackson, the architects sought to reformulate the nature of the living space as no longer centered around the housewife at the kitchen, facilitating efficiency and time-saving concepts, expressed particularly through the design of the kitchen and the separation of the service unit from the living space (figs. 28 & 29). On the other hand, the other central concept was "to organize an economic space with one aim: to vitalize the family as the most important cell of democracy"[61] for post-war times. Neil Jackson adds that "In the same way that Pei and Duhart had focused on the importance of the family, Charles Eames–himself, presumably, a student of human behavior–saw the family as the ultimate benefactor of industrialization."[62] Pei and Duhart designed the house (1943) prior to the Case Study houses (1945), which were all anticipating how in the United States during the postwar years the family unit would become such a highly regarded concept, with the suburban lifestyle and its clearly delineated gender roles.

61 Neil Jackson, "Metal-Frame Houses of the Modern Movement in Los Angeles: Part 1: Developing a Regional Tradition," *Architectural History* Vol. 32 (1989), 160, http://www.jstor.com/stable/1568566

62 Jackson, "Metal-Frame Houses of the Modern Movement in Los Angeles: Part 1: Developing a Regional Tradition", 162.

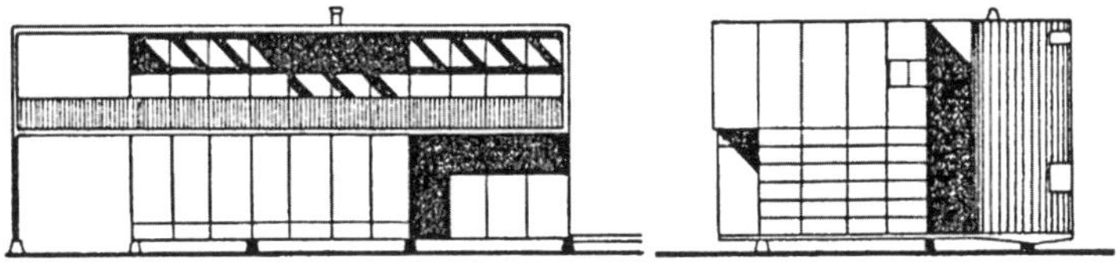

Figures 30 & 31: I. M. Pei and Emilio Duhart. Designs for Postwar Living Competition, elevations and interior perspective drawing, 1943.

Figure 32: I. M. Pei and Emilio Duhart. Designs for Postwar Living Competition. Perspective drawing of a kitchen, 1943.

STARTING A CAREER – THE UNITED STATES 1943-1944

Upon completing his studies at Harvard, Duhart worked for a short period with Gropius and Konrad Wachsmann on the Packaged House System at the General Panel Corporation. Subsequently, he moved to San Francisco for about a year to work with the architect Ernest Kump in prefabricated worker housing for the Kaiser Shipyards in California and other educational projects.

THE GENERAL PANEL CORPORATION

Gropius and Wachsmann had been preoccupied with housing's industrialization for decades. Gropius was involved in developing theoretical thinking about prefabrication since 1909, and as previously mentioned was involved in the design and construction of several structures in Europe inspired by that notion. Konrad Wachsmann, born in 1901 in Germany, was an architect noted for his contribution to the mass production of building elements. During the 1920s, he worked as the chief architect for the German company Christoph & Unmack, one of the most important European building companies that offered prefabricated components. Wachsmann was concerned with mass manufacturing by using standardized building units, which could be assembled in multiple ways with varying results. He knew Albert Einstein, for whom he designed a summer house in Brandenburg, Germany, using the prefabricated system by Christoph & Unmack. Einstein provided the connection, and Gropius invited Wachsmann to live in Lincoln, Massachusetts to escape from Europe, where he was in danger. By the end of 1941, Gropius and Wachsmann began collaborating on a prefabricated housing system called the Packaged House System. The prototype "featured an innovative framing system based on the 'wedge connector,' an X-shaped, cast-steel mechanism within wood-framed panels. The wedge connector could be configured in multiple ways and fastened together using only a hammer, eliminating the need for screws, nails, or bolts and making house assembly very fast and simple indeed: the company claimed a crew of eight workers could build a 1,000-square-foot, two-bedroom house in less than a day."[63] The system was an all-encompassing prefab scheme of a kind unique at the

63 "General Panel Residence," Los Angeles Conservancy, accessed July 7, 2020, https://www.laconservancy.org/locations/general-panel-residence

Figure 33: E. Duhart H., Walter Gropius, "Growing and Shrinking House", 1942-1945: Perspective.

time. It had evolved from a conception devised by Wachsmann in France right before emigrating to the United States. The basic blueprint had come from Wachsmann, who had been thinking in this direction for many years. However, Gropius was instrumental in providing the financial, conceptual, and logistical support to develop it. In September of 1942, the General Panel Corporation was established, and the manufacture of the Packaged House's prototype began. On February 23, 1943, it was mounted and unmounted in one day in Somerville, Massachusetts. However, by May 1945, the house had still not been produced. The company began searching for a plant for industrial production of the invention, raising funds to finally locate it in the former Lockheed Factory in Burbank, California, a repurposing of an aircraft fabrication plant. The factory production plant was ready by mid-1947, but the commercial aspect of the enterprise never took off. Only about 200 units of the Packaged House were produced and by 1950 the factory was closed.

Emilio Duhart did not provide any details of his time working at the General Panel Corporation. He only remarked that Wachsmann was a fascinating character and that he worked for a short period for the GPC, right after finishing his studies at Harvard (Spring 1943.) We can conclude that he was collaborating with the company beginning after the unveiling of the prototype in Somerville and until maybe the end of 1943 (fig. 33). The close contact with Gropius and Wachsmann must have represented an invaluable intimate look into both architects' minds in the context of practicing architecture.

Additionally, after his introduction to prefabrication at Harvard and his prefabrication competition project with I.M. Pei, this experience further immersed Duhart into this type of architectural approach. This involvement might have given him a unique insight at thinking about architecture from an entirely new perspective. It represented a systems thinking mindset in the sense that the elements with which structures were created were prefigured, yet they were open to multiple applications and in mutual interaction with one another.[64] In a way, this type of operation may function as a mechanical puzzle for space creation. At GPC, architecture was devised out of universal component parts to produce a variety of results. The materials with which architecture was to be assembled comprised pre-existing units that were utilized according to the aspirational outcome.

64 The connection between prefabrication and system thinking was inspired by Alicia Imperiale's paper at the 2012 ACSA Conference: https://www.acsa-arch.org/proceedings/Fall%20Conference%20Proceedings/ACSA.FALL.12/ACSA.FALL.12.8.pdf

THE WEST COAST – ERNEST J. KUMP, PREFABRICATION AND EDUCATIONAL ARCHITECTURE

Duhart's trip to the United States could not be completed without an exploration of the developments happening on the West Coast. Towards the end of his stay, Duhart moved to San Francisco, where he worked for approximately one year for the architect Ernest Kump. Through this experience, he added additional newfound expertise in modern educational architecture.

Of this phase Duhart remarked with vivid enthusiasm, "then I wanted to work in the working-class cities on the West Coast. A [whole] industry was being built out of nothing. In the three years of war, the United States tripled its industrial output, something that was incomprehensible and sounded like a wild revolution. And there I was in the middle of this phenomenon: entire prefabricated cities were built to be demolished later …."[65] Duhart was referring to the massive migration taking place within the United States and specifically when the West Coast experienced its most dramatic transformation. At this time California, Washington, and Oregon increased their population by forty percent, a reality that "resulted in economic and demographic shifts that permanently altered the nation's regional balance, giving the West Coast new-found status and independence."[66]

65 Pérez Oyarzun and Urrejola, "Series of interviews with Emilio Duhart," audio interview, Part 2 of 8.

66 Donald Albrecht, "Introduction," in *World War II and the American Dream*, XXII.

Of his work on the West Coast Duhart adds, "I had the opportunity to work on prefabrication, a topic that was very much in force during the war, which I got to know especially through my work in the workers' cities built in California for the Kaiser Shipyards …."[67] He added that, "everything was

67 Esparza Saavedra, "Emilio Duhart Harosteguy," 168.

prefabricated. It was fantastic. Thousands of workers were needed, along with their families, so it was necessary to create real cities from scratch and overnight[68] .... I did not work directly for the construction of ships, but in the new [settlements] for engineers and shipyard workers. I worked in housing and social equipment, schools, mainly in prefabrication. It was very interesting, but naturally, I also visited the shipyards in full operation .... I was dazzled, and I found the same enthusiasm of my youth for shipbuilding."[69] When Duhart went to San Francisco, he was immersed in an explosive new circumstance. In 1941, the Kaiser Shipyard located in Richmond, near San Francisco, turned into the largest shipbuilding operation on the West Coast, driving a meteoric rise of the population, from 23,600 in 1940 to 93,700 in 1943.[70] The new incomers were mainly sheltered in temporary structures, and between 1939 and 1945, worked to produce for the Kaiser Richmond Shipyard company about twenty-eight percent of the total ships commissioned by the U.S. Maritime Commission, an endeavor that was worth $1.8 billion.

68 Pérez Oyarzun and Urrejola, "Series of interviews with Emilio Duhart," audio interview, Part 2 of 8.

69 Camplá Lehmann, "Modernidad y Contextualidad Regional: El Caso de Emilio Duhart," 468.

70 "History of Richmond," City of Richmond, California, accessed July 9, 2020, http://www.ci.richmond.ca.us/112/History-of-Richmond.

As mentioned above, in San Francisco Duhart worked for Ernest Kump (1911-1999), an American modernist architect who became best known for his educational architecture. However, he was also notable for his many ideas and applications of prefabrication and modular structures. Kump studied as an undergraduate at the University of California, Berkeley, completing his degree in 1932, and then his master's degree at GSD in 1941. Under Gropius's supervision, he submitted a school design, the Fowler Grammar School, as his thesis project. He got early recognition when the Museum of Modern Art selected his Fresno City Hall project, a collaboration with partner Charles Franklin, as one of the most significant designs built between 1932 and 1944. In 1947 Kump participated in Princeton University's Bicentennial Conference with other distinguished architects such as Aalto, Gropius, Philip Johnson, Richard Neutra, Frank Lloyd Wright, William Wurster, and others. Among his outstanding works are Fresno City Hall (1941), United Airlines Airport Terminal in Merced (1947), Foothill College in Los Altos, California (1962), De Anza College in Cupertino (1967), the U.S. Embassy in Seoul, Korea (1959) and Crown College, University of California, in Santa Cruz (1967).

Referring to his work with Ernest Kump, Duhart reflected, "I got to work with an architect with whom I remained friends: Ernest Kump. He was a school specialist and his influence [in this matter] was very beneficial to me. It aided me a lot on my return to Chile [to handle] my first jobs in school [design]"[71] (fig. 34). In 1993-1994, remembering the first school he designed in Chile in 1948 with a group of colleagues, he observed

71 Pérez Oyarzun and Urrejola, "Series of interviews with Emilio Duhart," audio interview, Part 2 of 8.

Figure 34: Sergio Larraín G-M, Emilio Duhart and Ignacio Covarrubias, architects. Colegio Compañía de María, 1955-58.

> "because of what I had done in California with Ernest J. Kump, who was a great specialist in educational architecture, I came back [from the United States] strongly interested and also trained in school [architecture]. That I think is very important to mention, because I have a debt … he was a former Harvard student, too, but much older than me, with a great capacity for work and extraordinary dynamism. And it helped me because I learned a lot."[72]

72 Pérez Oyarzun and Urrejola, "Series of interviews with Emilio Duhart," audio interview, Part 2 of 8.

Although Duhart and Kump maintained an enduring friendship, his acknowledgement of Ernest Kump revealed something impending and is remarkable for two distinct reasons. One is the fact that this comment was made by Duhart many decades later, when a lot of his career trajectory had been accomplished. Looking back at his experience with Kump, he realized that he was indebted to him. Presumably, this reckoning is related to the lack of public recognition of Kump's influence. The second reason is that Duhart had moved to California for his expressed desire to work for the working class's new temporary cities springing up on the West Coast. However, through his contact with Kump, he encountered an entirely new field of interest: modern educational architecture, a field in which he would be invested later.

Duhart's time in the United States (1942-1944) was an intense phase in which he had to accomplish as much as possible compressed in as little time as possible. In 1942, a few months before leaving for Harvard, Duhart's wife had given birth to their first child, Michelle. The baby had been left behind with the grandparents, and the couple needed to go back to her promptly. After a stay of two years, the couple returned home.

ESTABLISHING MODERNISM IN CHILE 1944-1951

The years between 1944 until 1951 represent an intermediate phase in Duhart's career. It is characterized by the initiation of his work in academic and professional practice. He realized he was changed by the austere, demanding, and strict environment he had left, which resulted in an awareness that a discipline and a method had to be rigorously followed. In addition, he had also acquired considerable technical expertise: he had been professionalized. In contrast to his work as a student, where he could conceive real but utopian projects, he was going to apply the accumulated knowledge into a distinct reality. He was back into a place where he had done very little but where his seminal thoughts about architecture had been born, and he was eager to contribute. His understanding of the practice of architecture included that the forethinking of the project was the most important aspect and it entailed the consideration of "many things: from a whole cultural baggage and experience, the attention to life, the identity of the site, the identity of the client and his needs. Above all the identity of the fundamental references of place and time. And it is sometimes necessary in the conception [of architecture] to be aware that a stage had to be marked,"[73] indicating he was on a path that had to have specific demarcations. Seemingly, those demarcations were the expression of the thinking phase where the architect found himself, in time and space.

73 Pérez Oyarzun and Urrejola, "Series of interviews with Emilio Duhart," audio interview, Part 6 of 8.

He acknowledged the importance of his passage through the United States by saying that this experience was funneled into his architectural and academic practice. He was still looking for an authentic expression that involved nature, clarifying that "architecture is a thing that emerges from the physical world … [and] theory and poetry emerge from it,"[74] an analogy that makes reference to an inflorescence in a specific direction: from matter to theory and poetry.

74 Pérez Oyarzun and Urrejola, "Series of interviews with Emilio Duhart," audio interview, Part 2 of 8.

As for his experience in prefabrication, he concluded that it could also be applied beneficially in Chile. He said, "I felt that it was necessary to go in that direction. It was not easy because when I returned to the [Reconstruction and Relief] Corporation, [and] I realized all that effort I had made, with the adobe program and so on, had been lost like water in the sand."[75] He indicated that a fundamental preoccupation with housing for the dispossessed was somehow

75 Pérez Oyarzun and Urrejola, "Series of interviews with Emilio Duhart," audio interview, Part 2 of 8.

at the center of his thoughts, adding that "the needs [were] so immense, there was a problem not only of architecture as aesthetics but of architecture as an ethic."[76] This statement is crucial for his understanding of architecture as part of human subsistence and as part of a life support system.

76 Pérez Oyarzun and Urrejola, "Series of interviews with Emilio Duhart," audio interview, Part 2 of 8.

REFORMING ARCHITECTURE EDUCATION AND ACADEMIC LESSONS

As demonstrated by Verónica Esparza Saavedra, in her doctoral thesis called "Emilio Duhart Harosteguy—Un Arquitecto Integral: 1935-1992," one of the three pillars of Duhart's career was his academic work. Through it, he channeled important lessons to a student body who greatly benefitted from his firsthand contact with the epicenters of modernism. For that reason, he constitutes one of the crucial personalities in modern architecture in the country and an essential character of its lineage.

When Duhart returned to Chile in 1944, he was invited by his thesis professor at the Pontifical Catholic University at the School of Architecture, Sergio Larraín García-Moreno, to join him as his assistant in his fifth-year workshop, a position Duhart held until 1949. That same year he became professor of urbanism and later in 1951 he was appointed full professor in architecture.

Among his students he had the fame of knowing prefabrication and countless technical novelties which were unknown in Chile at the time. They referred to him with the moniker "the prefabricated monster," inspiring in them both respect and a degree of fear. In his teachings Duhart gave primacy to the mixing of contemporary architecture and urban planning, focusing as he stated it, on working-class housing to solve great economic and social problems, taking his students to fieldwork for project development.

Duhart's academic work marked the point of departure of his exploration in the field of urbanism. When he returned to Chile, he joined the faculty of the Pontifical Catholic University as an assistant professor with two colleagues, Mario Pérez de Arce and Manuel Marchant Lyon. The projects prepared by the students represented for Duhart and his young colleagues a theoretical laboratory where they could test their ideas on urbanism and low-income housing. These academic lessons were an important focus to Duhart, stating that, "urban planning and regional planning are increasingly important, and it is necessary to properly train the professionals responsible for this great architecture,"[77] a statement that altogether justifies his choice of academic themes.

77 Emilio Duhart H., "En Busqueda de la Tradicion Viva," *Architectura y Construcción* N°16, September 1949, 18.

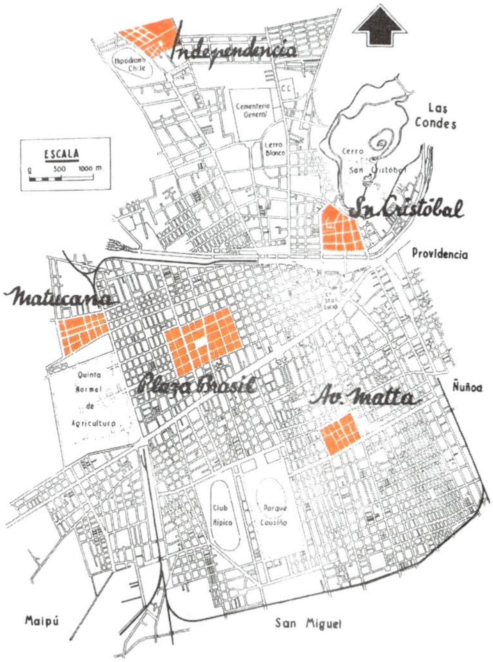

Figure 35: Left; Map of Santiago with 5 sectors to be intervened by students.

Figure 36: Above; Model showing the volumetric proposal in the Independencia sector.

The first academic exercises given to the students were projects aimed at realistically addressing the shortage of housing, choosing five representative sectors of Santiago for their critical urban problems, presenting interventions on the already-built ground (figs. 35 & 36). The proposals had to be economically viable, and each sector represented an urban unit with its own life. The projects included spaces for housing, green areas, recreation, parking, circulation, schools, churches, theaters, libraries, clubs, restaurants, grocery stores, post offices, among others. Each project was preceded by an in-depth study of the existing conditions and the communities' current forms of life and activities.

Another example of a project developed, this time independently by Duhart and his students, was a Beer Factory settlement, published in the September 1949 issue of the magazine *Arquitectura y Construcción*. It consisted of the proposal for a brewery factory and housing for workers in the Renca commune in Santiago (fig. 37). The project consisted of three areas: the factory, the urbanization for the industrial personnel and their families, and, for housing, prefabricated construction based on the General Panel Corporation system, simplified and adapted to a combination of wood and

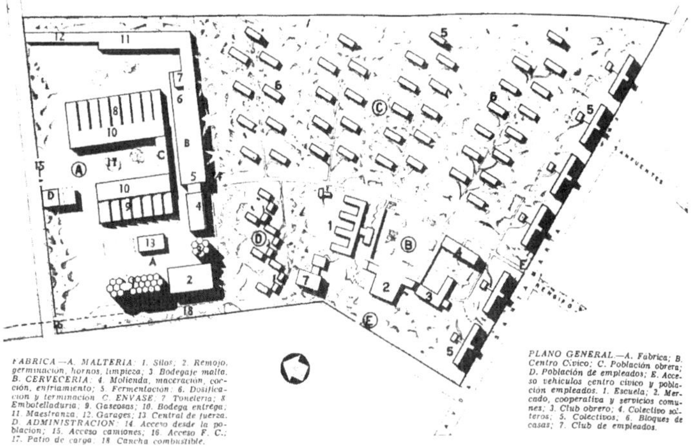

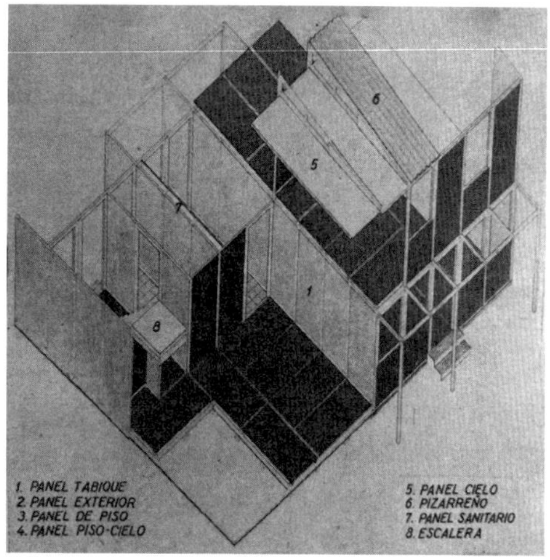

Figure 37: Left; Emilio Duhart's student workshop, brewery, general plan.

Figure 38: Above; Emilio Duhart's student workshop, brewery, prefabrication, perspective.

plaster (fig. 38). The factory was located on a 50.7-acre lot that had enough groundwater to supply the industry at a low cost. The housing sector was separated from the industrial sector by a line of trees and shrubs. It was secluded from the outside of the community and the orthogonal buildings were scattered in linear blocks within a park that was maintained with the water reclaimed from the brewery. Employees and workers were placed in separate areas and the school was located on the way to the factory. There was only one curved vehicular road with easy access to the market that, together with the workers' club, the public offices, and the theater (for supplementary use as a gym and art room) formed the civic center. The other routes of circulation were only for pedestrian use. The general distribution was functionally adopted considering expedited supply channels, access to both areas of the compound, the prevailing winds, and the surrounding physical existing conditions of the terrain. The students' projects achieved notoriety for their innovative nature and had a particular relevance in the architectural field because they were published in their entirety in the May 1946 issue of *Arquitectura y Construction*, a vital publication at the time.

Everything learned abroad converged in an academic career to which the architect assigned a lot of time and effort. Duhart's academic work brought him a very meager income, but it completed his architectural ambitions with significance. As stated by Duhart, it "duplicated our chores but gave greater insight and value to the ideas that we promoted."[78] This effort yielded results and Duhart observed that from 1950 onwards, the School of Architecture

78 Duhart, "Speech by Architect Emilio Duhart Harosteguy on Receiving the National Award for Architecture from the Chilean College of Architects," 5.

at the Pontifical Catholic University allowed the exercise of a new rigorous modern architecture and urban planning in the country.

Concerning education, these results are profoundly intertwined with parallel activities Duhart was invested in. Simultaneously to teaching, Duhart devoted himself for years to the struggle to bring about the pedagogical changes that he and his generation considered of fundamental importance. Returning from the United States, Duhart was full of knowledge and experiences that turned into a decisive contribution to the process of the school's educational reform. According to Duhart, Sergio Larraín García-Moreno and other professors were open to architecture with modernist inclinations, as he put it, a "modern style" he did not entirely agree with, but he considered that the professors' openness permitted some agency for the students' modernist leanings. However, starting around the middle of the 1940s, the school environment was embroiled with the discontent of the students and some professors who advocated for a modernist curriculum, fully rejecting the teachings of the French Beaux-Arts system. This initiated a long struggle that lasted about fifteen years. The desire for change mounted until it reached its peak in 1949, with the university in crisis, and the paralysis of all activities due to the total absence of the student body. This culminated in a grand theatrical rebellion where about 200 students brought their books on classical architecture, made a mound at the center of the court of the main campus, and set them on fire. The leadership of the university capitulated, changes began to take shape and consequently, Sergio Larraín García-Moreno was made dean of the school in 1952.

These dramatic developments were not unique to the Pontifical Catholic University. Similar events were unfolding at the University of Chile's School of Architecture, where students were also the generators of change. The reform document had been developed by a group of students who had sought the assistance of the Hungarian architect Tibor Weiner (1906-1965) who lived in Chile between 1939 and 1948, and who was an academic at the university at the time. Wiener studied at Bauhaus-Dessau and worked with Hannes Meyer, director of the school until 1931. Weiner provided advice and collaborated in the elaboration of the new curriculum, which as a result was profoundly influenced by the Bauhaus precepts. In 1946 a reform at the University was implemented, resulting in a much less contested struggle at this educational institution.

Between 1945 and 1947, Duhart and Alberto Cruz Covarrubias, his colleague and professor of the first-year workshop at the school, developed a close friendship with both being animated by the desire to change architectural education at the school. They spent countless evenings at Duhart's house, speculating about what that change needed to be. Of these informal gatherings Duhart recalled

> "I came with all the Bauhaus background and had many things up to date, I told Alberto [about] … a lot [of my interactions] with Walter Gropius, of all the Bauhaus people … [and] what was done at Harvard at that time, [about] contemporary teaching in architecture … [and] Alberto wrote and wrote on rolls of drawing paper …. [We were] trying to put all these ideas in order to create something that was coherent … through the years, let's say 45, 46, 47. In those three years I think we did … a reflection … [that was] very coherent about what the school could do."[79]

79 Pérez Oyarzun and Urrejola, "Series of interviews with Emilio Duhart," audio interview, Part 3 of 8.

Asked about what those reflections consisted of he explained:

> In recognizing that architecture was in a stage in which a fundamental re-examination of the pedagogical principles was required. For example, the adoption of a system to work on specific cases closely linked to reality and to the country's social, historical, and geographical landmarks. To prepare the new generations for the task that was ahead and that was dictated … [by] what the country needed … assuming its great regional and city problems, mainly social architecture problems. And a complete revision of the dogmas that made architecture a declarative thing for the privileged classes, [and instead] in search of an architecture that reflects the needs of the communities. In general, not an architect/client …. Now, the way of working was to privilege teamwork, a much greater participation of students in the preparation of programs, in the methodology adopted in each workshop, and a permanent search for what could be the architecture of our times in historical and geographical Chile. It is difficult to synthesize in two or three sentences.[80]

80 Pérez Oyarzun and Urrejola, "Series of interviews with Emilio Duhart," audio interview, Part 3 of 8.

Duhart was elaborating a new pedagogical paradigm for the education of Chilean architects, a curriculum based on his recent experience abroad, with the aim of resolving society's regional and urban problems.

According to Duhart the reform in architectural education of 1949 was a result of a shared inquiry of the vast majority students and professors who demanded a new curriculum, which by then was fully matured, and that originated from those long conversations between Duhart and Alberto Cruz. However, he remarked that the effort was collective, and he cited some of the professors that were involved in the struggle among whom were eminent figures of the modern movement in Chile like Alberto Piwonka, Mario Pérez de Arce, and Héctor Valdés.

In 1952, Alberto Cruz Covarrubias, the most progressive figure of the movement, seemingly causing additional conflicts at the Pontifical Catholic University in Santiago, left with poet Godofredo Iommi to found one of the most radical pedagogical institutes of architecture in the Latin American latitudes, in the city of Valparaíso. The Institute of Architecture at the Catholic University in Valparaíso, the School of Architecture of the University of Chile, and the School of Architecture of the Pontifical Catholic University, both in Santiago, constitute the three poles of tensions from which architectural modernity was channeled and established in the country. It is important to note that the Bauhaus had two distinct entry points during the Forties in the country: one through Duhart and his experience at Harvard in close proximity with Gropius and the other through Tibor Weiner and his participation in the elaboration of the reform of 1946 at the University of Chile.

Years later, in 1967, growing tension within the university faculty led to the resignation of Sergio Larraín García-Moreno as dean of the Faculty of Architecture. Simultaneously, in the late 1960s, Chile was experiencing momentous political changes. Salvador Allende would become president in 1970 with a government committed to implementing profound institutional, political, and economic reforms. The country had become polarized, and under internal and external pressure, the nation had become increasingly unstable. Duhart had lost his position at the university, and his clients had begun withdrawing some projects from among the many works in progress. Discouraged by these events and the need to distance himself from the tensions and competition within the profession, he accepted the offer of a teaching position at the École des Beaux-Arts in Paris in 1970. A new stage in his life began when, over a few years, he gradually moved to France, where he taught until 1983 and worked on numerous projects until 1992.

Figure 39: Emilio Duhart. Pinto Santa-Cruz House, 1944-45, Santiago, Chile. Perspective drawing, 1945.

Figure 40: Emilio Duhart and Sergio Larraín G-M. Partial model of Villa Presidente Ríos, 1947, photograph.

BUILDING A PROFESSIONAL CAREER IN CHILE

When Duhart returned from the United States to Santiago in 1945, he rejoined the Reconstruction and Relief Corporation, an organization that had kept his position during his absence. However, this affiliation was short-lived. As mentioned before, Duhart had carried out various investigations, both in the United States and in Chile, and aspired to use adobe for low-income housing in a contemporary way. To him, "this plan of the development of a contemporary construction using adobe was not accidental but [the result of the application of] simple and obvious logic … and the representatives [of the Corporation] rejected the idea,"[81] thus leading to his resignation.

81 Pérez Oyarzun and Urrejola, "Series of interviews with Emilio Duhart," audio interview, Part 2 of 8.

He went to work independently and then starting in 1945, also in association with Sergio Larraín García-Moreno, his most influential teacher at the university, turned friend and associate. The office of Larraín and Duhart was active between 1945 and 1957 and developed a series of projects which gave them prestige and recognition. Duhart commented that during the early period of the partnership, they both had to struggle with great difficulty to develop a contemporary architectural expression. He was alluding to the contemporary local resistance to the modernist architectural language. There were very few architects doing the same, but those who did were united in solidarity as a consequence of the limited reception of their modern stance in their environment. The office advanced a unified and skilled modern composition, adopted new building technologies, and after a few years became one of the main references of the modern idiom in the country.

Between 1945 and 1951, Duhart embarked on a period of intense professional activity, sometimes independently and others in partnership with Larraín, working in residential, institutional, educational architecture, and urban planning. Of those projects that stand out during this period, we can briefly highlight some of them, and others will be further analyzed in the upcoming section about Duhart's body of work. He designed about ten single-family houses, of which he remained especially fond of the first one, the Pinto Houses (1945) (fig. 39), a duplex dwelling in an architectural language that "definitely broke with the practice of styles [and] which was extremely austere, sparing, simple and refined,"[82] utilizing pre-manufactured and rationalized construction. The paired houses were controversial for their purist modern expression and gained notoriety for being a complete novelty. Over time they turned into a model that was endlessly reproduced in various forms, especially in middle to low-income neighborhoods. In 1946, Duhart independently designed President Ríos's New City (fig. 40),

82 Pérez Oyarzun and Urrejola, "Series of interviews with Emilio Duhart," audio interview, Part 2 of 8.

Figure 41: Emilio Duhart, Alberto Piwonka, Sergio Larraín G-M, and Mario Pérez de Arce, architects. Colegio Verbo Divino, 1948, Santiago.

between Concepción and Talcahuano (at about 350 miles from Santiago to the south), considered the first modern city built from scratch in Chile.[83] Finally, of the notable works Duhart did in partnership with Larraín before 1951 is the Colegio Verbo Divino (1948) (fig. 41). The architects also included Mario Pérez de Arce and Alberto Piwonka, who are now considered eminent figures of the modern movement in Chile. It was a school design that turned into a pioneering undertaking in this category of establishment. It was the result of its conceptual connections with the international debate on educational architecture: buildings had to be flexible, with proper sunlight and ventilation, with contact with nature, and in which predetermined dimensions for the classroom were the central units. This structure also turned into an archetype of reference for educational architecture in the country.

83 Berríos, *Emilio Duhart: Elaboración de un Espacio Urbano*, 65.

After eight years of abundant practice in Chile, Duhart felt the need for a sabbatical year to reconnect with Paris and his younger years. In 1951, he took advantage of a scholarship awarded by the French Government to travel to France and study at the Institut Supérieur d'Urbanisme de la Sorbonne in Paris, which he accepted.

AT THE SOURCE OF MODERNISM II - WORKING FOR LE CORBUSIER IN PARIS

Duhart started his classes at the Sorbonne, but they were interrupted after only two or three months. The program was not what he had expected. Having had a lot of experience with urbanism, many of the courses did not satisfy him. The program not only included architects but also engineers and urban administrators, which resulted in it being devoid of the focus and level of expertise that Duhart had expected. He realized that he would not get much from these studies and became disappointed and unmotivated.

At the same time, Gropius was also traveling to Paris to preside over the International Advisory Panel to create a new international headquarters of UNESCO in the City of Lights. The advisory panel also included Ernesto Rogers, Lucio Costa, Sven Markelius, and Eero Saarinen. They were summoned to determine how and where the new building was to be built.[84] Gropius and Duhart exchanged letters and agreed to meet in Paris. Duhart recounts that they saw each other along with some of Gropius's advisory panel colleagues a lot.

84 "UNESCO Building," Architectuul, accessed July 24, 2020, http://architectuul.com/architecture/unesco-building

Duhart, frustrated with his studies, had begun to look for other alternatives. He was aware of Le Corbusier's enormous influence and how challenging it would be to try to work for him. Candidates from the world over were waiting to be accepted to work at 35 Rue de Sèvres. However, in Paris, upon learning of Duhart's frustrated attempt to collaborate with Le Corbusier, and after seeing photos and drawings of his works in Chile, Gropius proposed to introduce him, and shortly after obtained an appointment with Le Corbusier for Duhart. Of their first encounter Duhart recalled that he

> "enter[ed] a 2.26 x 2.26 x 2.26-meter black cubicle, with a single reflector aimed at a polychromatic wood sculpture. With his glasses up, like a pioneer of aviation, he looked carefully at each photo and each drawing [of my work], making somewhat harsh and thoughtful comments: 'C'est très architecturé … ça manque un peu de chair …. Gropius m'a dit que vous saviez vous débrouiller …' ('it is very architectural … it lacks a bit of flesh …. Gropius told me that you know how to manage') he put my portfolio down and … told me briefly that my table would be waiting for me next Wednesday. Then

> I found myself installed under the great painting of the master at the end of a wide corridor that constituted the workshop. He called it l'Atelier de la recherche patiente (the Patient Research Studio.)"[85]

85 Emilio Duhart, "Recuerdos de Le Corbusier," *ARS* #6 September 1987, n/a.

Duhart left the Sorbonne and worked at the atelier Le Corbusier from the end of December 1951 to November 1952.

35 RUE DE SÈVRES – ATELIER DE LA RECHERCHE PATIENTE

Beginning in 1929 until the end of his days in 1965, Le Corbusier made more than a dozen trips to Latin America, maintaining a close relationship with his contemporaries from the world of architecture on that continent. He perceived Latin America as ripe territory for applying his theories, giving lectures on architecture and urbanism, and conceiving urban designs and other projects. This interaction led to numerous commissions that were mostly never realized but remained an essential legacy for the history of the field.

Especially after World War II, the Atelier Le Corbusier was a dominant pole of attraction for architects. It was a hub of cultural exchange, a generator of modernism throughout the world, and was extremely difficult to access. The introduction of Latin American architects to the atelier was made possible through several channels. It could be made through either a diplomat representing their countries in France, or artists living in Paris. It could also be initiated through meetings with Le Corbusier that occurred in their own countries, or through the Spanish architects Antoni Bonet and José Luis Sert, members of the CIAM. Finally, just a few introduced themselves by knocking at the door. Some Latin American architects accepted at Rue de Sèvres were of French descent such as Duhart, Roberto Matta (Chilean, 1911-2002), and Rogelio Salmona (Colombian 1929-2007),[86] for whom knowing the French culture and language greatly facilitated their integration into the studio.

86 Ingrid Quintana Guerrero, "La colonie latino-américaine dans l'atelier parisien de Le Corbusier," *Les Cahiers de la recherche aechitecturale urbaine et paysagère,* (February, 2018): 3.

The collaboration with young architects from Latin America at 35 Rue de Sèvres was prolific and, throughout the years numbered about twenty. It was one of the most numerous groups of foreigners who managed to be selected into Le Corbusier's studio (Greeks and Americans followed).[87] Among them, four Chileans were part of it: Roberto Dávila Carson (in 1932), Roberto Matta Echaurren (in 1935), Duhart (1951-1952) and Guillermo Jullián de la Fuente (in 1958), who became in a short period, head of the workshop until Le Corbusier died in 1965.

87 Ingrid Quintana Guerrero, "La colonie latino-américaine dans l'atelier parisien de Le Corbusier," *Les Cahiers de la recherche aechitecturale urbaine et paysagère,* (February, 2018): 2.

Figure 42: Le Corbusier in his painting studio, photograph, author unknown, circa 1960.

At the atelier the period between 1950 and 1959 is characterized by a crucial influx of work and a diversity of collaborators. André Wogenscky was the *chef d'atelier* until 1957, Fernand Gardien was technical coordinator (1946-65), Jane Heillbuth was the secretary, and Yannis Xenakis, an engineer and musician, who during his earlier years was exclusively in charge of structural and climate control related questions. Additionally, a core group of architects represented the more stable personnel that included two French, André Maisonnier (1947-59) and Jacques Michel (1952-56), two Colombians, Germán Samper (1949-52) and Rogelio Salmona (1948-54), one Indian, Balkrishna Doshi (1951-56), one Korean, Kim Chung-up (1952-1955), one Japanese, Yoshizaka Takamasa (1949-1955), one Greek, Georges Sachinidis (starting in 1953) and one Pole, Olek Kujawski (1949-55.)[88] All of them spent an important period of time at 35 Rue de Sèvres, ranging from four years to around a decade or more. The rest of the associates remained in the atelier for an average of one and a half years.[89] When Duhart worked there, the number of architects hired was reduced to thirteen, and in 1952 it progressively increased to twenty. They later gradually decreased in number until the end of Le Corbusier's days.[90]

88 Clara Elena Mejía Vallejo, "Rogelio Salmona y Le Corbusier: Sobre la Permeabilidad del Hacer" (PhD Thesis, Universidad Politécnica de Valencia, 2015), 58-60.

89 Ilario Leone,"Lo Studio di Le Corbusier nel Secondo Dopoguerra. Passaggi, Pratiche e Esiti," Parte I (PhD diss., Politecnico di Torino, Politecnico di Milano, 20013), 20-34.

90 Mejía Vallejo, "Rogelio Salmona y Le Corbusier: Sobre la Permeabilidad del Hacer," 55-56.

Le Corbusier was attentive to the skills and weaknesses of his collaborators. He assigned them the jobs that would achieve the best result according to their attributes, and fostered successful associations between them. In the atelier the work was shared, and the authorship diluted from the circulation of the projects through various hands.[91] The existing plans at the Le Corbusier Foundation that are signed by a single associate are very rare, with the number of architects who participated in a single drawing often reaching up to five.[92]

91 Mejía Vallejo, "Rogelio Salmona y Le Corbusier: Sobre la Permeabilidad del Hacer," 55-56.

92 Mejía Vallejo, "Rogelio Salmona y Le Corbusier: Sobre la Permeabilidad del Hacer," 55-56.

Duhart was one of the few Latin American associates who arrived at this office with ample professional experience. He joined Le Corbusier's team in late 1951, when all the atelier's efforts were focused on the project of Chandigarh.[93] Of his colleagues he remarked on their assignments:

93 Mejía Vallejo, "Rogelio Salmona y Le Corbusier: Sobre la Permeabilidad del Hacer," 56.

> All of them were mainly working on projects in India. The last stages of the Unité d'habitation in Marseille were entrusted to Wogenscky, the eldest of [Le Corbusier's] assistants. I remember, among others, Jacques Michel, in charge of Villa Sarabhai, Doshi the Indian, who developed the [Mill Owner's Association] Building in Ahmedabad, Samper the Colombian, who produced the Chandigarh Capitol Secretariat, Xenakis, engineer and music expert in acoustics … and Maisonnier ... I had great friendship with all of them and I met with them again decades later in Paris. The atmosphere of the workshop was simple and austere, continuously working all day, interrupted by a pause in the 'Café de l'Oiseaux' at the foot of the building.[94]

94 Duhart, "Recuerdos de Le Corbusier," n/a.

Duhart recalled that Le Corbusier usually arrived in the afternoons, devoting his mornings to painting and writing (fig. 42):

> The afternoons with him were intense. He went from table to table giving definitive shape to each of the stages of the projects. It was not easy, he was demanding, sometimes sarcastic but always truthful in the face of difficulties and his own doubts which he shared with everyone. From the relationships at work, rooted in the same rigor and passion for architecture, a direct relationship emerged, without compromises, of frankness tempered by humor and a background of gentleness. Sometimes briefly, he opened himself, confiding about his interrogations, the realizations of the work in the future …. India had impressed him strongly, he had immense respect for her and was nourished by his travel experiences which he shared with us. He wondered about Chile and Latin America, with which he felt great affinity.[95]

95 Duhart, "Recuerdos de Le Corbusier," n/a.

Duhart also added, "he was not a teacher, but in his own way he was a pedagogue; he was interested in problems … while working with him, he got involved, so it was very enriching."[96]

96 Pérez Oyarzun and Urrejola, "Series of interviews with Emilio Duhart," audio interview, Part 4 of 8.

During his time at 35 Rue de Sèvres, at first, Duhart was assigned some general interventions for the Chandigarh Capitol, but then he was entrusted with the development of the preliminary draft for the residence of Mr. Hutheesing in Ahmedabad, four to five hours away from Chandigarh. Surotam Hutheesing was president of the Mill Owner's Association in Ahmedabad, the textile center in the north-west of India where Le Corbusier built four projects: The Museum, the Mill Owner's Association Building, the Villa Shodhan, and the Villa Sarabhai. Hutheesing, Mr. Shodhan, and Mrs. Sarabhai were part of a group of rich and sophisticated patrons who "wished to convert their money into the more elevated currency of art."[97]

Three schemes were part of the development of the project, of which Duhart participated in the progression. The first sketch of the Villa Hutheesing shows a three-floor monumental orthogonal dwelling and as stated by Duhart it "was a kind of platform with overlapping cubicles protected by Colombian-type vaults on four slender pillars; the set oriented according to the prevailing winds of the region."[98,99] In this first sketch the vaults were suspended above the structure, and Duhart realized that because of the wind speeds, the hanging "parasols" would be in jeopardy. Re-thinking this design feature, Duhart added that, "after long studies of the initial solution, it was abandoned, and I looked for an alternative, remembering similar problems in seismic architecture, in the use of vertical plates instead of thin pillars. This profoundly modified the form of the first sketches, enriching the spatial relationships of the house, without betraying the first intentions."[100]

Cristián Berrios observes that at the Fondation Le Corbusier, in Plan 6463, there are three versions of the Villa Hutheesing [101] (fig. 65) where two more iterations of the original idea can be observed. In the second sketch the floor plan turns more square, and the suspended vaults are replaced by a plain slab. In the third sketch the floor plan is square, and the "roof" is a suspended platform. In all cases the overall structure is composed of cubic volumes intercepted by generous openings and brises-soleil to control shade, air, sunlight, and views.

The design for Mr. Hutheesing was developed at the same time as the house for the mayor of Ahmedabad, Chimanbhais, and both commissions ran into trouble. As stated by William Curtis, "the architect had spent three hard years working on the mayor's residence, even reaching to the point of choosing coloured marble inlays for the interiors .... The Chimanbhais seemed to think of the building in the most conventional of terms and tried to get Le Corbusier to change features that were to him integral to the conception.

97 William J. R. Curtis, *Le Corbusier: Ideas and Forms* (London: Phaidon Press, 1986), 202.

98 Duhart, "Recuerdos de Le Corbusier," n/a.

99 In their essay "Mid-20th Century Colombian Vaults, A Contemporary Tradition," García, Magdalena and Medina state that "Le Corbusier visited Colombia in 1950... the Casa Pizano...built by the local architect Francisco Pizano de Brigard. The house inspired Le Corbusier's two buildings covered with tile vaults: the houses Sarabhai (1955) and Jaoul (1955), which would be very influential in turn."

100 Duhart, "Recuerdos de Le Corbusier," n/a.

101 Berríos, *Emilio Duhart: Elaboración de un Espacio Urbano,* 88.

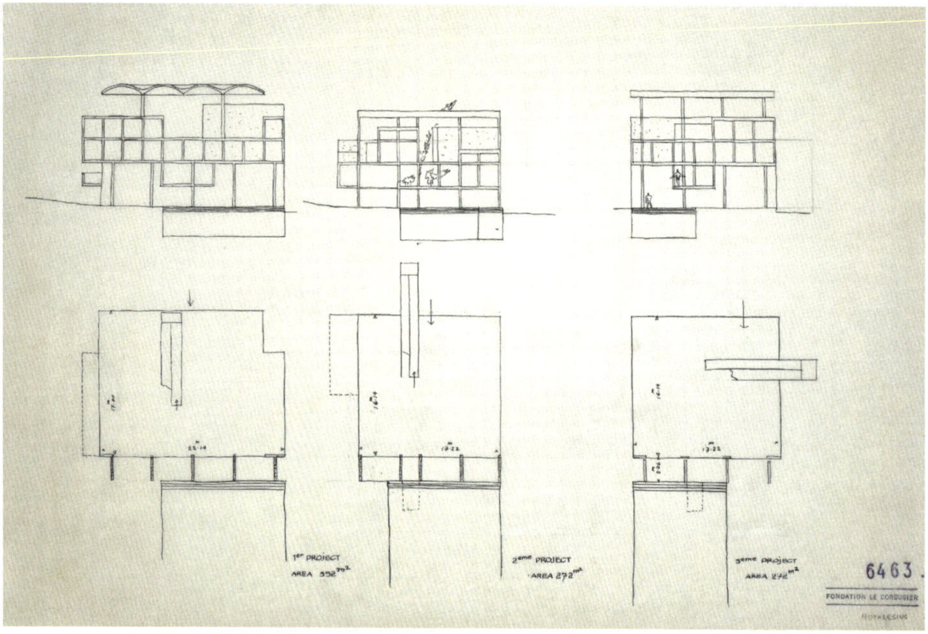

Figure 43: Le Corbusier. Three drawings of the different stages of development of the Villa Shodhan project, 1951-1954. Drawing FLC 6463.

Figure 44: Le Corbusier. Villa Shodhan, photograph, author unknown, 2015.

There were also squabbles over the late payment of fees and travel expenses. The Hutheesing commission encountered similar difficulties, and it became clear that the client did not wish to proceed."[102] The house commission for Hutheesing eventually was taken over by Shodhan and as stated by Duhart, the final construction plans of the house were resumed by Balkrishna Vithaldas Doshi (born 1927) since Duhart was returning to Chile. After his somewhat short but intense period of work with Le Corbusier, Duhart left with an enduring relationship with the master and a friendship that lasted until the end of his days. Duhart reunited with him for the last time in Paris in 1965, just a few weeks before Le Corbusier died.

102 Curtis, *Le Corbusier: Ideas and Forms,* 207-208.

The final realized Villa Shodhan (figs. 43-44) is, at first glance, a generically modern reinforced concrete yet porous mass. However, it could not be transplanted to any other region in the world and is the direct product of its specific locality. It is composed of a single, stereotomic, imposing square concrete volume with a parasol type of open roof. It features a complex integration of internal and external spaces, characteristic of traditional Indian architecture. The design allows occupants to experience the outdoors and the comfort of being indoors while remaining inside the home. The air flows throughout the interior spatiality. The work on the outer north-west and south-east walls is an iteration of the Corbusian brise soleil as a delicate response to the burning Indian sun and functions as parapets to the wind's direction. The brise soleil is amplified in size, turning into terrace-size features, and acting as a kaleidoscopic filter not only functioning as a heat reducer but deflecting sunlight to produce internal natural light. Moreover, the brise soleil fulfills the supplementary role as a barrier for high winds.

Le Corbusier had carefully observed the Indian architectural tradition in Ahmedabad to distill from it the features that he would consider accommodating in the design of Villa Shodhan, through their translation into his modern idiom. The residence is a dwelling that provides shelter for sun, wind, and rain allowing a smooth internal life under any of the prevailing weather conditions. It also subscribed to the vernacular Indian architecture. For instance, it provided a double-height entrance hall, a sign of status, and a feature of Ahmedabad's traditional wooden houses. The roof acts as a garden referencing the parasols existing in some traditional Indian temples.

As seen in the description of the house, such translation is not literal but rather conceptual and obscured, with a result where the final embodiment of the project (its representational side) is differentiated from its "being" (its ontological side). It constitutes an integration of certain specific regional characteristics drawn together with modernism, in such a way that forces you to look simultaneously at its ontological and representational planes and posing an inherent contradiction: it is made one way but presents itself in another. The hybrid result needs careful observation to distinguish what the arrangement is really accommodating.

Making a balance of the lessons learned at the atelier Duhart observed that "with 'Corbu' I learned a lot about architecture. He reinforced with his example my will not to weaken in the face of the hardships of the life of an architect and not allow myself to be invaded by compromises."[103] As the Hutheesing affair had been very frustrating and dramatic at the atelier, Duhart witnessed first-hand how difficult it was for Le Corbusier not to surrender to the client's will, to preserve the integrity of the project.[104] Being witness to this episode must have been a lesson of resistance and moral rectitude vis à vis the profession's practice.

103 Duhart, "Speech by Architect Emilio Duhart Harosteguy on Receiving the Nacional Award for Architecture from the Chilean College of Architects."

104 Pérez Oyarzun and Urrejola, "Series of interviews with Emilio Duhart," audio interview, Part 4 of 8.

However, above all, in the latter quote from Duhart, it is noticeable that he expressed having learned a lot about architecture, not urbanism or technicalities, a subtlety that deserves much attention. This enunciation also declared a crucial balance to his GSD education where the architect acknowledged having learned more about urbanism and technical advances. However, the participation in the development of the Villa Shodhan and the way Le Corbusier was interpreting the regional, intermingling it with his own modern idiom, seems to have been the enduring lesson Duhart obtained from his experience at the atelier. Additionally, it is compelling to reflect on what supplementary learnings Duhart might have gleaned from his contact with Le Corbusier.

In her thesis on the architect Rogelio Salmona, Clara Elena Mejía ventures to analyze Le Corbusier's working system.[105] She studied the body of work that the architect completed between 1944 and 1958 through the documents stored in the Fondation Le Corbusier and observed a clear consistency in the proceeding for developing his designs, a persistent method that she attributes to his capacity for high productivity. She posits that this method is at the base of his "patient search." She concluded that the development of the project began with recurrent basic floor plan configurations such as the high-density linear blocks (for homes and offices), the square-plan buildings (for homes, offices, museums, infrastructure projects and more), and buildings composed of parallel volumes (for low-density residential complexes). Le Corbusier then continued with the common progression which he rigorously followed, step by step, in every observed project documentation, progressing toward the

105 Mejía Vallejo, "Rogelio Salmona y Le Corbusier: Sobre la Permeabilidad del Hacer" 41-53.

structural system, followed by the volumetric configuration, continuing with the relationship with the landscape, to finally conclude with the material selection.

As denominated by Le Corbusier when he speaks of the "*atelier de la recherche patiente*," architecture creation requires search and patience, both of which imply time, a lot of time. In this systematic mode of working, the "patient search" method could perhaps be a profound productive insight that Duhart acquired and that he could apply and make recourse in his practice, taking away a very scientific and structured way of approaching architecture. This way of working was in stark contrast to the one postulated by Gropius's TAC where the developmental process was in the essence collective and did not come up from a single mind. As stated by Duhart, he did not abide by that way of working, believing instead that one person needed to conduct the undertaking to preserve the project's integrity.

Clear parallels can be traced between Le Corbusier and Duhart to his working methods as described in interviews with three of his collaborators in the CEPAL Building, Alberto Montealegre, Cristián De Groote, and Oscar Santelices. In his office, Duhart worked in a separate room. Every so often, as Le Corbusier used to do, he would go around the associates' desks to supervise the project's progress in one-to-one discussions.

According to Montealegre, the original ideas were always Duhart's, and the collaborating architects developed them under his supervision. Duhart was always involved in all stages providing regular instructions. He had control over everything done but was open to suggestions from his associates.

Duhart elaborated first on the project's conceptual proposition, and the general concept defined the rules of the game. Montealegre comments that "Emilio's office work ... was always very conceptual,"[106] adding that "you were never searching for a form. The project started with an idea, and the form appeared as a surprise based on the requirements ... the form surfaced from the project development. Emilio allowed himself to be governed by a certain rigor but with the flexibility to allow opportunities to appear."[107] Montealegre adds, "a plan was drawn ... that plan was analyzed ... [and a] solution was drawn. [the solution] was reached through several iterations."[108] There was no preconceived vision of what the architect wanted, but there was an exploration in which Duhart sought the convergence of the structural requirements and its form.

106 Cristián Izquierdo, "Interview with Alberto Montealegre," in "Traducciones: Intención/Palabra/Representación – Produccion del Anteproyecto para Naciones Unidas," in *Taller VII de Investigación*, Professor Fernando Pérez Oyarzun, 2005.

107 Izquierdo, "Interview with Alberto Montealegre," in "Traducciones: Intención/Palabra/Representación – Produccion del Anteproyecto para Naciones Unidas."

108 Izquierdo, "Interview with Alberto Montealegre," in "Traducciones: Intención/Palabra/Representación – Produccion del Anteproyecto para Naciones Unidas."

Furthermore, Montealegre adds that "the architect's way of working is complex, it is laborious, it means patience,"[109] suggesting that with Duhart, as in the atelier of Le Corbusier, the architectural process was a manifestation that emerged after countless hours of examination. Montealegre also describes the difficulties that his collaborators had to endure. He characterizes Duhart as a stubborn character who always "*t*ried to do the unrealizable."[110] Oscar Santelices reveals that Duhart "did not draw the plans himself, but rather dictated them."[111] He also gives us insight into the CEPAL project's evolution, revealing that it began with the square floor plan. The last thing made was the project's model, which draws a parallel with Le Corbusier systematic method unearthed by Clara Elena Mejía.

As previously revealed, Duhart's life made him a fortunate witness to the development of the twentieth century's modern architecture. His trajectory through the two epicenters of modern architecture of the twentieth century, the Graduate School of Design with Walter Gropius and the Atelier Le Corbusier, provided him with a privileged platform of direct contact with the two great masters of its creation. His encounter with Gropius helped develop his architectural thinking and interest in technique, focusing on urban planning, housing problems, and prefabrication. With Le Corbusier, Duhart got an insider view into the architectural process. He experienced the architect's systematic and patient method, presumably acquiring more in-depth insight into the discipline of architecture through a position of having observed the functioning of Le Corbusier's mind in action. With both Gropius and Le Corbusier, Duhart discovered that constructive dialogue and patience are two inescapable components of the practice of architecture. Although exceptional, these outstanding opportunities could have simultaneously presented themselves as significant overbearing challenges. However, he was not eclipsed by the masters and turned the lessons learned into a personal construct.

Finally, as previously indicated, there are a limited number of studies on this architect's life and work. Additionally, Duhart never comprehensively collected the thoughts that structured his architectural practice, such as in a publication, believing that his work spoke for itself. That explains the effort made in previous chapters to distill his thought process by reconstructing his bibliographical journey, opinions, and recollections scattered throughout interviews and miscellaneous written articles by the architect himself. In the following and final chapter, a survey of his body of work will be conducted through a critical analysis seeking to organize the total of his work under different perspectives, finding consistent threads, commonalities, divergences, and inconsistencies.

109 Izquierdo, "Interview with Alberto Montealegre," in "Traducciones: Intención/Palabra/Representación – Produccion del Anteproyecto para Naciones Unidas."

110 Izquierdo, "Interview with Alberto Montealegre," in "Traducciones: Intención/Palabra/Representación – Produccion del Anteproyecto para Naciones Unidas."

111 Cristián Izquierdo, "Interview with Oscar Santelices," in "Traducciones: Intención/Palabra/Representación – Produccion del Anteproyecto para Naciones Unidas," in *Taller VII de Investigación*, Professor Fernando Pérez Oyarzun, 2005.

LE CORBUSIER Paris, le 3 Novembre 1952

<u>A mes jeunes Amis architectes du Chili</u> :

Mes chers Amis,

Il paraît que vous êtes toute une bande de types épatants décidés à porter l'architecture sur son plan véritable qui est celui du service de l'homme.

Dès l'instant où l'on s'occupe des hommes, des femmes et des enfants dans tout ce qu'ils peuvent comporter d'attachant et d'admirable (défauts et qualités) on devient un architecte ~~extrêmement~~ complet. On laisse définitivement de côté les formules académiques et la moindre surface, la moindre distance, le moindre petit volume construit devient précieux comme le verre d'eau à l'explorateur dans le désert ou comme la réserve d'essence à l'aviateur à 6.000 mètres d'altitude.

Ce sens de la responsabilité des choses et de notre intervention vis à vis de ces choses est l'évènement sentimental moderne introduit dans l'architecture après une ~~son~~ éclipse d'un siècle presque.

C'est donc une question de sentiment; ce n'est pas une question d'argent et de bénéfice, mais une question de dévouement. Que ceux qui n'aiment pas cela, que ceux qui n'y trouvent pas leur compte se retirent en temps voulu et ne viennent pas encombrer de leurs désirs brutaux notre magnifique vocation.

J'ai pu finir l'Unité d'Habitation de Marseille grâce à vos jeunes camarades français ici, à Paris. Je ne vous souhaite pas de vivre toutes les difficultés que les cinq années de Marseille ont accumulées sous nos pas, mais quand vous rencontrerez des difficultés devant vous, ne vous détournez pas; saisissez-les au cou.

Et bonne chance !

Le Corbusier

LE CORBUSIER

35, RUE DE SÈVRES - PARIS (6e)
TÉL : LITTRÉ 99-62

Figure 45: Letter from Le Corbusier to his Chilean architect friends, 3 November 1952.

ARCHITECTURAL AND URBAN PLANNING CONCEITS IN THE LAND OF THE OCEAN

Analyzing the architectural work of Emilio Duhart in Chile, from 1940 until 1970, contains a certain level of complexity since, over time in its manifestations and at first glance, the work and its connecting threads are not easily revealed. Duhart's oeuvre is diverse and challenging to assess as a continuum, consisting more of a spiraling progression, where he adds successive elements to his conceptual toolset, leaving aside some aspects that will be revisited later, or creating entirely new approaches.

Of the challenge of appraising Duhart's oeuvre, José R. Camplá discerns "the difficulty of being able to establish common and permanent criteria [in Duhart's projects] over time, [and for] establishing clear stages."[1] He adds that Duhart's body of work represents a "variety of … projects in terms of programs, magnitudes, conceptual dimensions … different ways of approaching and materializing them."[2] Camplá remarks that this obstacle comes from "the limited bibliographic production about the work … [and] the lack of a written theoretical thought that could guide an interpretation and revision of his work today."[3] Nonetheless, in this book, his thoughts and theories on architecture and urban planning will be reconstructed to understand his body of work through a careful reading of the numerous writings on a variety of topics that the architect produced in specialized magazines and a limited number of interviews.

1 Camplá Lehmann, "Modernidad y Contextualidad Regional: El Caso de Emilio Duhart," 190.

2 Camplá Lehmann, "Modernidad y Contextualidad Regional: El Caso de Emilio Duhart," 190.

3 Camplá Lehmann, "Modernidad y Contextualidad Regional: El Caso de Emilio Duhart," 190.

In comprehending the architect's production as a whole, it is crucial to unveil how Duhart conceived of modernism and what were for him the fundamental concepts at the base of the disciplines of architecture and urbanism. Duhart regarded modernism in architecture as a manifestation demarking a new era. This nascent paradigm was a work in progress and a process made possible through a collective evolution. His work reflects the musings of a mind searching for possible answers to respond to an epoch that was still in development. In 1949 Duhart declared that modernism "will become [a phase] different from the previous [age], as was the Renaissance to the Middle Ages,"[4] and that it was "in a somewhat primitive gestation period."[5] He asserted that "architecture is made of slow, deep, and rigorous developments … [and is] a continuous process that suggests both sedimentation and erosion. From the accumulation of the different [collective] contributions, only those that are fundamental remain."[6]

4 Emilio Duhart H., "En Busqueda de la Tradición Viva," *Architectura y Construcción Nº16*, September 1949, 18.

5 Duhart H., "En Busqueda de la Tradición Viva," 18.

6 Emilio Duhart, "Una Mirada al Estado Actual de la Arquitectura," CA 28, Revista Colegio de Arquitectos de Chile, December 1980, 27.

About three decades later, he asserted that "modern times are made up of restless searches, of imbalances, contradictions and increasing accelerations of evolution,"[7] attributes that are reflected in his own work, itself a constant search echoed in the variety of his production. However, he also saw each design as a unique undertaking where the architect "must find the appropriate structures for each case and create prototypes, which will be refined with the creative contribution and sensitivity of generations of architects."[8] Duhart's ideas about modernism as a gradual elaboration and collective construct of a period may explain his constant quest and the application of multiple strategies to his output.

7 Duhart H., "En Busqueda de la Tradición Viva," 18.

8 Duhart H., "En Busqueda de la Tradición Viva," 18.

For Duhart, innovation and permanence were part of the equation, positing that the architect had to understand the constitutive elements of the world in which he lives and accept the correlation between "his art and his time."[9] As defined by him, the new era was "an overwhelming torrent that needed to be recognized with calm acceptance,"[10] and "the great current changes"[11] that the new paradigm would bring about would be essential for the profession's practice. He was suggesting that modernism was an unavoidable force and a defining period in history. Concurrently, Duhart proposed that the architect needed to reintegrate what he deemed the permanent values found in the architecture of the past (i.e., the Parthenon of Athens, the cathedral of Chartres, the drawing of Leonardo Da Vinci on the Vitruvian man) within the new era's framework. He was interested in finding the affinities, legacies, and lessons of past centuries, which could be integrated and re-applied.[12] Additionally, he declared that "adopting an unprejudiced and flexible position"[13] was fundamental to searching for "the foundations of a new historical cycle,"[14] conscious that the modern era had an expansive temporal permanence and finding the foundational and appropriate characteristic of the epoch was not necessarily evident.

9 Duhart H., "En Busqueda de la Tradición Viva," 18.

10 Duhart H., "En Busqueda de la Tradición Viva," 18.

11 Duhart H., "En Busqueda de la Tradición Viva," 18.

12 In a drawing for the Open Forum, Duhart makes a comparative study of his project with the Saint Mark's Square in Venice and with the Piazza Della Santissima Annunziata in Florence, Italy. He superimposes these squares' floor plans on those of the Open Forum, showing a willingness to establish correlations between them.

13 Duhart H., "En Busqueda de la Tradición Viva," 18.

14 Duhart H., "En Busqueda de la Tradición Viva," 18.

Decades later, responding to the advent of post-modernism, he outlined his conclusion on the evolution of modernism since the postwar years. He stated that the bygone "great masters announced or practiced the necessary transitions or spontaneous revisions [of modernism]: in particular in the later works of Le Corbusier (Ronchamps, La Tourette, Firminy) throughout the entire career of Alvar Aalto or that of Louis Khan. After them, a proliferation of constant creativity exists in contemporary architects: Sire and Pietilä in Finland, Utzon in Denmark, Tange, and Kikutake in Japan. Erskine and Sterling in England, Pei in the United States, Simounet in France, Kroll in Belgium, G. Böhm in Germany, and many others whose works fully reflect the evolution we are experiencing that respond validly and in various ways to the positive questions posed by … post-modernism."[15] In assessing the commonalities of these modern architects Duhart posited that "the architecture of the twentieth

15 Emilio Duhart, "Una Mirada al Estado Actual de la Arquitectura," CA 28, Revista Colegio de Arquitectos de Chile, December 1980, 27.

century shows … a natural evolution towards a growing incorporation of the expression of the geographical and historical values of each cultural region [reacting] against a trend towards international homogenization,"[16] inclinations he felt as constituent of his own practice and with which he agreed. He is also manifesting his awareness of one of the most critical perils of the movement, the erasure of local particularities when modernism is applied universally without discernment.

16 Duhart, "Una Mirada al Estado Actual de la Arquitectura," 27.

Furthermore, in modern times the discipline of architecture had to fulfill an additional objective. To Duhart, architecture had a role to play in the social order and was an art form for all and not the exclusive privilege of a minority. Through architecture, humanity could endow all people with solutions for a dignified existence. His commitment to practice urban planning as a tool for social transformation is best expressed when he declared "to avoid chaos and the formation of new oppressive forces, [there is an] imperative need to organize the territory and cities according to a harmonious and humane plan. Justice demands an order of urgency … reflected in the emphasis that the great programs of new human communities should have that will eliminate the universal plague of the slums. For these reasons, urban and regional planning are increasingly important. It is necessary to properly train the professionals responsible for this great architecture."[17] He believed that through architecture, one could exercise centralized planning to incite change and improve people's lives. Although seemingly a utopian view, the discipline was profoundly pragmatic to him, understanding architecture as part of a life support system for human subsistence.

17 Duhart H., "En Busqueda de la Tradicion Viva," 18.

On the other hand, a critical foundational notion about architecture was expressed by the architect when he stated that "the architect's fundamental thing is the construction."[18] This testimony highlights his alignment with a more contemporary notion where the language of architecture is analyzed through the physical reality of a building in addition to the way it is assembled, as Kenneth Frampton theorized in his book *Studies in Tectonic Culture* in 1995. Space-making, sign-making, and other emphasis that has been given by multiple architecture theories of the twentieth century were not mentioned as the prerogatives of his practice. Elaborating further, Duhart pointed out that "structure and materials will be our only means for now. With them, we will shape the space and comply with the programs."[19] He assigned more agency to architecture as a "thing," its physical realization, and its constructive means rather than the theoretical ones. However, he did not necessarily disavow the latter, which would infiltrate in many manners his intellectual disposition.

18 Duhart H., "En Busqueda de la Tradición Viva," 18.

19 Duhart H., "En Busqueda de la Tradición Viva," 18.

Under the above-described premises, the architect integrated both architecture per se and urbanism into his professional trajectory.

Figure 45-b: Emilio Duhart Harosteguy, photograph, c. 1970.

A DISTINCT GROUP OF PROJECTS

Examining the complete body of work of Duhart, a singular group of projects captivates the attention for being distinct from all the rest of his output. It is composed of a series of structures in which, in their physical embodiment, there is a dominant exploration of a regional tendency that commands the architectural expression. They are also the product of one of the internal poles of tensions of Duhart we formulated in the biographical section of this book, as a result of the architect's deep understanding of the conditions of the remote in being outside of the orbit of the cosmopolitan realm. It is also essential to mention that these projects were realized either outside of Santiago or in the provinces. They represent the currents that originated at the beginning of Duhart's career that resurfaced later under somewhat different forms. They are characterized by using mostly organic materials, such as stone, adobe, and wood, in addition to the consideration of traditional types and modes of construction. These projects are the expression of an independent search to codify the modern language through interweaving it with the regional culture. In these structures, there is a transfer of knowledge in the constructed result through bidirectional fluxes. On the one hand, there is international modernism and, on the other, the innovative use of local craftsman-like technologies and use of materials invoking the traditions of the place.

In these projects, the use of endemic elements is utilized from a purely rational perspective, the spaces were created from an analytical and strictly functional standpoint. When devising them, the impulse came from a logical line of thought and not from a nostalgic or romantic perspective. Duhart was working in an environment where modern technology was scarce, and the labor force had a wealth of knowledge ready to be utilized. Under both industrial constraints and lack of resources proper of Chile in the early 1940s and on, the invaluable resources at hand of stone, adobe, wood, and available workmanship could not be ignored and represented opportunities to be tried and evaluated.

This group includes the Fishing Base of San Quintín (1941); the Labbé House (1941); the Larraín House (1942); the Echeverría House in Zapallar (1953); Hostería de Ancud, Chiloé (1962); Hostería de Castro, Chiloé, (1962); and the Duhart House, in Ustaritz France (1976).[20]

20 Note: The latter is just mentioned here as part of the group. Nevertheless, this book will not analyze it for being outside of the range covered by this study.

Figure 46: Emilio Duhart and Mario Pérez de Arce, architects. Larraín House, 1942-1944, Requinoa, Chile. Perspective drawing.

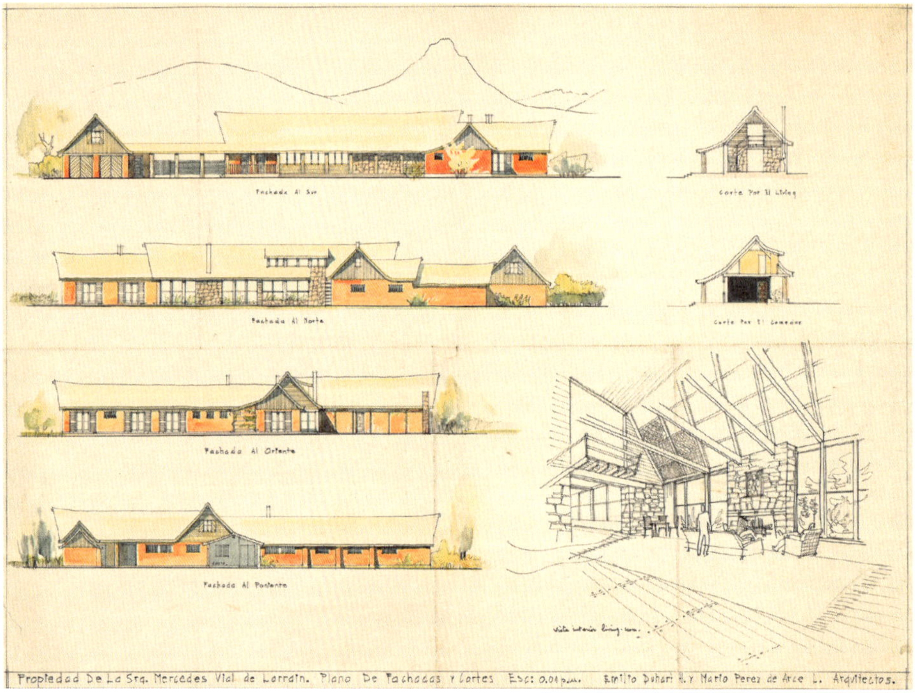

Figure 47: Emilio Duhart and Mario Pérez de Arce, architects. Larraín House, 1942-1944, Requinoa, Chile. Elevations and perspective drawing.

The Larraín House of 1942 (fig. 46 & 47) came from the same vein as the Labbé House and the Fishing Base project, two conceits which have already been addressed. The house, located about two hours south of Santiago, is more expansive (approx. 5,373 sq/ft,) and more traditional looking than the Labbé House. It responded to the Chilean farmhouse's typology, developed during colonial times. However, it makes parallel uses of adobe for bedroom and service areas as in the Labbé House. Stone is used for the foundation and terraces, the chimney, and adjacent walls in the living room area. The wall stone construction technique was random, uncoursed rubble masonry, a building mode that was not common in Chile, especially for internal walls. Presumably, it could have been a reference to French-Basque architecture. However, the stone use does not express a foreign quality since it is local, making the material speak mimetically with the landscape. On the other hand, wood was interlaced in areas between the adobe and stone walls, on the floor, and internal structural pillars.

The living and dining room is the modern area of the dwelling. It is spacious, with double height in the living room area, exposed structural beams, and no false ceiling. Above the dining room section, there is a second floor with a balcony allowing looking down over the living area. Like those of the colonial houses, which were never opened to the outside, the windows in the bedrooms and service area are small, creating introverted spaces. In contrast, those of the living room and dining room are large, opening the subject's internal experience to the surrounding environment.

In addition to the materials mentioned above (adobe, stone, and wood), initially a straw finish was specified for the roof, an utterly unorthodox decision for a modern house. This material finish for such application came from the traditional Mapuche house, the *ruka,* a type of dwelling with a circular base and conical shape, built with a structure of wood and organic materials for cladding and roof surfaces. These were finishes made of straw or reed fibers (coirón) used as thermal insulation and rain protection. As a solution to avoid the destruction of the houses under the stress of violent telluric movements, the material had intrigued Duhart for application on roofs due to its light-weight quality. In the Larraín House, although straw was originally specified for the roof, it was ultimately replaced by typical clay tiles. The construction had occurred while Duhart was in the United States, and his collaborator in charge of the project, Mario Perez de Arce, could not resist pressure from the owners not to use that material.

As in his exploration with adobe, Duhart's experiments with the straw roofs as a means to incorporate certain local materials and built environment references were met with fierce cultural resistance. However, in 1953 Duhart finally realized his aspiration to work with straw in the roof of the Echeverría House (figs. 48 & 49) he remodeled[21] for his family in Zapallar, a beach town about four hours north of Santiago. Decades later, during the 1970s and 1980s, it was not uncommon to find beach houses with straw roofs, mainly in coastal town of middle-class communities.

Figure 48, left: Echeverría Family House, built in 1906, Zapallar, Chile.

Figure 49, above: Emilio Duhart, architect. Echeverría House, remodelling 1953, Zapallar, Chile.

21 It was initially owned by Agustín Baeza and was built in 1906. Over the years, it was acquired by the father of Duhart's wife, Raquel Echeverría Baeza. It was remodeled in 1953, and as of 2023 still remains in the hands of the Echeverría family. Duhart was the first to use a straw roof in this coastal region and incorporated bamboo poles on the roof.

Zapallar is the same town where, without ever visiting Chile, in 1931 Le Corbusier had conceived a second house for the Chilean Ambassador in Argentina, Matías Errázuriz, whom he had met in Buenos Aires, in his first trip to Latin America in 1929. The Maison Errázuriz (fig. 50) was never realized; the client's expectations were different, assuming the design would be a classical Corbusian house. Instead, in his design Le Corbusier, for the first time, had explored ways of making architecture with local materials such as stone, wood, and clay tile, due to the lack of expertise in modern construction of the labor force of the region. This anecdotal development is relevant since, among architects, this project was well-known. Although there is no testimony from Duhart of when he learned about it, he certainly was aware of it since years later, after Le Corbusier's death in 1965, Duhart offered his assistance to pursue the project, but it finally could never be realized.

Figure 50: Le Corbusier. Errázuriz House, 1930. Drawing FLC 8980A.

In 1962, Duhart designed two hostels on the southern island of Chiloé, the Hostería de Ancud and the Hostería de Castro, built as part of a government tourism development program. They were in a rainy region where the architecture is characterized by its stilt houses, wood constructions with gable roofs and finished with cracked larch tiles. The architect integrated these elements in the two designs with a resolutely modern stamp in treating their layouts and spaces. In the Hostería de Ancud (figs. 51 & 52), Duhart dramatically used large interior logs as exposed structural pillars. The Hostería de Castro (fig. 53) stands out for recalling the southern mills' morphology and, above all, for its large window vertical opening on the roof that divides it from top to bottom into two parts, to illuminate the interior staircase and provide views of the natural landscape. In both projects he also conceived the interior design, including furniture, lamps, and rugs.

In the projects discussed above, the intent of Duhart to use organic materials of the local surroundings has an added value in the sense expressed by Frampton when he posited that "the propensity of mass form not only to gravitate toward earth but also to dissolve in its substance ... [is] never more evident than in mud brick construction, where the walls tend to fuse with the earth once they fall into ruin and disuse. However, untreated wood is equally ephemeral when exposed to the elements, as opposed to a well-bedded stone foundation that tends to endure across time and thus to mark the ground in perpetuity."[22] Although Duhart made use of stone foundations collected from the local environment, the use of adobe, wood, and straw speaks of structures

22 Kenneth Frampton, *Studies in Tectonic Culture: The Poetics of Construction in Nineteenth and Twentieth Century Architecture* (Massachusetts: MIT Press, 1995), 7-8.

Figure 51: Emilio Duhart, architect. Hostería de Ancud, 1960-66, Chiloé, Región de Los Lagos, Chile. View from the exterior, photograph, 1962.

Figure 52: Emilio Duhart, architect. Hostería de Ancud, 1961, Chiloé, Región de Los Lagos, Chile. Cut.

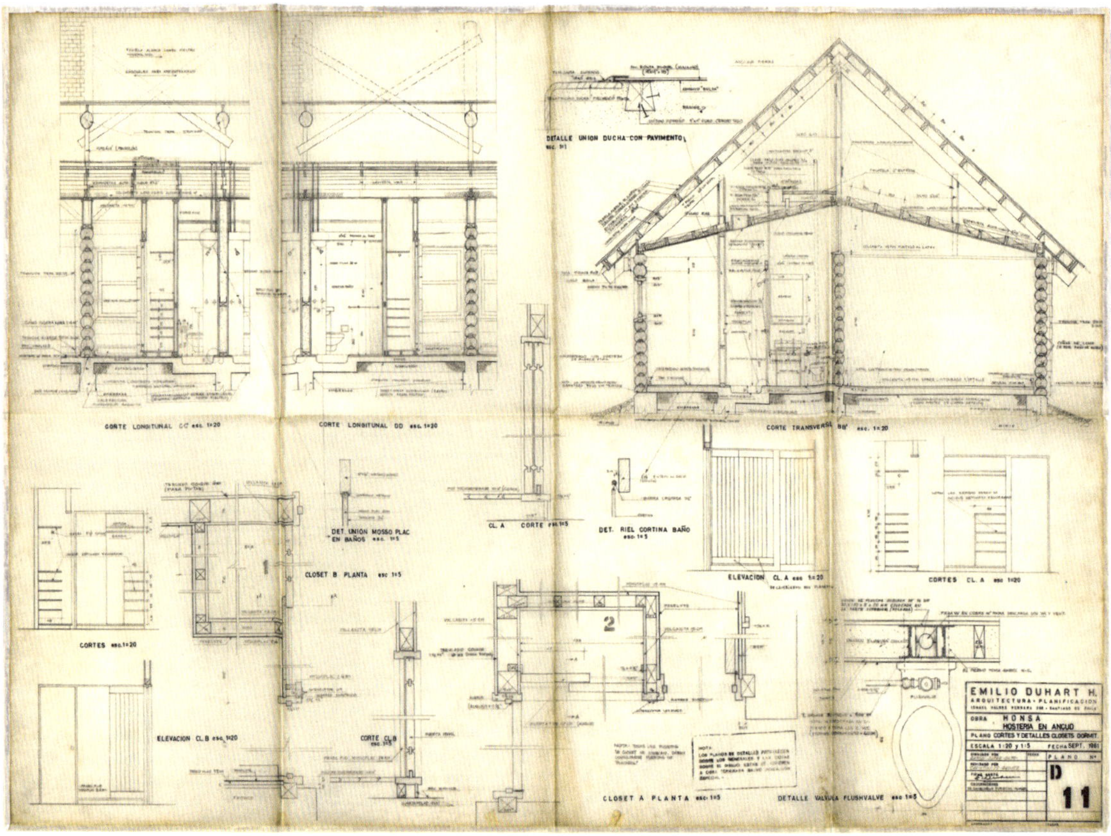

that were made with elements that in their degradation process would organically be reintegrated into their surrounding terrain in a benevolent connection with their ecosystem, implicitly conveying a more restrictive rather than enduring time of existence.

Duhart believed that architecture comes from the physical world and that the fundamental element of architecture is construction. Let it not slip from memory that he declared that "from its source, architecture is a thing that emerges from the physical world."[23] To this end, Frampton ponders that "the built is first and foremost a construction and only later an abstract discourse based on surface, volume, and plan … one may also add that building, unlike fine art, is as much an everyday experience as it is a representation and that the built is a thing rather than a sign."[24] From this perspective, through construction and materials, the human-made physical world is encoded with meaning. In this group of work, Duhart was establishing associations with the place, its materials, people, and memory of construction. He attempted to create a built environment with a physical discursive embodiment of elements that came from the earth and with the craftsmanship knowledge at hand. However, rationality and functionality were the driving force of spatial organization. Innovation was expressed in different novel features, such as the indoor/outdoor double exhaust chimney and the ceiling to floor extra-large living room window of the Labbé House. In the Larraín House, the living and dining area's spatiality, and second floor, with its balcony looking down at the living room in addition to the large windows, are modern gestures (fig. 54). Furthermore, in the Hostería de Castro, the innovative roof window that splits it into two parts should be highlighted for its inventive design.

23 Pérez Oyarzun and Urrejola, "Series of interviews with Emilio Duhart," audio interview, Part 1 of 8.

24 Frampton, *Studies in Tectonic Culture*, 2.

Above all, the projects alluded to a pursuit of a tectonic expression that physically included the endemic culture, linking contemporary architecture with ancient or past regional societies. However, as stated above, this line of thought was curtailed by a categorical cultural rejection by the local communities, especially coming from the upper and the lower classes. It motivated Duhart to look for alternative solutions, turning to a more explicit modern international idiom, and threading the regional in a more conceptual way.

Figure 53: Emilio Duhart, architect. Hostería de Castro, 1960-66. Chiloé, Los Lagos Region, Chile.

Figure 54: Emilio Duhart and Mario Pérez de Arce, architects. Larraín House, 1942-1944, Requinoa, Chile. Detail of perspective drawing, interior of living room, 1942.

INTRODUCTION OF NEW TYPOLOGIES OF BUILDINGS

When back in Chile in 1945, Duhart concentrated on developing a contemporary architectural expression, fiercely fighting against the prevailing architecture that was "a formal setting for a society culturally fixed in the nineteenth-century convention."[25] He was profoundly motivated to use his profession to advance society and to implant modernism in Chile. He was a pioneer with an opportunity given by the historical reality of a country where modernism had not yet been established. From 1945 to 1951, after Duhart attended Harvard and before working at the Atelier Le Corbusier in Paris, he incorporated the first typology of various types of structures. During this period, all his projects were profoundly influenced by Walter Gropius, and the international modernism of the United States, and in the case of educational buildings, by Ernest J. Kump. Among this series of projects is the first modern duplex house, the Pinto House of 1945 (fig. 55), and the first modern industrial city, the President Rios New City of 1947 (fig. 56). He was also involved in the first modern educational facility inspired by the new educational architecture ideas, the Colegio Verbo Divino of 1948 (fig. 57). In 1954 after returning from Paris, he realized the first high-rise structure, the Plaza de Armas building (fig. 58).

25 Pérez Oyarzun and Urrejola, "Series of interviews with Emilio Duhart," audio interview, Part 1 of 8.

Before traveling to France in 1951, he also realized about ten single-family houses, which all shared both many design features that also appeared in the students' work at GSD and some general common characteristics such as light-weight appearance, simplicity, functional design, and rational construction. They were made with reinforced concrete materials, filler brick, natural varnished wood, and glass. They had adequate ventilation and exposure to sunlight and allowed the flow of space between indoors and out. They also included terraces and flat roofs. Nevertheless, each project has its own way of integrating the local surrounding and culture in a specific way.

The primordial example of this type of dwelling is the Duhart House (figs. 59 & 60) built in Santiago in 1946. The Duhart House was a one-story modern house built on a nearly square piece of land, 72.8 feet wide and 68.9 feet wide. It was initially destined for the architect's mother. The house turned out to be the one in which Duhart, his spouse, and six children lived for 30 years.

Figure 55: Emilio Duhart, architect. Francisco Pinto Santa Cruz House, 1944-45, Santiago. Photograph by Marcos Chamudes, 1945.

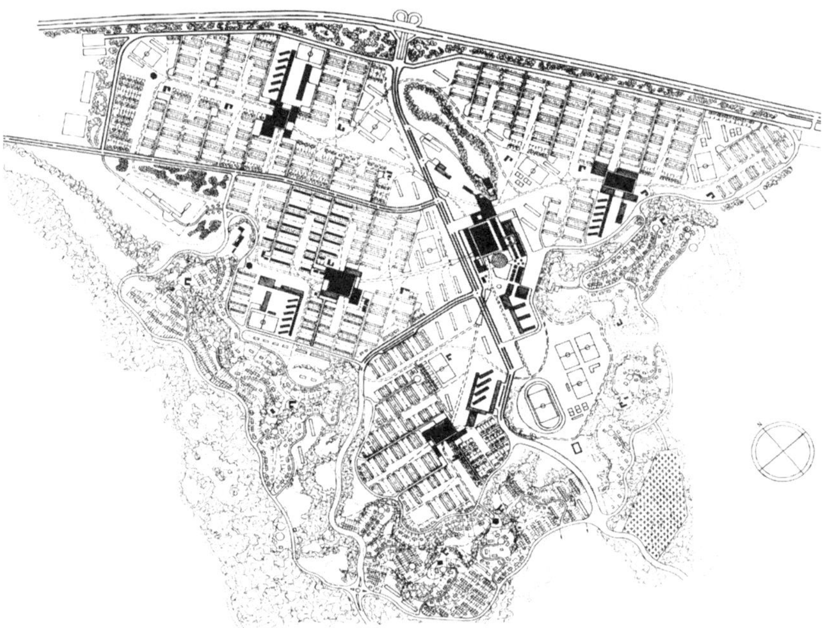

Figure 56: Emilio Duhart and Sergio Larraín G-M, architects. Nueva Ciudad Presidente Ríos, 1946-53, Huachipato, Chile. Urban plan, 1946.

Figure 57: Sergio Larraín G-M, Emilio Duhart, Alberto Piwonka and Mario Pérez de Arce, architects. Colegio Verbo Divino, 1948, Santiago.

Figure 58: Sergio Larraín G-M, Emilio Duhart, Jaime Larraín, Osvaldo Larraín and Jaime Sanfuentes, architects. Plaza de Armas building, 1953-58, Santiago.

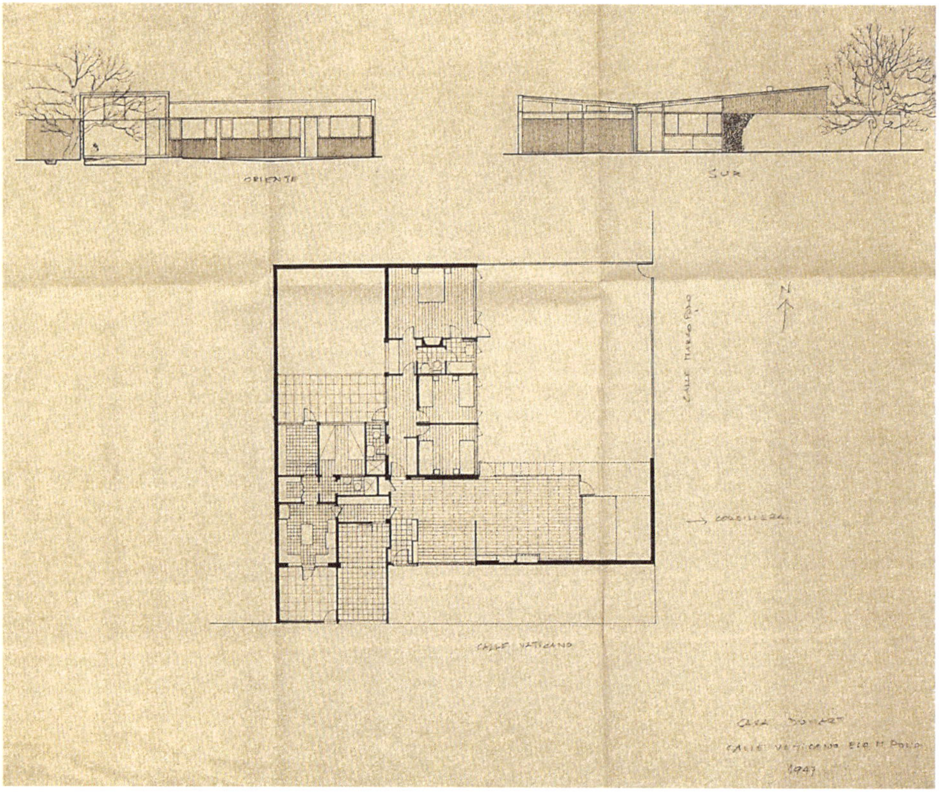

Figure 59: Emilio Duhart, architect. Duhart House, 1946, Santiago. Facade view, photograph.

Figure 60: Emilio Duhart, architect. Duhart House, Santiago. Ground floor, plan, 1947.

The 2,465-square-foot house was a reductive linear structure located on the corner of a block. It was composed of two intersected parallelepiped volumes with a low angle V-shaped roof to the front and a perpendicular discrete gable roof toward the back. It was made out of brick masonry walls, reinforced with concrete beams and pillars, wooden and metal roofing, and exterior pebble-covered walls. The interior finishing materials were stucco, tongue and groove wood paneling, cardboard plaster, and planked wooden floor (fig. 61).

The frontal exterior wall adjoins the sidewalks of the street (figs. 62 & 63) in reference to the typical colonial houses of Santiago. It resulted in an introverted house composed of several internal courtyards that make reference to both the internal courtyards of colonial houses and the Three Patios House designed by Mies van der Rohe in 1938. Duhart used the small-sized land, dispersing the four enclosed yards within the scheme, resulting in a larger interior spatial sense for the user. The colonial patio is transformed and subdivided into several self-enclosed compartments spread out within the property. Duhart named these as the Walnut Patio, the Fig Tree Patio, the Orange Trees Patio, and the Service Patio, and each contained the type of trees that their name designated. These names make an allusion to both the past rural condition of the land and southern Chile, incorporating the trees into the vistas from the interiors towards the patios, a nostalgic reference by the author to his southern past.

A complete modern novelty at the time, the house is an outstanding example of the architect's early work. Henry-Russel Hitchcock selected it for the 1955 MoMA exhibition titled *Latin American Architecture since 1945.* In the catalog of the exhibition, it is stated that "its thin membering and crisp definition reflects the architect's experience with Gropius and with Pei in the States, [however] the planning is definitely Latin American." This project also represents a foundational model in how the architect began to find ways to integrate the regional quality into a modern outcome, pivoting toward the memory of the place, local spatial notions, and local vegetation elements to index the regional in a more abstract conceptual manner, a strategic move that was consistent in his work from then on.

Figure 61: Emilio Duhart, architect. Duhart House, 1946, Santiago. Interior.

Figures 62-63:

Emilio Duhart, architect. Duhart House, 1946, Santiago. Access views.

AESTHETICS AS A BY-PRODUCT

Another ubiquitous conceit of Duhart's is the unique way he formulated his take on aesthetics, which profoundly affects his architecture's formal appearance. Formalism was not the focal point in the architect's conception of architecture, explaining why his projects' formal aspects are not always homogeneous. To understand his views, we need to make recourse to his own words. In an interview published in 1979, illustrating the architect's role, Duhart referred to a metaphor given to him by Walter Gropius while studying at Harvard: "Gropius told me: 'I have no recipes to give you. However, I will tell you a bit about my opinion of what an architect should be. The architect is like a driver of a chariot, a Roman chariot that has four horses' …. If four horses pull in unison, the chariot moves along. If one of them fails, the chariot tips aside and overturns. No one should override the other, and the more robustly and faster they pull, the more the chariot advances."[26] Those four horses referred to form, function, technique, and economy, "economy in the Greek sense of the word, of the available elements,"[27] which implied a careful use of means. However, to Duhart, one of the all-encompassing precepts pervasive throughout his work is that the function, technique, and economy of a project pave the way to its form. The form is a by-product, and in function, technique, and economy lies the essence of the work.

26 Damián Bayon and Paolo Gasparini, *Panorámica de la Arquitectura Latino-Americana* (Barcelona: Blume, 1977), 121-122.

27 Bayon and Gasparini, *Panorámica de la Arquitectura Latino-Americana*, 122.

His encounter with the "epidermal" kind of architecture he first came across in Santiago in 1935 ingrained in him a profound disdain for structures whose raison d'être was to present a gratuitous aesthetic, unjustified and foreign to a locality. Presumably, this contempt might have further developed at GSD, where people considered aestheticism a taboo subject. That led him to think about form in a specific and elaborated way. To Duhart, form's relationship to beauty is secondary, citing Plato to explain further when he said, "beauty is the splendor of truth"[28] to support his view. In the architectural program, the search for truth and honesty was paramount and intimately related to a specific regional reality. He further reasoned that there needs to be a "relationship and coherence to be established between form and 'being' – [in the sense that in architecture] 'being' [is] spatially realizable. This 'being' is related to the project's pursued end and its program …. This 'being' is also in the project itself, in its intrinsic quality."[29] The architect should devise "places

28 Duhart, "Speech by Architect Emilio Duhart Harosteguy on Receiving the National Award for Architecture from the Chilean College of Architects," 8.

29 Duhart, "Speech by Architect Emilio Duhart Harosteguy on Receiving the National Award for Architecture from the Chilean College of Architects," 8.

[where] we experience wellness."[30] In Duhart's conception, the human sense of wellness is prioritized over beauty, in the sense that Salingaros defined it, to "make human beings feel at ease; make them feel psychologically comfortable so that persons can carry out whatever functions they have to unselfconsciously, without being disturbed by the built environment in any way."[31] Furthermore, if architecture involves a language and communication, "it is not explained: it only 'is,'"[32] emphasizing that architecture is first and foremost a "thing." Duhart added that the architect "has to understand the deep 'reason for being' of the architecture, its character and its needs, its meaning, and its usefulness. Thus, pregnant at the same time with matter and meaning, technique and spirit, a piece of architecture is born and lives."[33] He believed that the form of a structure needs to be preceded by a slow, patient, and demanding analysis and synthesis as a fundamental proceeding. He indicated that "this takes us very far from the motto 'form follows function,'"[34] the famous maxim coined by architect Louis Henry Sullivan. To Duhart, form follows much more than function. He believed that the main focus of architecture is not the form but rather that form follows all the project's needs, being the end result of a long search that involves research, exploration, interpretation, analysis, and synthesis.

Architecture without aesthetics is an oxymoron, but as described above, Duhart's method to achieve a form is distinct, inevitably leading to multiple formal results. Nevertheless, in certain types of buildings but not exclusively, primarily educational and high-rise buildings, the presence of an aesthetic continuity is easily detected. This is related to the Bauhaus grid, a geometric expression learned at Harvard with a definitive impact on the final appearance of a number of his structures.

The language of abstraction is a derivative of the second phase of the Bauhaus. Since 1922 the school adopted the grid as a fundamental structuring framework representing the age of art and technology, the new binary unity postulated by the institution. As a new professor at the Bauhaus, the painter László Moholy-Nagy (1895-1946) paved the way for the new direction with significant consequences for architecture. In his paintings, influenced by El Lissitzky, he "[explored] the intersection of abstract forms in abstract space … inhabited by floating planes without mass and of varying degrees of transparency …. The model is no longer perspectival, an image of things seen, but rather the idiom of descriptive geometry."[35] According to Leah Dickerman, Moholy-Nagy, additionally influenced by de Stijl and Constructivism, brought "painting closer to the language of architecture … [and] also implicitly [proposed] a new model of architecture, in which planes slide past one another on a three-dimensional grid rather than closed

30 Duhart, "Speech by Architect Emilio Duhart Harosteguy on Receiving the National Award for Architecture from the Chilean College of Architects," 9.

31 Nikos A. Salingaros, *A Theory of Architecture* (Nepal: Vajra Books, 2013), 222.

32 Duhart, "Speech by Architect Emilio Duhart Harosteguy on Receiving the National Award for Architecture from the Chilean College of Architects," 10.

33 Duhart, "Speech by Architect Emilio Duhart Harosteguy on Receiving the National Award for Architecture from the Chilean College of Architects," 8-9.

34 Duhart, "Speech by Architect Emilio Duhart Harosteguy on Receiving the National Award for Architecture from the Chilean College of Architects," 9.

35 Leah Dickerman, "Bauhaus Fundaments," in *Bauhaus 1919-1933: Workshops for Modernity*, ed. Barry Bergdoll, Leah Dickerman (New York: The Museum of Modern Art, 2009), 20.

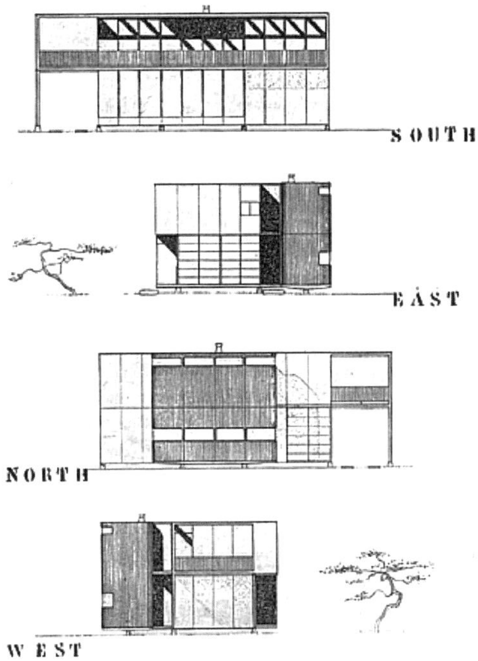

Figure 64: I. M. Pei and Emilio Duhart. Designs for Postwar Living competition. Elevation, 1943.

boxes of traditional architecture [and] here one sees the ascendancy of … *elementarization*, the distillation of fundamental forms and the right angle, and the use of primary colors plus black, gray, and white; and *integration*, the binding of these forms together in a new, encompassing whole."[36]

36 Dickerman, "Bauhaus Fundaments," in *Bauhaus 1919-1933: Workshops for Modernity*, 20-21.

This description could be applied to several of Duhart's projects. It first appeared in the Designs for Post War Living Competition of I. M. Pei and Emilio Duhart in 1943 (fig. 64). From then on, the latticework scheme, the presence of elemental forms, mostly orthogonal, the right angle, and the colors white and gray dominating the color palette, are elements present in numerous projects such as in the Pinto House (1945) (fig. 55); the housing complex of the President Rios New City (1946) (fig. 65); the Verbo Divino School (1948) (fig. 57); the Arturo Prat Building (1954) (fig. 66); the Lycée Alliance Française de Saint Exupéry (1956) (figs. 67, 68 & 69); the University City of Concepción (1957-1969) (figs. 70 & 71), and more. What is noteworthy in some of these structures is their atectonic quality. The term *atectonic* is used in the sense that "the expressive interaction of load and support in architecture is visually neglected or obscured,"[37] by conveying a visual impression of weightlessness, in contradiction to the heavier nature of the structure and the construction of the building.

37 Frampton, *Studies in Tectonic Culture*, 20.

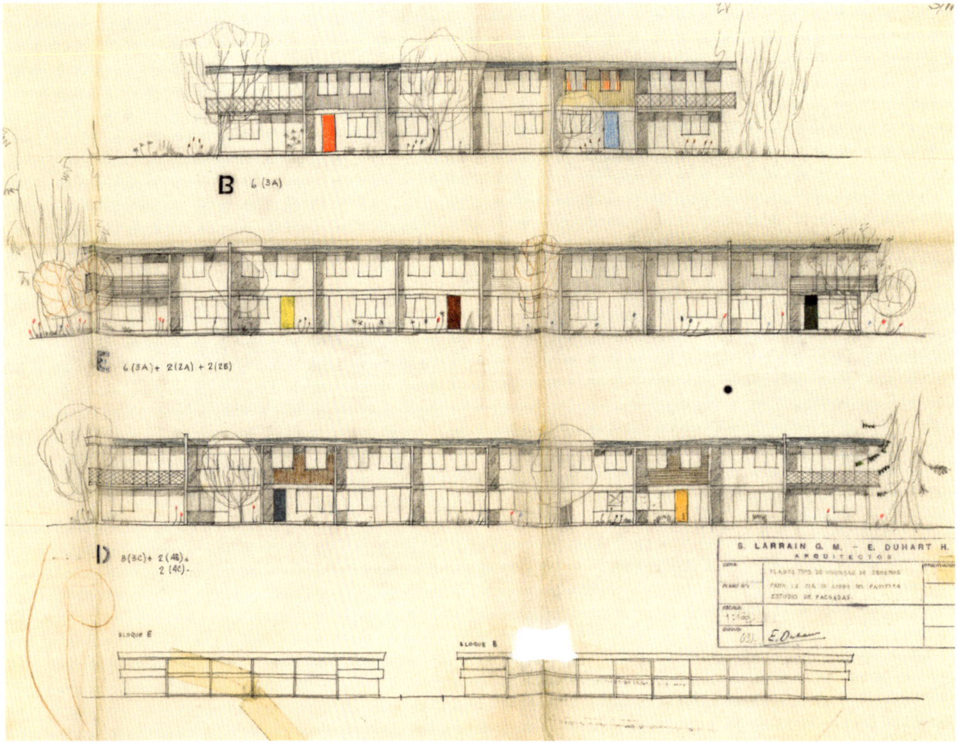

Figure 65: Emilio Duhart and Sergio Larrain G-M, architects. Nueva Ciudad Presidente Ríos, 1949-53, Huachipato, Chile. Study of facades and elevations.

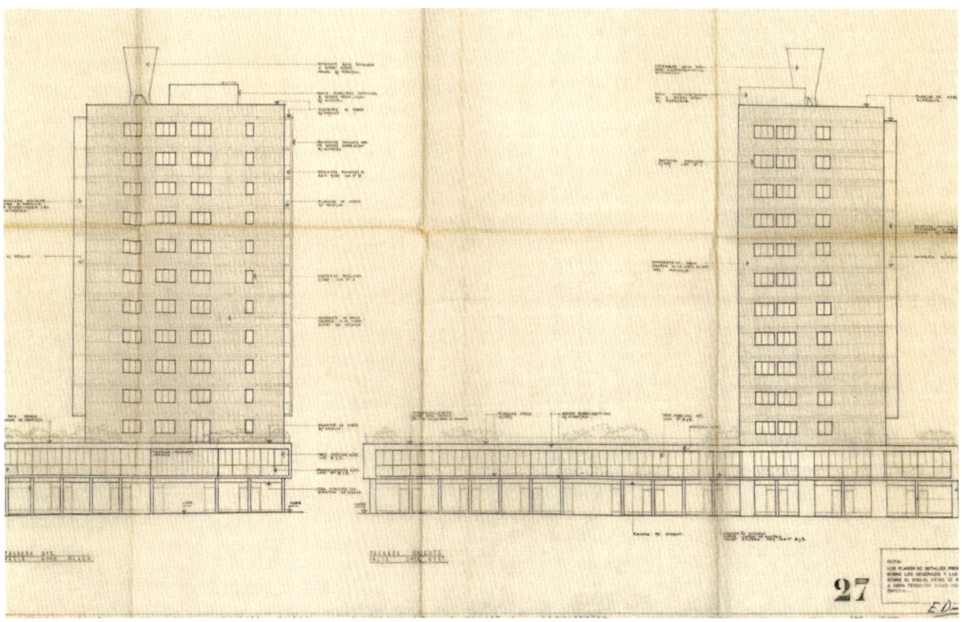

Figure 66: Sergio Larraín G-M, Emilio Duhart, and Ignacio Covarrubias, architects. Arturo Prat Building, 1953-57, Santiago. Elevations.

Figure 67: Sergio Larraín G-M and Emilio Duhart, architects. Lycée Alliance Française, 1954, Santiago. Photograph, 1959.

Figure 68: Sergio Larraín G-M and Emilio Duhart, architects. Lycée Alliance Française, 1954, Santiago.

Figure 69: Sergio Larraín G-M and Emilio Duhart, architects. Lycée Alliance Française, 1954, Santiago.

Figure 70: Emilio Duhart and Roberto Goycoolea, architects. University of Concepción. Façade of the Institute of Chemistry, 1958, Concepción, Chile.

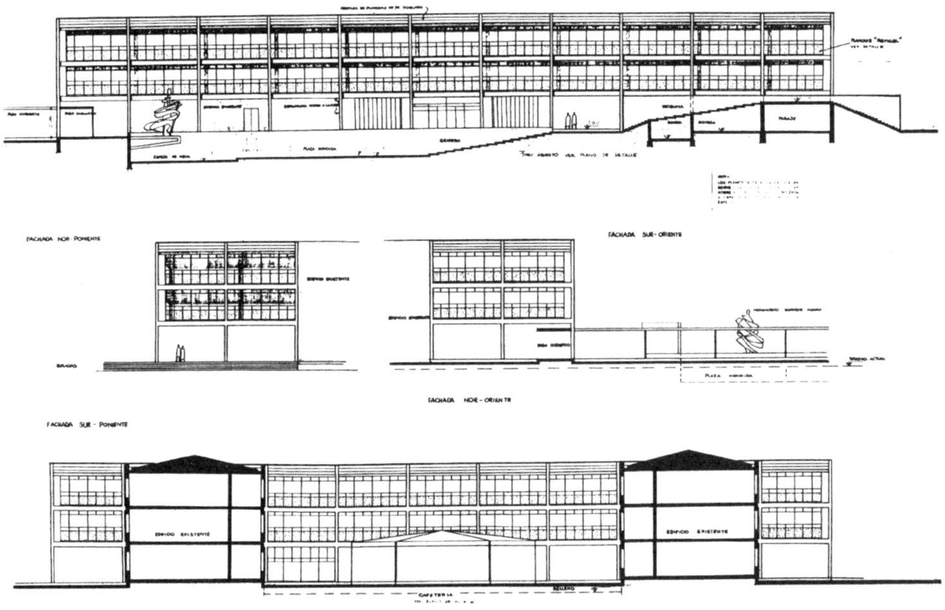

Figure 71: Emilio Duhart and Roberto Goycoolea, architects. Campus Universidad de Concepción. Facades of the Chemistry Building, Concepción, Chile. Elevations, 1958.

To this end Frampton comments regarding German architects of the early twentieth century, “that the central preoccupations … will shift away from the tectonic to the abstractly atectonic, bordering on the graphic,”[38] a characteristic that could be applied to Gropius and what Duhart learned at Harvard. That quality might be the trait that Le Corbusier noticed when reviewing the architect’s portfolio in their first encounter, when he commented that Duhart’s projects lacked “a little bit of flesh”[39] (see the Pinto House (fig. 55) or the Arturo Prat Building (fig. 66), for example). Only after Duhart’s passage through Le Corbusier’s atelier is the grid softened, and discrete integration of the curve is incorporated.

Alberto Montealegre, a Chilean architect and author who worked for Duhart for ten years, qualifies Duhart’s work in the following way: “[Duhart] always maintains an intellectual control of sensitivity ... there is a language reduced to an economy of means and the indispensable, in which nothing is expressed beyond what is strictly necessary.”[40]

38 Frampton, *Studies in Tectonic Culture*, 19.

39 Duhart, “Recuerdos de Le Corbusier,” n/a.

40 Alberto Montealegre Klenner, “Emilio Duhart y la Originalidad Posible,” unplublished manuscript.

A SEARCH WITH AN UNORTHODOX EVOLUTION: ADOBE, PREFABRICATION, SYSTEM THINKING

In Duhart's research on the different possibilities facing architecture in a region of scarce resources, a particular progression of thoughts is present: the unorthodox connection between adobe and prefabrication, and which over the years converged into system thinking. On several occasions working in adobe led Duhart nowhere, despite the architect's intention of employing it. We also saw how, in his visit to the United States, prefabrication was an essential subject of attention. However, apart from having been a focal point in his academic work, he could not develop in Chile an important application strategy for prefabrication in his own work.

In the United States between 1942 and 1945, Duhart was immersed in an architectural scene where prefabrication was broadly debated, tried, and evaluated. He was acutely interested in its possible applications as one of the alternatives for low-cost solutions in an underdeveloped country, as was Chile in the 1940s. However, upon his return in 1945, prefabrication came to be "an almost absolute failure at that time ... simply [because] the matter was not mature,"[41] due to the scarcity of capital and financing, shortage of technicians, and lack of systems of industrialization. In assessing the Chilean reality with its available labor force in need of work and the availability of raw materials, he concluded that the matter needed to be carefully pondered, concluding that "we should ... think of our own solutions, employing the maximum of manpower, [and helping to] develop it 'within' the work [without] pretending to reduce the workforce to increase mechanization. So, the matter of prefabrication must be looked at quite carefully."[42] This call from the local reality converged in Duhart in system thinking, the substratum of the lessons on prefabrication. That meant to detect the elements among the industrial components already available in the Chilean industry, those open for multiple applications in reciprocal interaction with one another for the ultimate goal in producing low-cost outcomes.

41 Bayon and Gasparini, *Panorámica de la Arquitectura Latino-Americana* (Barcelona: Blume, 1977), 116.

42 Bayon and Gasparini, *Panorámica de la Arquitectura Latino-Americana* (Barcelona: Blume, 1977), 117.

As a professor, Duhart was known for his prefabrication expertise. Through academic lessons, he transferred his knowledge to his students, and as already mentioned, the result of one of his students' workshops was highlighted in

1949 in the *Arquitectura y Construcción* magazine. Part of the project was a workers' housing complex for a brewery factory, representing a readaptation of the General Panel Corporation system. It consisted of prefabricated construction in a combination of wood and plaster, the materials available at the time (fig. 56). As one can infer from this example, Duhart was teaching his own version of prefabrication in the sense that the brief to the students specified conceiving of prefabrication as a system devised with pre-existing materials, a lesson he deemed essential to transmit.

However, in 1957 Duhart embarked on a project he worked on for more than a decade, an urban development and construction of new university buildings for the University of Concepción, a project in which he applied system thinking in its maximum expression. In this project, the architect "draws a modular grid over the entire university field, trying to systematize the project's measurements at all its scales."[43] The plan included the elevations of the surrounding hills, the existing buildings and vehicular lanes, and the city streets' layout to the southwest and northwest of the campus. Along two different orientations, the planning was finally governed by a normal general plot of 25 feet by 25 feet, and another at an angle of 40 degrees in respect to the first. As mentioned by Cristián Berríos, the modular grid's adoption most certainly was influenced by Mies van der Rohe in his project for the Illinois Institute of Technology in 1939, in which Duhart had used a modulated lattice to organize the whole complex.[44] Most notably, at the University of Concepción the standard measurement was comprehensively applied to all the new building structural work. The architect proposed a 25-foot modular steel structure, specified for weight considerations, economy, and flexibility for prospective future construction, to achieve a more expeditious rationalization of the whole's construction and overall consistency.[45] The use and dimensions of the steel structure were also considered for convenience due to the proximity to the then largest steel manufacturing plant in the country located nearby and its dimensional industrial capacity. He was applying system thinking not just for the sake of it but for preserving the integrity of the design of the campus for the future, concurrently utilizing a new steel technology that was manufactured at hand in the region, adapting the design to the industrial capability of the plant in a reciprocal type of relationship.

43 Berrios, *Emilio Duhart: Elaboración de un Espacio Urbano*, 211.

44 Berrios, *Emilio Duhart: Elaboración de un Espacio Urbano*, 215.

45 Berrios, *Emilio Duhart: Elaboración de un Espacio Urbano*, 219.

THE SITE, THE RELIEF, AND THE SUB-GROUND

Addressing the topographic field, we have frequently conveyed Duhart's awareness of the site as a microcosmic part of larger forms and features of the land surface. Paying attention to the three-dimensional variations of the territory, in particular the nearby mountains or hills, he oriented and designed the projects in such a way that the landscape could be contemplated (fig. 92). As indicated by Frampton, "through the concept of the site and the principle of settlement, the environment becomes ... the essence of architectural production ... this is an act of knowledge of the context that comes out of its architectural modification,"[46] a notion that is present in Duhart's mind even before traveling abroad. The architect always attended to the larger context of the site, which included its formations but also its history and its people. The site was seen as including a binary nature/human reciprocal relationship, binding each party in a mutual exchange of privileges.

46 Frampton, *Studies in Tectonic Culture*, 8.

The site, in some cases, has intricate characteristics that continually threaten the longevity of architectural masses. In this sense, a transversal component of Duhart's architecture is related to the geological condition of the Chilean territory that profoundly defines the architectural construct, not just for him but also for every practicing professional in the land. Three telluric plates, the South American plate, the Nazca Plate, and the Antarctic Plate, meet in the Chilean territory forming a continuous geological fissure from north to south. The land is one of the world's highest seismic hazard zones, records an average of three significant earthquakes every decade, and has experienced the largest instrumentally recorded quake in the world (in 1960, magnitude 9.5).

In such an unpredictable dramatic environment, architecture is not exclusively related to the relief of the project's specific terrain. The earth's crust's structure also influences it with its sudden and unexpected violent motions. The built environment needs to be in accord with engineering knowledge to absorb the shock waves of telluric movements. The structural mass of a building constantly experiences compression forces due to gravity. However, during an earthquake, additional compressive stress is introduced alongside tensile and shear forces, wich compromises all the components of the bulding's structure. The nature of the site's terrain, the projected structural components, the joints, and materiality are all assessed and defined by this geological condition, permeating the whole tectonic architectural mass from foundation to finishes. The relation to the topography and the nature of the soil must be carefully studied. The sub-surface, the ground, and the foundations play a significant role in earthquake-resistant construction. Seismic architecture has an additional and different construction idiom that penetrates the entire structure.

Furthermore, to achieve a stable result, the choice of materials is in close relationship with anti-seismic architecture. To this end, over the years, Duhart developed a glossary of materials that can be used in anti-seismic constructions, each one with specific characteristics and to be used conscientiously according to the types of volumes to be built. Among them are adobe, brick, cement blocks, stone, wood, steel, iron, reinforced concrete and ferrocement. His architecture evolved over the years towards the use of reinforced concrete, and ferrocement, typical materials utilized comprehensively in modern architecture in Latin America.

Duhart devised an array of responses to earthquake challenges. He asserted that seismic architecture "does not require anything other than applying the rules of ... constructing properly according to the prescriptions of the project."[47] Two of many examples are the University of Concepcion, where Duhart used steel structure and longitudinal and transverse triangular blades in many buildings (pgs. 258-265), and the Industrial Carozzi Complex (1960). This was a food factory built in cement and painted in white in which the main building characteristics are the anti-seismic reinforced concrete, reticulated triangulations of the façade (pgs. 189-192). The triangular framework systems play the same role as bracing frame structures. Alberto Montealegre adds that these systems "are more expressive of the efforts of resistance a structure exercises against seismic movements. In reality, conventional frames are more elastic and deformable than triangular solutions, which are more rigid and resistant."[48] On the other hand, it offered the advantage of greater wall transparency to fulfill the aim of allowing internal natural lighting to show the industry's inner operation from the outside. For the silos of the factory, a sliding formwork technology[49] was applied. It is a firm and continuous structure resistant to earthquakes made of homogeneous concrete material.

47 Émile Duhart H., "Architecture Parasismique," *Techniques & Architecture, Nº 334*, 1981, 136.

48 Alberto Montealegre, email exchange with the author on December 19, 2023.

49 "The main principle of the sliding formwork technology is the process of continuous lifting of the formwork structure vertically, simultaneously with the implementation of general working processes: installation of formwork, reinforcement, concreting and final surface treatment," Sliding Formwork," TMX, accessed December 20, 2020, http://thm-holding.ru/en/sliding-formwork/.

In a schematic section of a reinforced concrete volume that Duhart published in an article called "Architecture Parasismique,"[50] without identifying the project, it is possible to observe the use of internal mushroom posts without bracing blades. The posts built in such way provide stability to the floor surfaces, without which the lack of horizontal rigidity of the floors would destroy the structure under the tremors of an earthquake. Moving upward in the building, the height of the floors decreased to reduce the overall compression forces.

50 Émile Duhart H., "Architecture Parasismique," *Techniques & Architecture, nº 334*, (1981): 141.

Duhart was also involved in the Endesa Building conceived between 1961 and 1968, a tall open-plan high-rise that was a structural challenge for the time. It was "a binuclear body made up of two boxes, with specific spans linked together by an H-shaped structure"[51] based on the principle of the rigidity of the vertical core that would reduce the impact on the structural design and conception that sustained it, and the reinforced concrete constitution of its walls (fig. 97). In the CEPAL headquarters, Duhart figured out an innovative anti-seismic method for the main square ring building inspired by bridge engineering in the form of a suspended pendulum-like structure supported by twenty-eight columns attached to the foundation (fig. 76). For the round conference room building, a continuous, reinforced concrete veil was realized.

51 Marcos Barrientos, "Terrenos, Arquitectura y la Norma Chilena NCh433. Of.72. Cálculo Antisísmico de Edificios (1959-1972,)" in *Anales de Arquitectura UC*, https://www.researchgate.net/profile/Marco-Barrientos/publication/358191875_Terremotos_arquitectura_y_la_Norma_Chilena_NCh433_Of72_Calculo_Antisismico_de_Edificios_1959-1972/links/61f481da11a1090a79bb1e7d/Terremotos-arquitectura-y-la-Norma-Chilena-NCh433-Of72-Calculo-Antisismico-de-Edifcios-1959-1972.pdf

Figure 72: Emilio Duhart and Luis Mitrovic, architects. Carozzi Industrial Complex, 1960-65, Santiago.

The Carozzi Industrial Complex, a flour-based food factory, was a project that Duhart held dear, given his family's history with the milling industry in southern Chile, which he knew well.

Figure 74 (above): Emilio Duhart and Luis Mitrovic, architects. Carozzi industrial complex, 1960-65, Santiago.

The site, close to the capital, was located just off the Pan-American Highway that connects Santiago with southern Chile. Because of its location, it was an unavoidable showcase for the brand, exposed to the view of anyone passing along the road.

Figure 75 (left): Emilio Duhart and Luis Mitrovic, architects. Carozzi Industrial Complex, 1960-65, Santiago.

The factory is a concrete structure, painted white, with sixteen silos arranged in two rows, a mill, and a manufacturing plant. The programme also included offices and laboratories.

Figure 76: Emilio Duhart with Christian de Groote, Roberto Goycoolea, and Oscar Santelices, architects. View of the back of the building, ca. 1968.

Building for the United Nations Economic Commission for Latin America and the Caribbean (CEPAL), 1960-66, Santiago.

ARCHITECTURE AND THE CORPOREAL EXPERIENCE

The body as a perceptual being, and topography, or more precisely the site, are linked in the work of Duhart foremost by pervasively offering structures of contemplation of the surrounding landscape. Examples abound, like the placement of the San Quintin Fishing Base overlooking Mount Valentin, the Labbé House looking at the Andes Mountains, the Lycée Français and the Ziegler House oriented toward the Manquehue Hill and so on. To this end Frampton argues that the architectural work is also an experience lived by the body, constituting itself a metaphor in "a human process by which we understand and structure one domain of experience in terms of another of a different kind … rather than being solely a linguistic or rhetorical trope."[52]

52 Frampton, *Studies in Tectonic Culture,* 11.

The structures of contemplation that Duhart conceived oriented for humans to free their minds by looking up and out toward the horizon where the visual is not directed toward the architecture but away from it in an experience where, as described by Tim Inglod, "the mental and the material, or the terrains of the imagination and the physical environment, run into one another to the extent of being barely distinguishable."[53] His architecture offered an experience where the landscape is turned into a repository for thought and as a visual stimulant for metaphysical contemplation, to "channel and focus the restless churning of the human mind."[54]

53 Tim Ingold, *Being Alive: Essays on Movement, Knowledge and Descriptions* (London, New York: Routledge, 2011),198.

54 Tim Ingold, *Being Alive,* 199.

Going further into Frampton's interpretation of what he names the "corporeal metaphor,"[55] Duhart's conception of the human body included his care for the human experience; for instance, in the Labbé House, by providing a parking space set away from the property to create an intermediate experience to flush out the remnants of city life before entering the weekend house. It is also present in much of his urban planning, placing rows of trees to protect the body from the sun and including porticos to shelter from the rain in the design of the campus of the University of Concepción. Moreover, he devised a pedestrian zone for the heart of the city of Santiago (1957), for the body that walks, and likewise he created a sinuous urbanization in Jardín del Este to insulate the

55 Frampton, *Studies in Tectonic Culture*, 10.

human body from the city traffic allowing a less noisy and busy neighborhood experience (fig. 77). This consideration permits that "the body reconstitutes the world through its tactile appropriation of reality."[56] Additionally, although never opposed to the technological era he was immersed in, Duhart on innumerable occasions referred to the importance of the human scale as a physical relation to architecture and urban planning to elicit in humans a feeling of comfort and ease, many times insulating the experience from high-density automobile traffic.

56 Frampton, *Studies in Tectonic Culture*, 10.

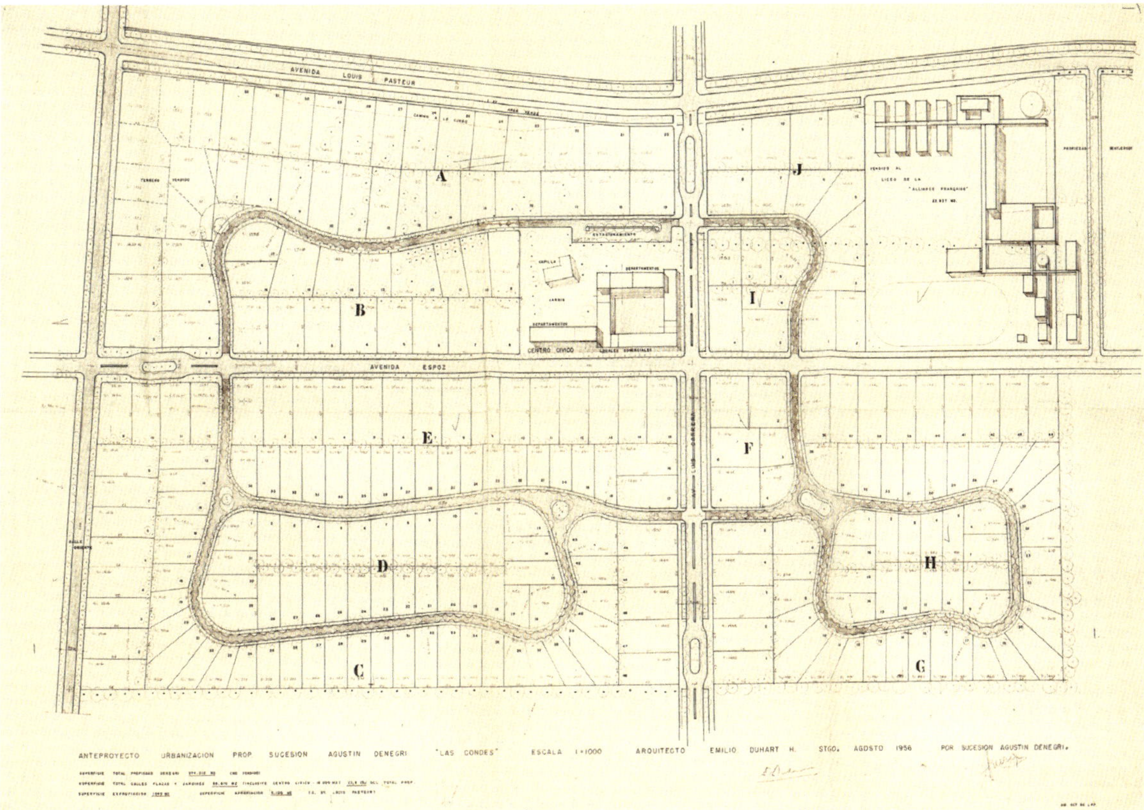

Figure 77: Emilio Duhart. Jardín del Este development. Surface area of succession, plan, 1956.

A PROTO-ECOLOGIST

Duhart expressed being touched by "the historical destruction of human groups and cultures. Entire regions of the [Chilean] southern canals and the northern highlands, [are] now empty, [and] currently will not be able to develop because their natural inhabitants have disappeared and nobody can or wants to replace them in those areas now depopulated."[57] Related to this issue, by the end of his speech for the reception of the National Prize of Architecture in 1977, he remarked, "Chile conquered its unity throughout its extraordinary geography; now it is time for us to stop the process of … destroying its particularities. Everyone must be able to live and express themselves and finally acknowledge the richness and diversity implicit in this wonderful 'Land of the Ocean',"[58] a telling metaphor for his enduring appreciation of the exuberant natural resources of the country.

Duhart envisioned architectural practice as a means to intervene in the universal erosion of the earth, the homogenization of the landscape, and the continual suppression of cultural variety and particularities.[59] His conception of the site and of the topographic field was more than a mere relief on the crust of the earth but also contained history, culture and people. The site was an entity in close equalitarian interchange with the human in which there should be an implied assumption that they both have value. These thoughts, in addition to the many design details in his entire trajectory, attend to nature in many ways and may affirm him as a proto ecologist.

57 Duhart, "Speech by Architect Emilio Duhart Harosteguy on Receiving the National Award for Architecture from the Chilean College of Architects," 12.

58 Duhart, "Speech by Architect Emilio Duhart Harosteguy on Receiving the National Award for Architecture from the Chilean College of Architects," 12.

59 Duhart, "Speech by Architect Emilio Duhart Harosteguy on Receiving the National Award for Architecture from the Chilean College of Architects," 11-12.

A CONCEPTUAL INTEGRATION OF THE REGIONAL CULTURE

The period from 1953 until 1970 represents Duhart's mature phase. Since 1945 he had been working in partnership with Sergio Larrain García-Moreno; however, in 1958, he ended this partnership and opened his own office called Emilio Duhart H. Architecture and Planning.

Of this time, Duhart declared, "the decades of the 50s and 60s were those with the greatest opportunities I had as an architect and urban planner ... I had then achieved greater maturity and autonomy to give the necessary substance and coherence to the works. I had achieved a synthesis between spontaneous sensitivity of the early years and the formal and technical discipline of later years."[60] During this phase Duhart designed approximately eighty projects, including competitions and unrealized projects, including educational, industrial, institutional, residential, religious, and high-rises. Of them, approximately thirty private homes mostly located in Santiago were involved, in addition to several educational facilities in Santiago and Concepción. Residential architecture is a group of interest since Duhart thought that its design "can serve as a laboratory, a 'banc d'essai' (test bench),"[61] a statement that very well might constitute a focal point to lead to further in-depth analysis of his residential work, an effort that has not been realized yet. Among this group of work, the Larraín House (1942), the Pinto Houses (1945), the Duhart House (1946), the Dittborn House (1948), the Andrade House (1959-1960) (fig. 80), the Ziegler House (1960) (fig. 78), the Denegri House (1962-1963) (fig. 79), and the De La Fuente House (1964) are among the most-worthy of examination. Following this group in number are the educational projects. The most important, to which he dedicated more than a decade, is the campus of the University of Concepción (1957-1969).

60 Duhart, "Speech by Architect Emilio Duhart Harosteguy on Receiving the National Award for Architecture from the Chilean College of Architects," 6.

61 Bayón and Gasparini, *Panorámica de la Arquitectura Latino-Americana*, 110.

During this phase, Duhart's response to architecture and the region becomes more intricate and aligned with the lessons learned at the Atelier Le Corbusier and specifically related to his work for Villa Shodhan (1951-1956), and the intellectual illumination that the experience afforded him. The way in which Le Corbusier elaborated the conjugation of the regional with the universal in this project might have appeared to Duhart as an alternative model to the

Figure 78: Emilio Duhart, architect. Ziegler House, 1960-62, Santiago.

Figure 79 (below): Emilio Duhart, architect. Denegri House, 1962-63, Santiago. Photograph, 1965.

Figure 80: Emilio Duhart, architect. Andrade House, 1959-60, Santiago.

solutions that he had already tried. Following Duhart's experience with Le Corbusier, a pivoting toward a similar conceptual approach in the integration of the local culture can be observed in his work. Additionally, although Duhart never abandoned the grid with its right angles, in some cases he softened it (Ministerio del Trabajo Building, Santiago, 1969), incorporated the curve (Hotel International, Santiago, 1969; Santiago International Airport, 1970-1992), rounded edges, and the like. Furthermore, his architecture previously in some cases atectonic, became more gravity-friendly and in others upfront stereotomic: the Ziegler House, Santiago, 1960 (fig. 78) and the Carozzi Industrial Complex, Santiago 1961 (fig. 72).

Yet, in the CEPAL headquarters of 1960, Duhart consolidated everything he had learned about architecture throughout the years into its maximum expression. Of this undertaking, Duhart declared, "when I did the project, I did not think of any architect, of any history, [or] of any geography. The project came out … at an extraordinary speed,"[62] and added that for him the CEPAL Building "was a deep impulse into which I poured everything I had inside."[63] He also commented that "in this project, I summarized all I had amassed in terms of love for the geography of Chile, the destiny of Latin America, and the teaching of my masters."[64]

The United Nations Economic Commission for Latin America headquarters (pgs. 206 - 228), locally known as the CEPAL Building, is a monumental piece of architecture. It was designed in 1960, completed in 1966, and built

62 Pérez Oyarzun and Urrejola, "Series of interviews with Emilio Duhart," audio interview, Part 4 of 8.

63 Pérez Oyarzun and Urrejola, "Series of interviews with Emilio Duhart," audio interview, Part 4 of 8.

64 Duhart, "Recuerdos de Le Corbusier," n/a.

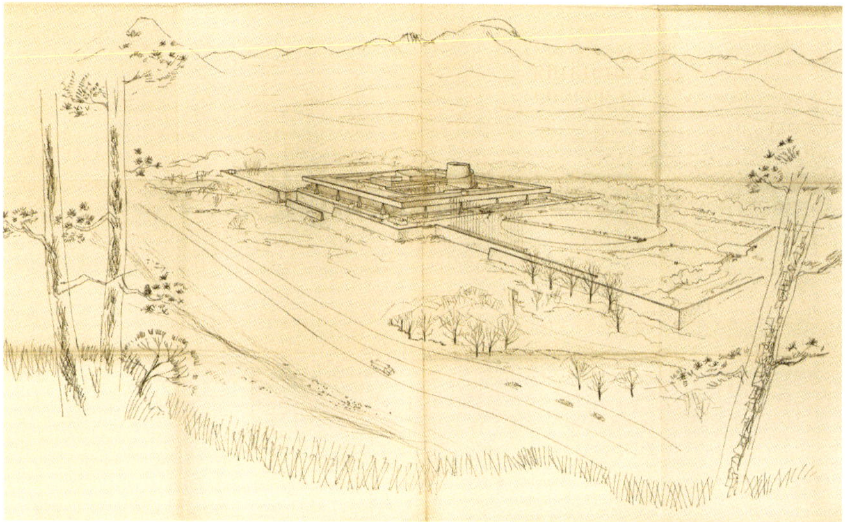

Figure 81: CEPAL Building, 1960-1966. Perspective.

on a 153,215 square-foot flat land located in the eastern part of Santiago, near the Manquehue Hill and adjacent to the Mapocho River (fig. 102). The headquarters is a compound that encompasses 55,775 square feet. Duhart developed the project in collaboration with a group of young architects who included Roberto Goycoolea (1928-2018), Christián de Groote (1931-2013), and Oscar Santelices.

This project represented the epitome of Duhart's career, consolidating him as a pivotal figure in modernism in the country and the continent. The CEPAL Building, now a landmark of modern architecture, was widely published, endowing Duhart with sharing the Latin American architectural limelight with other distinguished continental colleagues of the times. Valerie Fraser cited the CEPAL Building because it "can serve as a paradigmatic example of Latin America's own brand of architectural modernism,"[65] in a publication whose primary purpose was to argue that in Latin America, architects developed their own interpretation of modernism.

65 Fraser, *Building the New World: Studies in the Modern Architecture of Latin America 1930-1960*, 16.

The CEPAL headquarters is a dramatic modernist structure made predominantly out of reinforced concrete. It oscillates between its brutalist aspect, its unique layout, and its gravity-defying anti-seismic structural construction, simultaneously being an imposing stereotomic mass (pgs. 208, 209, 211). The CEPAL Building is an utterly modern structure completely permeated by regional cultural references integrated through abstract or conceptual operations in exercises consonant to prestidigitation procedures.

What one sees is not necessarily what it is. The translation of the modern lexicon integrates a variety of local and continental attributes tightly clustered together in such a way that its representational aspect is what you see, and its ontological aspect is concealed, and in some ways contradicts its appearance. Except for the shape of the twenty-eight pilotis, in a stylized and elongated form of the Mayan and Aztec temples that sustain the peripheral square ring, at first inspection the modern idiom takes precedent. The more the meanings of its components are unveiled, the more gravitas the structure captures, containing multiple layers of forethought that require careful study and observation to decipher its inner workings and design.

Upon entering the site, the viewer is faced with an expansive esplanade, a low orthogonal horizontal structure preceded by a grand elliptical water reservoir located diagonally to the face of the building and positioned asymmetrically to the right (pg. 207). In the background are the Andes Mountains. The overall design could be read as an iteration of the School of Art and Ballet complex project that Duhart designed at GSD, a square floor plan building with an internal patio where the ground floor outer edge appeared transparent. The CEPAL complex was conceived in a similar manner. It is composed of an autonomous one-story "floating" square ring of approximately 314 by 314 square feet with an interior quadrilateral opening of 218 by 218 square feet. Inside that internal space it contains three large independent structures. The three inner facilities (one of them never built for lack of funding) and the outer ring are linked to each other with covered walkways and bridges also free of support, which in turn form four open-air patios, smoothly relating both the ground and upper levels (pg. 215). The design contemplated a strictly functional and rational distribution with each division dedicated to functions common to the various bodies to be operating in the headquarters, each with their own name: The Ring was for offices, the Nucleus (a rectangular cuboid of rounded corners,) for administration, press, and technical equipment, the Diamond, never realized, for smaller meeting rooms (a volume with a polyhedral configuration and a folded slab roof), and the Caracol (Snail) for the general assembly (pg. 214). The modern conception of the Ring was "functionally … a one-level continuous [office] floor with standardized ceilings, floors and partitions, without any interference from structural elements,"[66] an open-plan flexible space.

As stated above, regional references abound in the design. Three of them were at the base of the architectural planning, two of which are common heritage to Latin American countries. These are the block's dimension of the Hispanic grid,[67] the template of the colonial Hispanic house with its internal patios

66 Emile Duhart, "Édifice des Nations Unies pour l'Amérique Latine," *Architecture d'Aujourd'hui*, Décembre 1967 – Janvier 1968, 54.

67 Approximately 328 square feet, which is the approximate dimensions of the Ring.

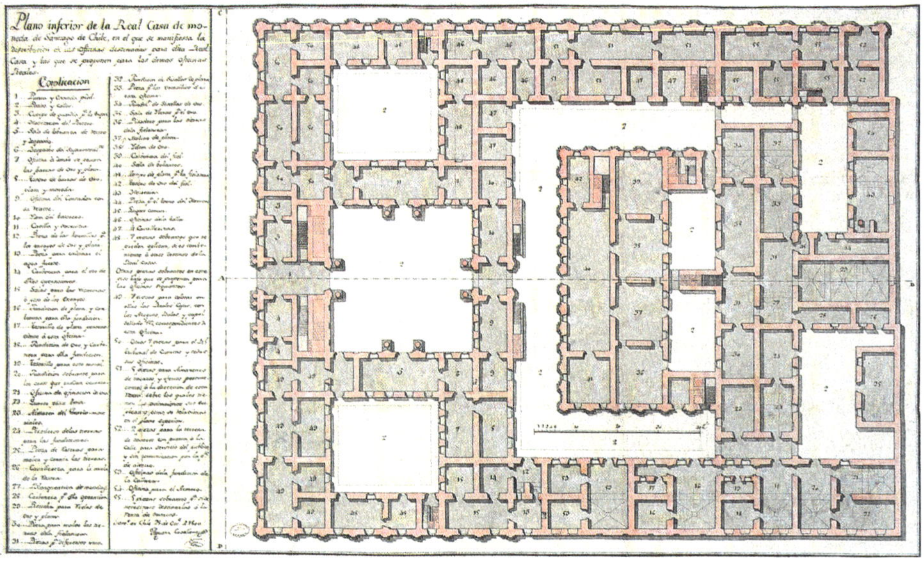

Figure 82: Agustín Caballero. La Moneda Palace. Floor plan, plan. 1800.

surrounded by the dwelling; and the layout of the Moneda Palace (1784-1805), the presidential palace of the Republic of Chile (fig. 82). Although in an updated and synthesized scheme, the presidential palace was considered by Duhart for being an institutional structure with many offices distributed around patios and circumscribed within a typical block. According to Duhart, "the sculptural volumes of the center [the Nucleus, the Diamond and the Caracol] are reminiscent of the mountainous masses which are … a characteristic element of the topography of the country."[68] The Caracol, the imposing rounded concrete volume one sees from outside the entrance, has a conical shape cut flat at the top, and houses two conference rooms superimposed one on top of the other. This structure, for the assembly meetings, is charged with meaning in its shapes, inscriptions, and details evocative of the Andean peaks. The external cement wall is inscribed with forty-eight low-relief symbols drawn by the architect, taken from iconography of the Americas from pre-Hispanic to contemporary times (pgs. 229-241). When positioning oneself at the center of the terrace-like roof and speaking at the top of the Caracol, a whispering-gallery type of wave is created, and the echo of the voice is heard when sound travels back around a slightly concave floor surface. It is a device to listen to one's voice above the plenary room, a space where talking and listening are essential.

68 Duhart, "Édifice des Nations Unies pour l'Amérique Latine," 54.

The four courtyards were each designated with their own name and are each distinct from the other in their specified botanical species. These were the Patio of Honor, the Green Patio, the Cactaceae (Cactus) Patio and the Flowers' Patio. As expressed by Duhart "the gardens [were] designed according to the climate of Santiago and the [country's] native flora."[69]

69 Duhart, "Édifice des Nations Unies pour l'Amérique Latine," 54.

The design of the building complex is permeated by an idiosyncratic way of addressing the elements of wind, light, and water, gathering, distributing, reflecting them, a focus reminiscent of the process of designing of the Villa Shodhan. The main façade confronts the predominant southwest wind flows that penetrate the courtyard through the entryway. A large set of windows of multiple sizes with outward protruding frames, also referred to as Winds Takes and located on the left of the Nucleus door in front of the entrance gather some of the currents, produce cross-ventilation, and redistribute the air flows throughout (pgs. 216-217). Additionally, according to José R. Camplá "these windows known as 'Winds Takes' … minimize the work of the air conditioning … in the months of greater solar exposure."[70]

70 Camplá, "Modernidad y Contextualidad Regional: El Caso de Emilio Duhart," 382.

With regards to lighting, in the original design of the Caracol, inside the large assembly room the lightwork gets much more intriguing and unique even if not completely realized. The plenary room has the option of being partially illuminated with natural light through two vertical interstices that are easy to manipulate to produce flush lighting on the curved walls. The initial design included a circular eye, the existing oculus, located towards the north, and the never realized double mirror heliostat (presumably inspired by the sacred pillar of Intihuatana in Machu Pichu, Peru) designed to capture and concentrate the sun's rays, directing them towards the inverted fiberglass dome. The dome called "the moon," hangs from the ceiling and is a mobile component with artificial lighting that serves as a light diffuser and acoustic buffer (pg. 227). Additionally, of the Nucleus, more light-play can be observed. Located in the interior to the right of the Nucleus entry door, the large set of windows of multiple sizes with outwardly protruding frames you can observe from the outside (already mentioned as Wind Takes) compose an unorthodox fenestration design with stained glass in multiple colors that produces dynamic lighting effects inside the interior hall of the Nucleus.

The presence and use of water in the CEPAL complex is by far the most surprising feature and runs through it as both a concealed and exposed system, somewhat hidden but for everyone to see at the same time. Rainwater is collected on the terraces of the Ring and the Nucleus roofs, and is guided by gutters to reach exhaust channels (pgs. 218-219, 222-223). From there it goes down through sixteen rain spouts, falling into their respective concrete receptacles in the shape of troughs measuring 9.2 feet by 4.6 feet (some with stones for slow water distribution). At ground level, the water converges into a main channel and then circulates between the four patios, watering the vegetation through irrigation ditches, a characteristic feature of the internal patios of the Chilean colonial house. Following their route, water reaches the great reservoir in front of the headquarters. This same water is then reused for the air conditioning system of the building's complex. The water circuit can be understood as a "hydrography that is inserted in the architecture through routes and pieces that make up 'the walk of the waters.'"[71] It can also be perceived as attesting to the profound love of nature that Duhart so insistently proclaimed, as well as his preoccupation with the economic use of resources.

71 Daniela Arancibia, "El Lenguaje del Agua en el Edificio de las Naciones Unidas" in *Emilio Duhart Obra Completa, Taller VII de Investigación,* Professor Fernando Pérez Oyarzun, 2005.

The twenty-eight columns of the Ring are pyramidal in shape, reminiscent of some of the Incan, Mayan, or Aztec pre-colonial architecture. Engaging with the materials surrounding the premises, both these columns and the headquarters' frontal walls are made out of a mixture of cement with stone balls brought from the nearby Mapocho River. The stones were left visible on the surface, suggesting the proximity of the waterway (pg. 213). Finally, Duhart imprinted the hands of the workers involved in the construction of the building in the access wall to the compound (pg. 228).

Adding even more complexity to the structural design, the CEPAL Building is a testament to the architect's audacity to devise a heavy and suspended structure in a country constantly battered by telluric forces. In the case of the headquarters of the Economic Commission for Latin America and the Caribbean, Duhart explored original solutions with anti-seismic technologies rarely adopted in the country before. The Ring is hanging on a structure with oscillating capabilities supported by twenty-eight columns attached to the foundation, and with specially designed shock absorbers between them (pg. 213). This method, inspired by bridge engineering, was employed to prevent horizontal collapse. The novel solutions also involved the structural support for the cantilevered access canopy (pg. 212), the placing of the Diamond quarter perched above the ground on four thick pedestals, and the Caracol that is slightly tilted to one side. From a technological point of view, this building represents a milestone in structural engineering, and despite having endured multiple earthquakes, is still in good condition.

The CEPAL Building was conceived as an architectural body both for contemplation of the landscape and to be contemplated itself. The frontal water reservoir doubles the building as a mirror, reflecting its inverted image, duplicating its presence, and exalting it at night with artificial lighting.

The human experience of the building is enhanced by additional special features. Duhart's architecture always fostered the contemplation of the landscape that surrounds it. In this case, he conceived an observation deck on the roof of the Caracol that faces the Andes Mountain Range to the east and the Manquehue Hill to the north, and an open-air auditorium on top of the Nucleus, both for contemplative use (pg. 224).

Once the project was accepted Duhart felt specially indebted to Le Corbusier. He sent him drawings with an accompanying letter. According to the architect, Le Corbusier immediately responded with some courteous lines. When Duhart visited Le Corbusier in Paris in 1965 right before his death, Le Corbusier reminisced of his multiple United Nations design frustrations, in Geneva, New York, and Paris.[72] This ended with Le Corbusier commenting about the United Nations building in Santiago and saying, "this is the revenge of the Latinos."[73] Of this comment Duhart remarked on the "strange utterance [from Le Corbusier] that even today leads me to reflection. That this work was carried out despite the economic and bureaucratic difficulties filled [Le Corbusier] with pleasure."[74]

72 Le Corbusier's proposal for the Palace of the United Nations Headquarters in Geneva was not approved. In the 1930s, the Palace of Soviets in Moscow was finally commissioned to the Institute of Architecture of the Soviet Union (IOFAN). In 1946, Le Corbusier was among the selected group of architects for the design of the United Nations Headquarters in New York; however, the process ended in disagreement. By 1951, he was excluded from the team of architects who designed the UNESCO Headquarters in Paris because the US representative vetoed his participation due to the controversies from the previous New York project.

73 Duhart, "Recuerdos de Le Corbusier," n/a.

74 Duhart, "Recuerdos de Le Corbusier," n/a.

However, Duhart was firm in his rejection of considering the project solely Corbusian:

> I am a bit bored with the question of Europe, the centers, and the periphery. [In] the United Nations [building] there was a pre-Columbian era as present as Corbu and others. Chile too … and there is colonial Chile as well. But here in Chile, [people] always usually refer to the architects of modern history or of European countries, or of American influence … Yes, of course, but why leave aside the things typical of here, of the continent? It's curious. It e will be no Chilean architecture of its own.[75]

75 Pérez Oyarzun and Urrejola, "Series of interviews with Emilio Duhart," audioeo interview, Part 4 of 8.

The above declaration squarely aligns with the ideas animating this book. The value assigned to a work of architecture should not only rest on the influences that could come from hegemonic foreign ideas but also on those that come from regional circumstances. Furthermore, it is due to the application of modernity without giving agency to the particularities of the local that the worldwide architectural landscape has flattened, with the resulting cultural loss and diminished sense of belonging that this engenders.

United Nations Economic Commission for Latin America and the Caribbean (CEPAL)

BAS RELIEFS CONFERENCE ROOM, CARACOL BUILDING - CEPAL

The forty-eight symbols displayed below were inscribed on the exterior wall of the Caracol within the CEPAL complex, designed by Emilio Duhart between 1960 and 1966.

In July 2024, the author of this book sought more information about these bas-reliefs and reached out to Alberto Montealegre Klenner, an architect who had collaborated with Emilio Duhart for about a decade. Montealegre joined Duhart's office during the construction of the CEPAL Building. During my conversation with him, Montealegre revealed that, under Duhart's guidance, he was responsible for most of the drawings used to inscribe these symbols on the façade of the Caracol. This critical detail had previously been unknown.

Isabel García Pérez de Arce, the director of the Archivo de Originales at the Pontificia Universidad Católica de Chile, and José Pérez de Arce, who holds a PhD in Latin American studies, later interviewed Montealegre to document his insights about the bas-reliefs. During the interview, Montealegre explained that Duhart selected the images based on the criterion that these inscriptions should serve as 'icons' or 'cultural traces' reflecting the history and culture of Latin America and the Caribbean. This selection was intended to help integrate the Caracol building as a 'landmark' for a shared continental history. Montealegre further noted that the drawings were primarily based on bibliographical sources rather than original ones. He also mentioned that the drawings were created while building construction was already in progress. To convert these sketches into a physical form, he took them to a carpenter who made templates from thin pressed wood planks and plywood. Montealegre then transported these templates to the construction site to be embedded into the fresh concrete.

For this publication, José Pérez de Arce was commissioned to write the explanatory texts for the forty-eight signs published here. As a whole and in chronological order, they tell a continental historical narrative of Latin America and the Caribbean from the perspective of Emilio Duhart. Pérez de Arce's texts are drawn from direct observation of the icons in the CEPAL Building, from photographs he took in situ, from drawings housed in the Emilio Duhart Documentary Fund, and from the bibliography either indicated in the original diagrams, Montealegre's accounts, or from relevant new sources identified by Pérez de Arce.

The texts accompanying the symbols on the following pages were written by José Pérez de Arce, PhD in Latin American Studies.

Duhart, E. 1965. *Fell's Cavern.*
Drawing #1 on tracing paper.

THE FIRST HUMANS

Fire, the remains of an extinct horse, and stone artifacts represent the first human presence in the Chilean territory. Thanks to the findings in Monteverde, we know that 14,800 years ago, there were villages where shamanic rituals were celebrated. Hunting the mastodon, the horse, or the mylodon required a lot of group coordination. All the cultures that would develop in the following 14,000 years began there.

Duhart, E. 1965. *Guanaco Scouting.*
Drawing #2 on tracing paper.

THE GUANACO AND THE ANDEAN MAN

Rock carvings of guanaco inscriptions found in caves in Patagonia represent guanaco hunting 8,000 years ago, perhaps by scaring and diverting prey from the herd to hunt it more easily. The guanaco was the main animal for its meat and skin. Its family structure is a social model of mutual care, with a father and several mothers and offspring. It lives only in South America and has become extinct in much of the territory.

Duhart, E. 1965. *Hands: Cave Canyon.*
Drawing #3 on tracing paper.

ROCK PAINTING IN PATAGONIA

The drawing is copied from inscriptions found in the Painted Hands Cave in Argentine Patagonia, where 7,300 years ago, the inhabitants of that area rested their hands on the rock and, blowing colored earth, left their footprints. The hand imprints were probably from hunting ceremonies, as an act of reciprocity where the hunters paid with their art, the first we know of on the continent.

Duhart, E. 1965. *Magical Dance.*
Drawing #4 on tracing paper.

THE PETROGLYPHS OF TORO MUERTO, AREQUIPA

These rock engravings, totaling more than 6,000 blocks in the Majes Valley, were made between 800 and 1,500 A.D., or perhaps even earlier. It's important to note that their interpretation is speculative; some images suggest dance actions with headdresses or masks. By ethnographic association, it is assumed that the stone was considered a living being which, through appropriate rituals, made communication with the tutelary spirits of animals and plants possible.

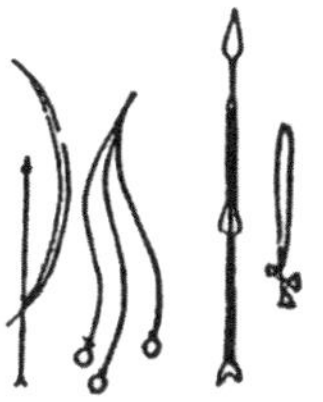

Duhart, E. 1965. *Arms.*
Drawing #5 on tracing paper.

THE ESTÓLICA, THE BOLEADORA, AND THE BOW

The drawing represents the weapons used when there were only wild animals, and hunting was a form of relationship with the environment. The estólica allows shots with force, speed, and precision, capable of killing large animals. The bow slowly replaced it with less power but greater control. The boleadora lets the animal be captured alive by entangling its legs. Over time, these weapons will become symbols of power.

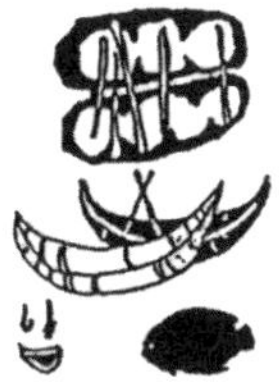

Duhart, E. 1965. *Fisher People.*
Drawing #6 on tracing paper.

PRE-HISPANIC BOATS

The drawing depicts navigation 4,000 years ago on the northern coast of Peru, with boats made of reeds still in use. The raft made out of inflated wolf hides was used 1,000 years ago on what is now the northern coast of Chile. It continued to be used until the beginning of the twentieth century by the changos that loaded saltpeter onto ships.

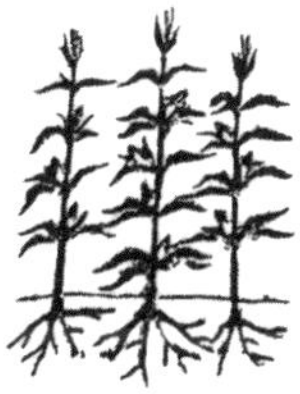

Duhart, E. 1965. *Maize.*
Drawing #7 on tracing paper.

MAIZE

The choclo, maíz or elote, was domesticated in Mexico about 9,000 years ago. From there, it spread throughout the Americas thanks to its ease of adaptation. According to legend, the first Mayans were made from corn. The domestication process produced many varieties of flavors, colors, and uses. Over time, the plant lost the ability to reproduce without human help.

Duhart, E. 1965. *Irrigation: Diagram of Canals and Crop Lands. Outside of Vurú, Valle del Santa.*
Drawing #7A on tracing paper.

MOCHE AGRICULTURAL IRRIGATION PLAN

The drawing represents the irrigation system with sinuous furrows used in the arid coastal areas of northern Peru 3,500 years ago. They allowed production to increase in the densely populated valleys of the Moche civilization, helping to conserve soil moisture and prevent erosion. A similar system was used in Tiwanaku, in the Bolivian highlands, 1,400 years ago.

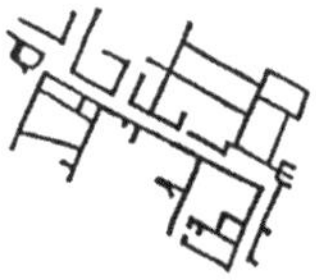

Duhart, E. 1965. *Atacameño Village Near Solor.*
Drawing #8 on tracing paper.

PLAN OF AN ATACAMEÑO INCA VILLAGE

The drawing corresponds to the floor plan of an Atacama town in northern Chile. It is probably Incan due to the complexity of the enclosures, squares, and streets in orthogonal layouts, typical of a large dairy farm. The tambos, accommodations and warehouses at the service of the Inca Trail (Kapak Ñam), were only utilized by officials, soldiers, or priests of the empire.

Duhart, E. 1965. *Venus of Tlatilco.*
Drawing #9 on tracing paper.

THE TLATILCO CIVILISATION

The small ceramic female figurines, with intricate headdresses and painted bodies, were part of a complex ritual system associated with the agricultural cycle of Tlatilco (the place of hidden things) in central Mexico 3,200 years ago. Along with obsidian, jade, and cinnabar, they were part of the abundant trade with various peoples that extended from the Pacific to the Atlantic.

Duhart, E. 1965. *Shepherd and Llamas.*
Drawing #10 on tracing paper.

THE LLAMA AND THE ANDEAN MAN

This pictograph alludes to llama livestock, a central element of the Andean civilization. Its wool allowed for cultural development in textiles. It was the only sizeable domestic animal in America, with behavior similar to humans in several aspects. Today, they are celebrated in festivals in the highlands of Chile and Bolivia.

Duhart, E. 1965. *Feline Divinity, Ceremonial Mortar.*
Drawings #11, 11a, 11b and 11c on tracing paper.

THE CHAVÍN FELINE-SNAKE

The image of the feline with large fangs, both a snake and an eagle, spread as part of the Chavín civilization 2,900 years ago from the northern mountains of Peru to the entire Central Andes. The drawing corresponds to a stone mortar used to grind visionary plants that would allow the shaman to transform into a powerful animal and communicate with the powers of nature.

Duhart, E. 1965. *Megalithic Stele, San Agustín, Colombia.* Drawing #12 on tracing paper.

THE JAGUAR-MAN OF COLOMBIA

In San Agustín, Colombia, enormous stone sculptures were made 2,500 years ago as part of the site's transformation into the region's main necropolis. Processions came from distant towns to bury their rulers in large tombs with mounds, sculptures, and temples. This figure, with a skull hanging on his chest, may have been represented in those rituals.

Duhart, E. 1965. *God or Priest with Coas.* Drawing #13 on tracing paper.

THE SUN-FELINE OF TIWANAKU

The drawing synthesizes two images of the sun-feline Tiwanaku, which dominated the high Andean region of Titicaca 1,500 years ago. The legend says that he was born from the lake and that corn, condors, pumas, llamas, and seeds sprouted from his face like the sun's rays, and that his staffs broke the earth and made it arable. Tiwanaku's knowledge is based on complementarity and balance, and radiated to Peru and Chile.

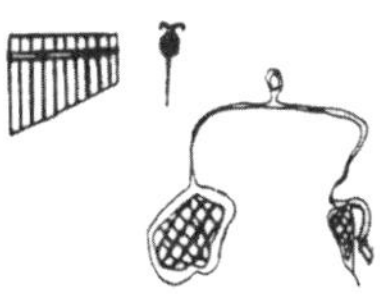

Duhart, E. 1965. *Transpacific Relationship: Pan Flute, Pin, Scale.* Drawing #14 on tracing paper.

THE ANTARA, THE TUPU, AND THE PORTABLE SCALE

These three objects, the antara, the tupu, and the portable scale, are not just artifacts. They are unique representations of widespread and diverse pre-Hispanic traditions, each with a rich and awe-inspiring history. The antara, also known as the Andean pan flute, is not only the oldest but also the most abundant and varied pan flute in the world, a testament to the ingenuity of ancient Andean cultures. The tupu, a silver pin, underscores its historical significance with its age and widespread use in the Andes. The portable wooden scale, with its hanging meshes, symbolizes reciprocal balance in Andean trade, a tradition that commands respect.

Duhart, E. 1965. *Ecuadorian Raft.* Drawing #15 on tracing paper.

THE PRE-HISPANIC ECUADORIAN RAFT

Large rafts loading up to fifteen tons in pre-Hispanic Ecuador could navigate to Mexico. Made of balsa wood, they had up to six keels, two large oars, and several sails to maneuver. They were in use until 1858, when this drawing was made for a French magazine.

Duhart, E. 1965. *Easter Island, Petroglyph.*
Drawing #16 on tracing paper.

THE BIRD-MAN, RAPANUI

The engraving of the Tangata Manu, or bird-man, holding an egg, is a powerful symbol of the complex ritual practices of Easter Island. In this ritual, the bird-man played a crucial role, symbolizing the delicate balance between man and nature in the island's ecosystem. The ritual itself was a challenging one, requiring a swim to the Motu Nui islet, the retrieval of the first egg of the manutara bird, and its transport to the summit of the Ranu Kau volcano. The individual who accomplished this feat was revered as the ruler for a year.

Duhart, E. 1965. *Sacrifice to the Sun, Stele of Santa Lucía, Cotzumalhuapa, Guatemala.*
Drawing #17 on tracing paper.

THE MAYAN STELE OF COTZUMALHUAPA

The seven stelae of the Mayan city of Cotzumalhuapa, Guatemala celebrated the ball game ritual 1,400 years ago. The scene shows the part of the solar deity with bird claws, and below a hand offering a head. Missing is the cosmic reptile from which the god emerges, the ball player who sings alongside the god of death, and the two glyphs that allude to the ruler.

Duhart, E. 1965. *Nahua Glyphs.*
Drawing #18 on tracing paper.

AZTEC WRITING

The Aztec glyph system in the Nahuatl language was developed from the oldest writing system of Mexico. It could represent sounds, letters, words, and sentences using shapes, sizes, colors, and positions. With Nahuatl being an official language of the Viceroyalty of New Spain, its writing was prohibited and eradicated after the Hispanic invasion.

Duhart, E. 1965. *Astronomical Observatory.*
Drawing #19 on tracing paper.

THE AZTEC READING

The drawing dominated by the calendar sign calli ("house") from some Aztec codex has been interpreted as an astronomical observatory. Only an elite would have been acquainted with the writing of glyphs. They knew how to arrange, from left to right and top to bottom each part's color, position, and size to read phonetic sounds, words, or concepts.

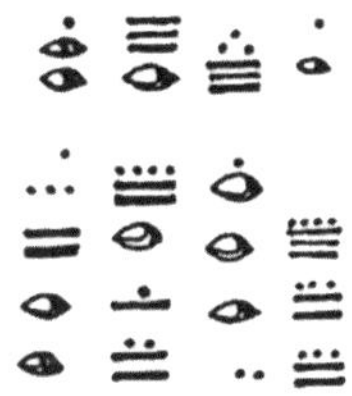

Duhart, E. 1965. *Mayan Numbers.*
Drawing #20 on tracing paper.

MAYAN MATHEMATICS

The Maya in Guatemala created a mathematical system in which a dot represented the number 1, a dash represented 5, and a shell represented 0. Moving up one row of a number multiplies the number by 20, and two rows then by 400 (20x20) and then three rows by 8,000 (20x20x20). It was used for calendrical calculations based on the solar and lunar calendars. The Spanish colonizers burned all Mayan codices.

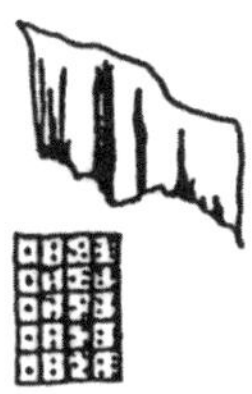

Duhart, E. 1965. *Ábaco and Quipus.*
Drawing #21 on tracing paper.

THE KIPU AND THE YUPANA

The kipu was an Incan textile writing system. Using knots of different shapes and positions in twisted wool or cotton threads of chosen colors, they wrote Quechua. After the Hispanic invasion, its reading was lost when the colonizers systematically eliminated all traces of interpretation. The yupana was an Incan abacus that used squares and pebbles to calculate large amounts.

Duhart, E. 1965. *Suspension Bridge.*
Drawing #22 on tracing paper.

THE INCA ENGINEERING

The simppachaca ("rope-bridge") were hanging bridges that allowed the Incan road network to extend across the complex Andean geography. The textile solution allowed for a collective, collaborative construction based on plant cords that were braided until thick cables that resisted the weight were achieved. The material required repeating the process every two years through mitas, which were work, parties, and competition rituals. Today, only a few remain as tourist attractions.

Duhart, E. 1965. *Water Tank (Sacsauhuamán), Crop Terraces.*
Drawing #23 on tracing paper.

THE INCA URBANIZATION OF SACSAYHUAMÁN

The large circular structure of Sacsayhuamán, interpreted as an agricultural pond, is today known to be part of a multi-story stone tower from the fifteen or sixteen century. From its base, water flowed into five fountains, and spiral stairs connected the upper floors, which had a panoramic view of Cusco. The Andean platforms represent the ecological and integrated system of the agricultural domain of the hills.

.Duhart, E. 1965. *Quetzalcoatl, the Feathered Serpent.*
Drawings #24A and 24B on tracing paper.

QUETZALCOATL – THE TOLTEC FEATHERED SERPENT

This figure of Quetzalcoatl, the feathered serpent covered in snails, appears in the Pyramid of Xochicalco ("the place of the house of flowers"), built in 664 AD. Quetzalcoatl was a man-bird-snake, lord of learning, who invented the calendar, writing, metallurgy, and agriculture. The pyramid is covered with names, dates, events, and characters associated with ball game rituals.

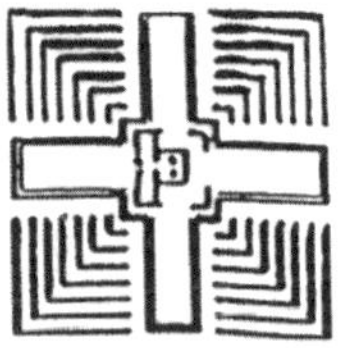

Duhart, E. 1965. *Plant of the Kukulcán Temple in Chichen-Itza.*
Drawing #25 on tracing paper.

PLANT OF THE KUKULCÁN PYRAMID

The Pyramid of Kukulcán was built in the twelve century AD in Chichen Itzá, the great Mayan city of the Yucatán. The complex double calendar of 260 and 365 days governed its construction, oriented towards the equinoxes and solstices, generating lights and shadows with its steps, facades, staircases, and other elements. Every 52 years, the two calendars coincided, and a new pyramid was built on top of the previous one.

Duhart, E. 1965. *Chimu Head. Brochure Economic Commission for Latin America and the Caribbean (CEPAL): Symbols of Latin America and the Caribbean* (page 20).

THE MOCHE PORTRAIT

The Moche civilization developed in northern Peru between 100 BC until 700 AD. Each valley was independent, but together, they constituted a powerful cultural focus, with large pyramids and urban centers. Within its ceramic art, hundreds of portraits stand out, all different, of great realism, and probably related to funerary customs.

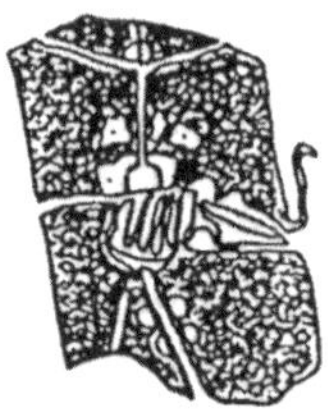

Duhart, E. 1965. *Tenochtitlán.*
Drawing #27 on tracing paper.

TENOCHTITLÁN – THE AZTEC CAPITAL

Tenochtitlán was the capital of the Aztec Empire of Mexico. Thanks to the record of the amazement that the Spanish felt when they arrived in 1519, we know that it was one of the largest cities in the world, with a vast market, avenues, drawbridges, piers, canals, aqueducts, and two-story houses with gardens and drinking water. A year and eight months later, as a consequence of the colonizing war and the plague, the Aztec capital was destroyed.

Duhart, E. 1965. *Caravels.*
Drawings #28a, 28b, 28c and 28d on tracing paper.

THE ARRIVAL OF CHRISTOPHER COLUMBUS

In 1492, Christopher Columbus's three ships arrived at Guanahani Island in the Bahamas. By taking possession of the island, calling it San Salvador, and naming its inhabitants *Indians,* the era of colonial rule based on the ignorance of the locals was inaugurated, which continues to this day.

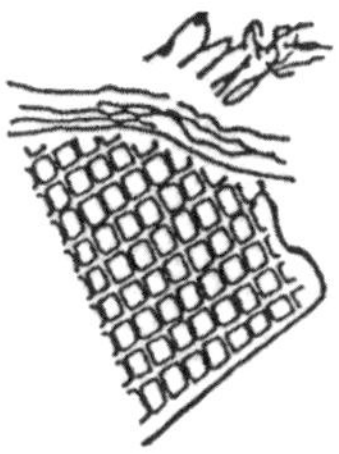

Duhart, E. 1965. *Santiago del Nuevo Extremo.*
Drawing #29 on tracing paper.

SANTIAGO DEL NUEVO EXTREMO

The map of Santiago and Pedro de Valdivia's signature symbolize the beginning of colonial rule in Chile. In 1540, Valdivia proclaimed land ownership and founded Santiago over the Incan city.

Duhart, E. 1965. *Fusion of races.*
Drawing #30 on tracing paper.

THE SOUTH AMERICAN MESTIZAJE

Latin America is the continent with the most mixed population in the world due to the introduction of Europeans and Africans as the foundation of the colonizing process. Over time, this generated a multiethnic, multicultural, and economically segregated population.

Duhart, E. 1965. *Religious Orders.*
Drawing #31a and 31b on tracing paper.

THE CATHOLIC MISSIONS

The shields of the Jesuit, Augustinian, Dominican, Franciscan, and Mercedarian orders that arrived on the continent represent the process of evangelization and Catholic education of the indigenous people. They were effective agents of colonization to replace vernacular knowledge. But paradoxically, we owe the little we know about pre-Hispanic cultures to them.

Duhart, E. 1965. *Chapel and image of Fray Pedro de Gante*. Drawing from the Aztec Codex. Drawing #31a on tracing paper.

COLONIAL EDUCATION

This image, taken from some Mesoamerican colonial codex, represents a chapel, an image of Fray Pedro de Gante, and a cactus. Fray Pedro de Gante was one of the first missionaries dedicated to indoctrinating the Aztec nobles in Texcoco in Catholic teaching and obedience to the king. The nopal, a Mexican cactus, is a central symbol of the Mayan and Aztec civilizations, and it is today present in the coat of arms of Mexico.

Duhart, E. 1965. *San Marcos University.* Drawing #32 on tracing paper.

NATIONAL UNIVERSITY OF SAN MARCOS

The shield of this university represents the first university in South America, founded in 1548 to imbue the Christian faith and submission to the king. It became a university in 1551 under the strict control of the Inquisition. Over time, it gradually became autonomous from the Church, supported independence from the Spaniards, and continued its educational role in the twentieth century.

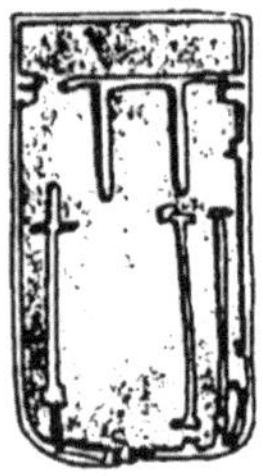

Duhart, E. 1965. *Sao Joao Del-Rei Architecture (Carmelita Church)* Drawing #33 on tracing paper.

PLAN OF SÃO JOÃO DEL-REI CATHEDRAL

The Cathedral of São João Del-Rei was built between 1774 and 1809 according to the conventional colonial plan, with a central nave, side altars, and choir. But its architects, especially Aleijadinho, gave it a marked local style. The baroque style with gilding, sculptures, and curved stairs made it an icon of Brazilian baroque art.

Duhart, E. 1965. *A Montgolfiere.* Drawing #35a on tracing paper.

THE AIR BALLOON

The drawing represents the unmanned hot air balloon that the expedition of Jean François de Galaup, Count of la Pérouse, raised in Talcahuano, Chile in 1786 in honor of Don Ambrosio O'Higgins. Appearing three years earlier in France, they became widespread through shows and fairs, and to this day they are still used both for entertainment and scientific purposes.

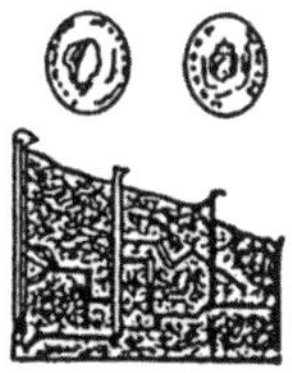

Duhart, E. 1965. *Mining and Trade.*
Drawings #34a and 34b on tracing paper.

MINING AND TRADE

The 1773 gold coin represents the global economy with the image of King Charles III. The image of mining pits represents Chile's main economic activity, which is represented by gold, silver, saltpeter, and copper.

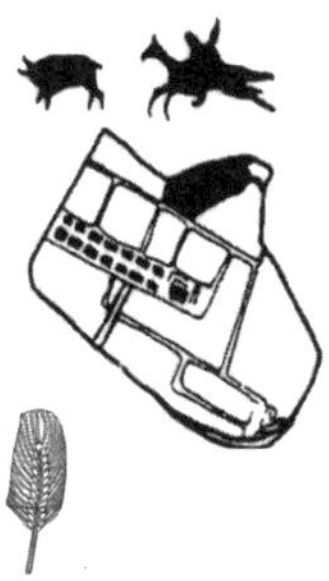

Duhart, E. 1965. *Agriculture (a Hacienda in Chile.)*
Drawing #35 on tracing paper.

PLANT OF A COLONIAL HACIENDA

A colonial hacienda, a huaso (a Chilean cowboy) herding cattle, and an ear of wheat symbolize the agricultural boom caused by wheat export between 1687 and 1879 to Peru, California, and Australia. On the hacienda, based on the Andalusian model, a landowning family governed a population of tenants, laborers, and also enslaved Mapuche or Huarpe people.

Duhart, E. 1965. *Independence.*
Drawing #36 on tracing paper.

INDEPENDENCE

The drawing represents the Independence of Latin American countries through the Mauser rifle as technology of war, the Phrygian cap that symbolizes the ideas of freedom of the French Revolution, and the five-pointed star, a symbol of Freemasonry that through the Lodge Lautaro promoted the libertarian process. Between 1803 and 1836, all the countries of South America became independent except Puerto Rico and Cuba.

Duhart, E. 1965. *The Constitution and the Printing Press.*
Drawing #37 on tracing paper.

THE LAW AND THE PRINTING PRESS

The scales and the sword symbolize justice in colonial times and until today. The printing press used in 1811 by Camilo Henríquez represents the first publication of the thoughts of the independent government. This allowed the ideas of freedom and independence to be disseminated among the small intellectual circle that knew how to read and write in Chile, beginning the era of the newspaper that would gain greater importance until the twentieth century.

Duhart, E. 1965. *The Bandeirantes: The conquest of the territory.* Drawing #38 on tracing paper.

THE *BANDEIRANTES*

The drawing represents the bandeirantes, adventurers who entered Brazil during the seventeenth century, expanding their territory from Sao Pablo to the interior. They were slave traffickers who captured Guaraníes to sell them to plantations or mining and searched for gold and silver. Their primary opponents were the Jesuits, who defended the Guaraní populations. In Brazil they are considered colonizing heroes, and in Sao Paulo, they have a grand monument.

Duhart, E. 1965. *European Immigration XIX Century* Drawing #39a and 39b on tracing paper.

REPUBLICAN COLONIZATION

The Immigrant Hotel built in Buenos Aires in 1888 represents the accelerated pace of European immigration promoted by Latin American governments. This allowed Western dominion to extend over the indigenous territories, considered "deserts." The incessant European colonization has generated a mestizo territory of great complexity and enormous inequalities.

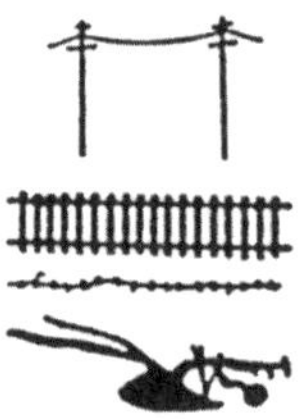

Duhart, E. 1965. *Electricity, Railways, Barbed Wire, Plough. Brochure Economic Commission for Latin America and the Caribbean (CEPAL): Symbols of Latin America and the Caribbean* (page 28)

ELECTRICITY, RAILWAYS, BARBED WIRE, AND THE PLOW

These developments, namely electricity, railways, barbed wire, and the plow, symbolize Latin American countries' transformative progress. The electrical revolution, for instance, brought about a profound change with the introduction of lighting, the tram, industrial motors, and electronics. The railway, on the other hand, revolutionized communication between regions. Fences, a simple yet crucial invention, demarcated the property of settlers occupying new territories, and the plow, a symbol of agricultural progress, produced economic value in these new territories.

Duhart, E. 1965. *Alberto Santos Dumont in "The Demoiselle."* Drawing #42 on tracing paper

THE *DEMOISELLE*

This plane was a model designed by Alberto Santos Dumont, of Brazilian origin. Its first flight was made in 1906, three years after the first flight of the Wright brothers, and through successive improvements, it was able to participate in international competitions in Paris, Brazil, and other countries. Over time, the plane would become the main transport connecting Latin America with the rest of the world.

Duhart, E. 1965. *Education, suffrage and planning. Brochure Economic Commission for Latin America and the Caribbean (CEPAL): Symbols of Latin America and the Caribbean* (page 29)

EDUCATION, VOTING RIGHTS, AND PLANNING

These have been basic factors of development. The right to vote has been incorporating men, women, indigenous people, and Afro-descendants into political decisions. Education has been reinforcing the basis of official culture, and planning is the tool to move towards a preconceived future.

Duhart, E. 1965. *Blast Furnace.* Brochure *Economic Commission for Latin America and the Caribbean (CEPAL): Symbols of Latin America and the Caribbean* (page 30)

INDUSTRIAL DEVELOPMENT

The diagram of a blast furnace in the steel industry refers to steel produced from iron oxide, from which oxygen is extracted through coal at high temperatures. In Chile, steel was used since 1872 in the Central Market, the Malleco Viaduct, and other buildings. In 1950, Siderúrgica Huachipato was inaugurated, which, in its peak period, became one of the most essential steel producers internationally.

Duhart, E. 1965. *Brasilia.*
Drawing #45 on tracing paper.

BRASILIA

Brasilia, the federal capital of Brazil, was built in the interior of the country between 1956 and 1960 by a team led by urban planner Lucio Costa, architect Oscar Niemeyer, and landscape designer Burle Marx. Its cross-shaped plan indicates the possession and conquest of the territory, and its avant-garde architectural design includes administrative, functional, and residential areas linked by highways. The cathedral stands out, with its curved shape that opens to the sky.

Duhart, E. 1965. *Demographic Explosion. Brochure Economic Commission for Latin America and the Caribbean (CEPAL): Symbols of Latin America and the Caribbean* (page 31).

THE DEMOGRAPHIC EXPLOSION

The drawing alludes to demographic growth accelerated by a birth rate higher than the mortality rate, an increment achieved by increasing life expectancy and reducing infant mortality. Since the middle of the twentieth century, there is a danger that the population will exceed the planet's capacity to sustain it.

URBANISM AS COMMUNITY BUILDING

Duhart's urban planning is a group of work of a different category and should be analyzed separately to distill the all-encompassing notions that motivated it. As previously discussed, the discovery of the field of urbanism prompted Duhart to study architecture. This interest was evidenced first in his degree project and then continued throughout his professional career. His deep admiration for airplanes during his youth sparked dreams of aerial views of the landscape. These reveries may have inspired him to imagine the topographic fields from above, culminating in his involvement in studying cities, questioning their forms and functions, and opening a new area of interest. Morshed writes, "the advent of flight ushered in new kinds of visual and spatial perceptions,"[76] recounting that Le Corbusier sketched his urban designs for Rio de Janeiro in 1929 when flying in an airplane over the bay, informing his ideas about modern planning.

Motivated by his significant conceptual preoccupation with aerial, topographical, and social awareness, Duhart conceived around a dozen urban and urban-related projects, some of them never realized. Additionally, in 1951 he founded and directed the Institute of Planning, Urbanism, and Housing to develop research and a working method that contributed to the more expansive knowledge of Chile's regional and urban problems, an endeavor he led for six years and an added task to his multiple endeavors.

Duhart's urban planning projects are roughly divided into small-scale cities or neighborhoods, city regulatory plans, and university cities. These projects are united by a common aim centered on the human scale and urban arrangements that promoted community building.

Duhart got involved in urbanism because he was deeply touched by the contrasting social reality he observed in Chile when he first arrived from Paris in 1935. His observations reflected a broader context developing in the country. At the onset of the twentieth century, due to industrialization a massive migration towards urban centers was initiated, driven by the changes of the macroeconomy.[77] The Great Depression of 1929 had devastated the economy of Chile, increasing poverty and social malaises. This was aggravated by the earthquake of 1939 that caused immense devastation.

76 Adnan Morshed, "The Cultural Politics of Aerial Vision: Le Corbusier in Brazil (1929)," *Journal of Architectural Education*, Vol. 55, Nº 4 (May, 2002):201, http://www.jstor.com/stable/1425721

77 As stated by Beatrix Aguirre and Salim Rabí in "La Trayectoria Espacial de la Corporación de la Vivienda," "In Santiago, in the same year, approximately 350,000 people live in tenements, 'cités' and houses that were sublet by pieces. This figure represents 65,000 families, that is, 30% of the city's population at that time. The number of inhabitants living in slums, is estimated at 75,000, corresponding to 6.25% of the population of Santiago. Santiago absorbs 57.92% of the urban population of the country. The annual growth rate of the urban population of Santiago corresponds to 3.1% in the period 1940-1952."

These crises resulted in overcrowding and saturation of the urban infrastructure, developments that prevented large segments of the population access to decent housing. As exposed by the Chilean architectural magazines during the period 1930-1950, city planning and the lack of low-income housing were the problems most debated,[78] attesting to a deep preoccupation within the profession about a grave situation.

78 Hugo Mongragón López, "Project on Social Engineering: The debate on Housing Plan in Journals, Santiago, 1930-1950," *AUS* 17, first semester 2015, 30, http://revistas.uach.cl/pdf/aus/n17/art06.pdf.

Duhart, like many of his generation, was influenced by new concepts in architecture and planning that were widespread internationally and which had a tremendous impact on Chilean architecture. In the international arena, starting in the late 1920s, modern architecture was being fundamentally changed by the advent of modern urbanism elaborated by the International Congresses of Modern Architecture (CIAM,) founded in Switzerland in 1928. The CIAM was an affiliation of European avant-garde architectural professionals that met regularly. The ideas discussed by the CIAM up until 1933 converged around "the new international ideal of urban living conditions for the urban masses."[79] According to Eric Mumford, the general view was that the "industrial cities should be designed with the purpose of improving the living conditions of the majority of the population, increasing economic efficiency through improvements in transportation systems, and protecting the natural environment as a site for mass recreation."[80] In 1933, at their most consequential congress for modern urbanism's fate, the CIAM came up with its most far-reaching and long-lived notion: the concept of the Functional City with the rational territorial distribution of the four basic functions of dwelling, work, recreation, and transportation. The second crucial concept elaborated by CIAM introduced for the post-war years was the notion of the Heart of the City, a fifth function that had escaped previous postulates. This notion of the Heart of the City (CIAM 8, 1951) considered civic and cultural space as sites for pedestrians and public life in the planning of urbanizations. The CIAM was a polyphonic organization, with a spectrum of opinions on the same general theme. However, some voices had more significant weight than others, including those of Gropius, Le Corbusier, Sigfried Giedion, and Josep Lluís Sert, the Spanish architect and president of CIAM from 1947 until 1956.

79 Eric Mumford, "El Discurso del CIAM Sobre el Urbanismo, 1928-1960," *Bitacora: Urbano/Territorial,* accessed August 21, 2020, 98, https://revistas.unal.edu.co/index.php/bitacora/article/view/18632/19528

80 Mumford, Eric, "El Discurso del CIAM Sobre el Urbanismo, 1928-1960," 98.

Duhart's focus on the human factor explains his adoption of another concept to which he paid close attention. It relates to the neighborhood units, a precept first developed by the American urban planner Clarence Perry (1872-1944) and later adopted by Josep Lluís Sert in his influential book *Can Our Cities Survive?* Under this schema, the neighborhood unit's basic principles included a semi-independent residential assemblage of a predetermined size (in this case 5,000 to 10,000 inhabitants) secluded from the large traffic arteries and sharing open spaces. Duhart's concern in breaking down the city scape into smaller assemblages is associated with "the topography concept of the bounded domain or place, as opposed to the space endlessness of the megalopolis,"[81] where an amorphous city formation feeds human alienation with no sense of belonging and from which developing more permanent human contact becomes a challenge. Although the exact source of information is unknown, the Fishing Base degree project (1941) was inspired by the early ideas of the CIAM. It is essential to point out that the Fishing Base's urban organization was centered around a central core of community buildings anticipating by more than a decade Josep Lluís Sert's notion of the Heart of the City.

81 Frampton, *Studies in Tectonic Culture*, 22.

Duhart was particularly interested in the international developments in urban planning, and in a note on social awareness, he declared that "the … human must be preserved: we must defend the poor man of the twentieth century, a little lost among [the] … machines that harass him … It is essential to recover a social sensibility appropriate to human nature, with full and fair use of the new physical forces that technical progress provides us,"[82] a statement that signaled the architect's desire to invest himself in urbanism. The result was a series of works that combined functionalism and rationalism as central to their approach, along with a strong emphasis on human-centered urban planning.

82 Duhart H., "En Busqueda de la Tradicion Viva," 18.

In 1946, as previously mentioned, Duhart and Larraín designed President Ríos New City, considered to be the first modern industrial city built in the country. The new city was created to house a population of 35,000 workers for the Compañía de Acero del Pacífico (Pacific Steel Company.) Its organization was based on four neighborhood units that provided essential community services (schools, markets, recreation, and more) and converged on a central point, the civic center. According to Veronica Esparza,[83] the fundamental contribution of this urbanization was the interpretation of international references, specifically the Charter of Athens, adapted to the specific social reality of the community of workers, prioritizing social rather than functional considerations.[84]

83 Author of the doctoral thesis "Emilio Duhart Harostegui, un Arquitecto Integral: 1935-1992."

84 Verónica Esparza Saavedra, "Villa Presidente Ríos en Talcahuano, 1947-1951," Academia, accessed August 12, 2020, https://www.academia.edu/22618385/VILLA_PRESIDENTE_RÍOS_EN_TALCAHUANO_1947_1951_SERGIO_LARRAÍN_G_M_Y_EMILIO_DUHART_H

One of the early examples of urban planning Duhart created was the Achupallas Urbanization Housing Project (1953), for the Valparaiso Workers' Union Confederation, to be realized on a 2,259-acre piece of land to accommodate a group of 25,000 inhabitants. Although never built for lack of funding, Duhart assigned great personal importance to this project, affirming

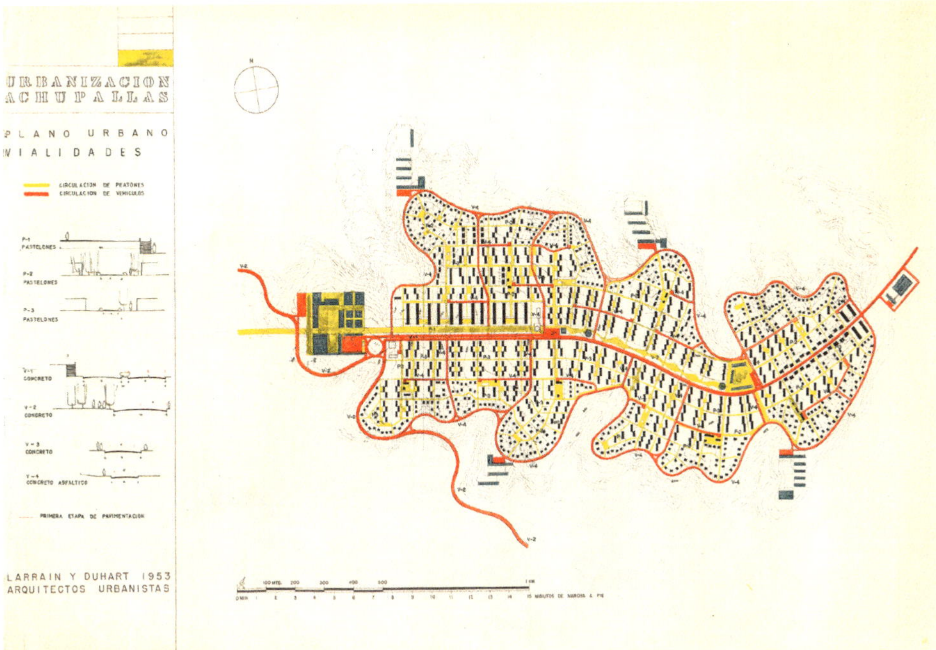

Figure 83: Emilio Duhart and Sergio Larraín G-M, architects. Urbanización Achupallas, Viña del Mar, Chile. Urban plan, Vialidades, 1953.

that it was "a beautiful project that could have been a model for Latin America."[85] The urbanization was to be located on the crest of the hills, oriented towards the ocean, between Valparaiso and the neighboring city of Viña del Mar, in a geographical area where the Pacific meets the coastal mountain range. The urban proposal was a settlement organically shaped and deposited on the hills' peaks, a design that responded to the natural topography (fig. 83). An axis divided the plan into two relatively equal parts with a central primary street, framed on one side by a roundabout with a sizeable civic center and a large esplanade, and on the other side a shopping center with a second plaza. The housing complexes were situated to both sides and were organized around eleven neighborhood units, each with its corresponding services and green areas. The urban planning prioritized contact with nature, easy access to services (food, education, social services, recreation), independence for family life, economy, and ease of maintenance. This proposal reveals an emphasis on community life creation where the functionality of the urban development is at the service of its inhabitants' lives.

85 Pérez Oyarzun and Urrejola, "Series of interviews with Emilio Duhart," audio interview, Part 5 of 8.

Figures 84 & 85: Emilio Duhart and Sergio Larraín G-M, architects. Achupallas Urbanization Housing Project, Viña del Mar, Chile. Perspective from Avenida Central, 1956.

To Duhart "architecture is life, not a means of words [but] concrete things … above all people's life."[86] He expressed that it meant building a true community from a human perspective. Summarizing this project, in a socioeconomic vein, its ethos is singularly revealed through Duhart's inclusion of numerous sales posts for craft throughout the urbanization. One can speculate that the architect was thinking of providing the community, especially women, with outlets to sell crafts as additional income. With its grand scale vistas of the Pacific Ocean (figs. 84-85), the central avenue could have been thought of as a place for public gathering of an outside population attracted by the views and which could at the same time activate the community's internal economy.

86 Pérez Oyarzun and Urrejola, "Series of interviews with Emilio Duhart," audio interview, Part 5 of 8.

In 1957 Duhart participated, on behalf of the School of Architecture of the Pontifical Catholic University, in the first all-encompassing study of the metropolis of Santiago as an urban center. The Greater Santiago Seminar, established as a one-time think tank, was sponsored by the Chilean Ministry of Public Works, and was organized by the Institute of Cultural Extension of the University of Chile. The discussions presented led to the Intercommunal Plan of Santiago of 1960, the regulatory body which enacts urban-regional planning in Chile. For this event, Emilio Duhart prepared a presentation with his fifth-year architecture students that included fifty-seven diagrams.

After a comprehensive examination of historical, geographical, and existing conditions (pg. 250), Duhart's proposal ascertained that Santiago's expansion was chaotic, concluding that the capital could not continue its growth at the expense of using the best agricultural soil in areas located towards the mountains. The inquiry recommended organizing the metropolis based on the independence and strengthening of the surrounding small cities to address the continual population increase. These cities could constitute smaller units with individual life and personality, which could partially absorb the region's demographic and industrial enlargement. Each small city needed to have a surrounding green "lung" belt that nurtures it, and a space that supplies the cultural needs for its inhabitants' physical and mental balance.

Additionally, for the city of Santiago itself to be divided in neighborhood units (pg. 251, below), the propositions included the development of a connecting north/south artery (pg. 252), and given the flow of winds, the relocation of polluting industries to the north of the city to avoid smog concentration in the Santiago valley (pg. 253, above). The proposal included the joining of the north and south railway networks. Furthermore, it suggested creating a ring road system inserted in the larger metropolitan territory that would distribute traffic, link peripheral communes to each other, and limit the areas of density as a means to define and control the city's growth (pg. 251, above). It also included the renovation of old drinking water and sewage networks in the old city area. The downtown area needed remodeling with the conservation of historic buildings, to convert it into the new civic center, conceived as the heart of the city (pg. 249), envisaged as an area for pedestrians, free from vehicular interference, and with increased green areas. The civic center was surrounded by a ring of vehicular arteries with underground parking lots. Inside the civic center, a line of low speed and silent electric cars would be provided for internal zone transport. Finally, Duhart dedicated a couple of diagrams to what he called "Operation Air" and "Operation Green," with recommendations for the city to clean its air and proposed a large ring of green areas around the city center. To the loss of the city, none of Duhart's recommendations were taken into consideration except for the north/south connection artery that today links the territory. Santiago would have significantly benefitted if many of the other propositions had been taken into consideration.

Following pages:
Emilio Duhart.
Regulatory Plan for the Santiago Metropolitan Area. Historical and geographical studies, documents, 1957.

Regulatory Plan for the Metropolitan Region of Santiago de Chile

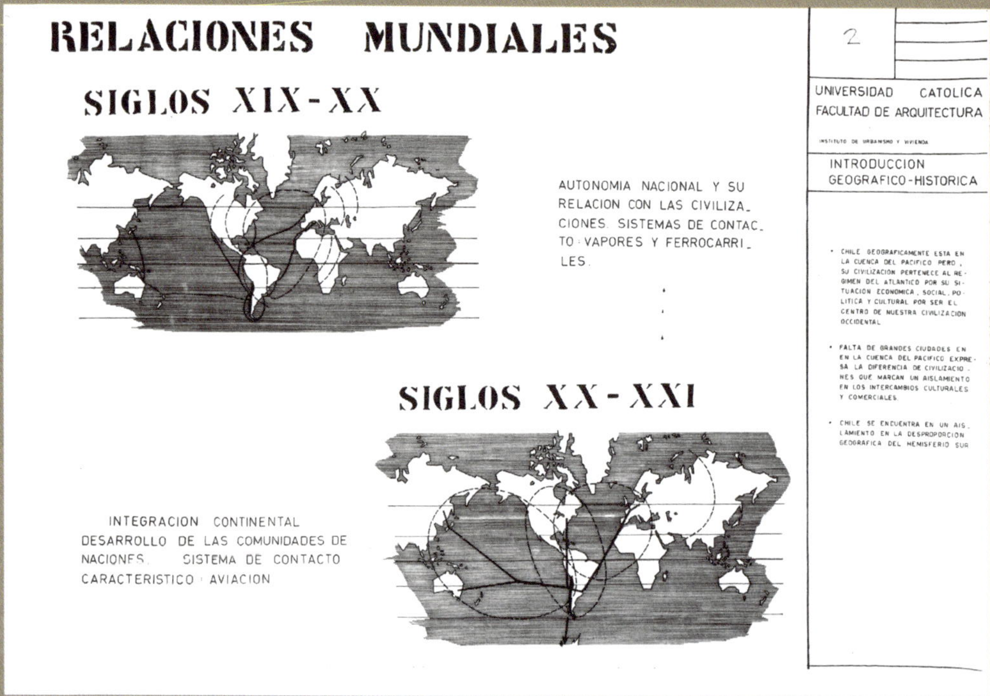
RELACIONES MUNDIALES
SIGLOS XIX-XX
AUTONOMIA NACIONAL Y SU RELACION CON LAS CIVILIZACIONES. SISTEMAS DE CONTACTO: VAPORES Y FERROCARRILES.
SIGLOS XX-XXI
INTEGRACION CONTINENTAL
DESARROLLO DE LAS COMUNIDADES DE NACIONES. SISTEMA DE CONTACTO CARACTERISTICO: AVIACION
2
UNIVERSIDAD CATOLICA
FACULTAD DE ARQUITECTURA
INTRODUCCION
GEOGRAFICO-HISTORICA
• CHILE GEOGRAFICAMENTE ESTA EN LA CUENCA DEL PACIFICO PERO, SU CIVILIZACION PERTENECE AL REGIMEN DEL ATLANTICO POR SU SITUACION ECONOMICA, SOCIAL, POLITICA Y CULTURAL POR SER EL CENTRO DE NUESTRA CIVILIZACION OCCIDENTAL
• FALTA DE GRANDES CIUDADES EN EN LA CUENCA DEL PACIFICO EXPRESA LA DIFERENCIA DE CIVILIZACIONES QUE MARCAN UN AISLAMIENTO EN LOS INTERCAMBIOS CULTURALES Y COMERCIALES.
• CHILE SE ENCUENTRA EN UN AISLAMIENTO EN LA DESPROPORCION GEOGRAFICA DEL HEMISFERIO SUR

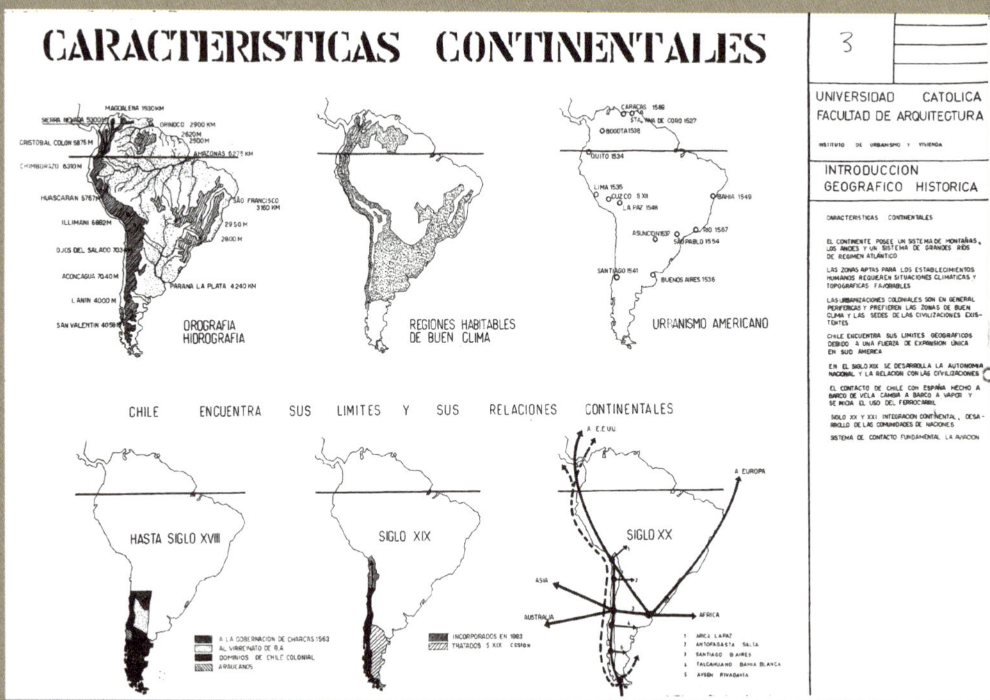
CARACTERISTICAS CONTINENTALES
OROGRAFIA
HIDROGRAFIA
REGIONES HABITABLES
DE BUEN CLIMA
URBANISMO AMERICANO
CHILE ENCUENTRA SUS LIMITES Y SUS RELACIONES CONTINENTALES
HASTA SIGLO XVIII
SIGLO XIX
SIGLO XX
A EUROPA
ASIA
AUSTRALIA
AFRICA
3
UNIVERSIDAD CATOLICA
FACULTAD DE ARQUITECTURA
INSTITUTO DE URBANISMO Y VIVIENDA
INTRODUCCION
GEOGRAFICO HISTORICA
CARACTERISTICAS CONTINENTALES
EL CONTINENTE POSEE UN SISTEMA DE MONTAÑAS, LOS ANDES Y UN SISTEMA DE GRANDES RÍOS DE REGIMEN ATLÁNTICO
LAS ZONAS APTAS PARA LOS ESTABLECIMIENTOS HUMANOS REQUIEREN SITUACIONES CLIMATICAS Y TOPOGRAFICAS FAVORABLES
LAS URBANIZACIONES COLONIALES SON EN GENERAL PERIFERICAS Y PREFIEREN LAS ZONAS DE BUEN CLIMA Y LAS SEDES DE LAS CIVILIZACIONES EXISTENTES
CHILE ENCUENTRA SUS LIMITES GEOGRAFICOS DEBIDO A UNA FUERZA DE EXPANSION ÚNICA EN SUD AMERICA
EN EL SIGLO XIX SE DESARROLLA LA AUTONOMIA NACIONAL Y LA RELACION CON LAS CIVILIZACIONES
EL CONTACTO DE CHILE CON ESPAÑA HECHO A BARCO DE VELA CAMBIA A BARCO A VAPOR Y SE INICIA EL USO DEL FERROCARRIL
SIGLO XX Y XXI INTEGRACION CONTINENTAL, DESARROLLO DE LAS COMUNIDADES DE NACIONES
SISTEMA DE CONTACTO FUNDAMENTAL LA AVIACION

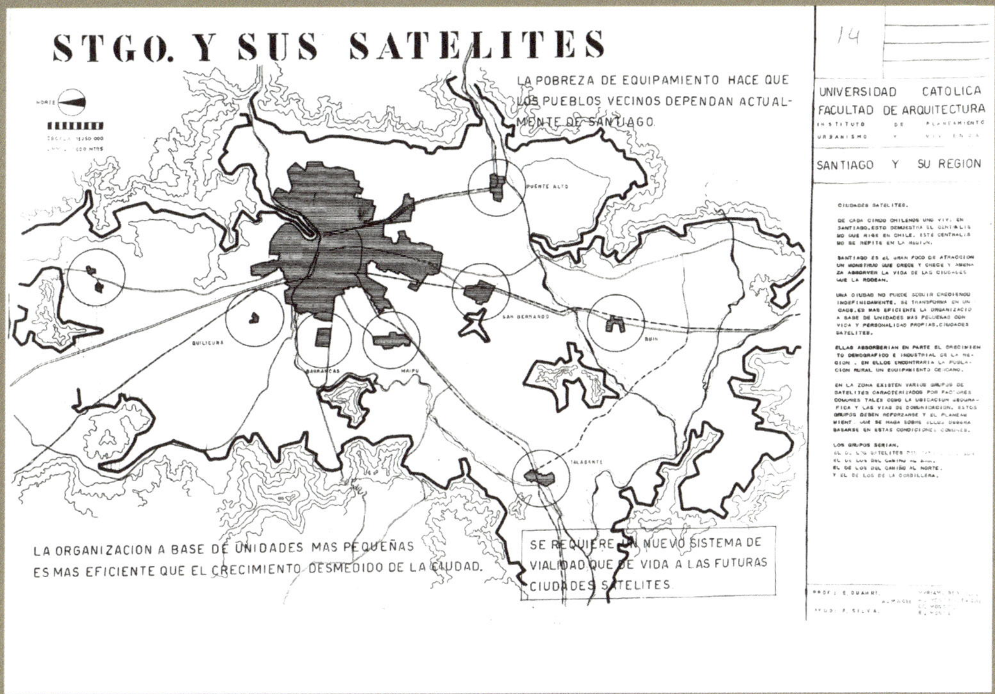
STGO. Y SUS SATELITES
LA POBREZA DE EQUIPAMIENTO HACE QUE LOS PUEBLOS VECINOS DEPENDAN ACTUALMENTE DE SANTIAGO.
14
UNIVERSIDAD CATOLICA
FACULTAD DE ARQUITECTURA
SANTIAGO Y SU REGION
LA ORGANIZACION A BASE DE UNIDADES MAS PEQUEÑAS ES MAS EFICIENTE QUE EL CRECIMIENTO DESMEDIDO DE LA CIUDAD.
SE REQUIERE UN NUEVO SISTEMA DE VIALIDAD QUE DE VIDA A LAS FUTURAS CIUDADES SATELITES

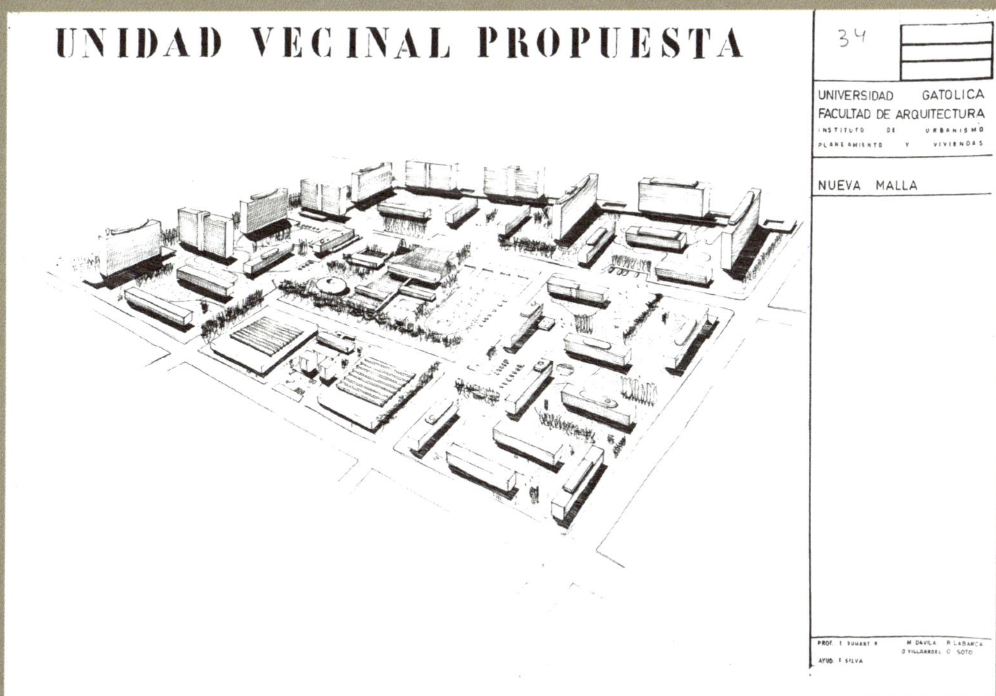
UNIDAD VECINAL PROPUESTA
34
UNIVERSIDAD CATOLICA
FACULTAD DE ARQUITECTURA
INSTITUTO DE URBANISMO
PLANEAMIENTO Y VIVIENDAS
NUEVA MALLA

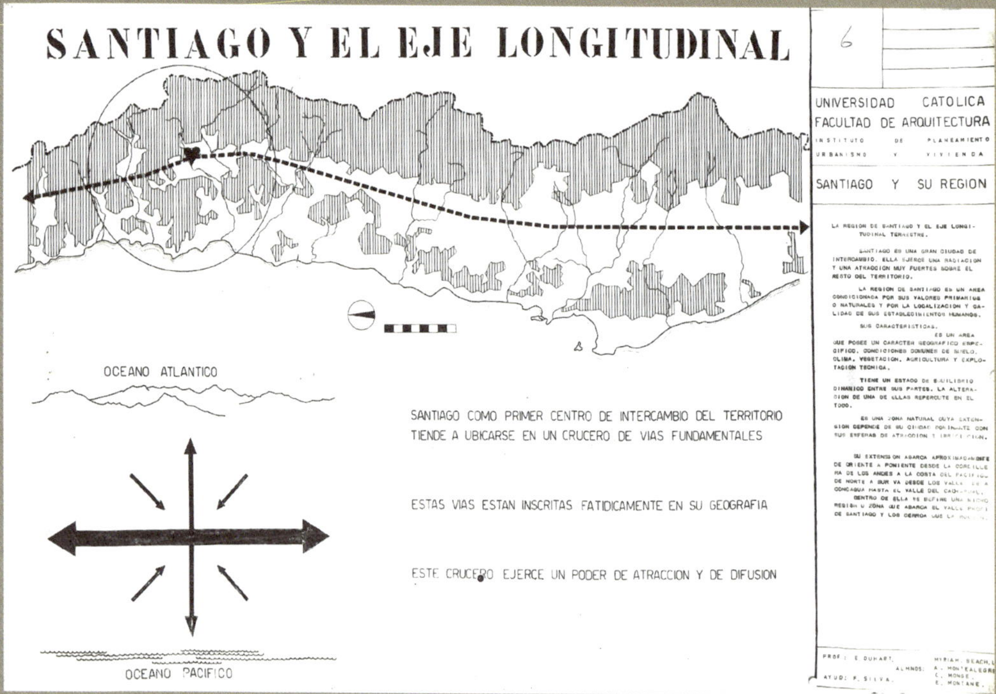
SANTIAGO Y EL EJE LONGITUDINAL
6
UNIVERSIDAD CATOLICA
FACULTAD DE ARQUITECTURA
INSTITUTO DE PLANEAMIENTO URBANISMO Y VIVIENDA
SANTIAGO Y SU REGION
LA REGION DE SANTIAGO Y EL EJE LONGITUDINAL TERRESTRE.
SANTIAGO ES UNA GRAN CIUDAD DE INTERCAMBIO. ELLA EJERCE UNA RADIACION Y UNA ATRACCION MUY FUERTES SOBRE EL RESTO DEL TERRITORIO.
LA REGION DE SANTIAGO ES UN AREA CONDICIONADA POR SUS VALORES PRIMARIOS O NATURALES Y POR LA LOCALIZACION Y CALIDAD DE SUS ESTABLECIMIENTOS HUMANOS.
SUS CARACTERISTICAS.
ES UN AREA QUE POSEE UN CARACTER GEOGRAFICO ESPECIFICO, CONDICIONES COMUNES DE SUELO, CLIMA, VEGETACION, AGRICULTURA Y EXPLOTACION TECNICA.
TIENE UN ESTADO DE EQUILIBRIO DINAMICO ENTRE SUS PARTES. LA ALTERACION DE UNA DE ELLAS REPERCUTE EN EL TODO.
OCEANO ATLANTICO
SANTIAGO COMO PRIMER CENTRO DE INTERCAMBIO DEL TERRITORIO TIENDE A UBICARSE EN UN CRUCERO DE VIAS FUNDAMENTALES
ESTAS VIAS ESTAN INSCRITAS FATIDICAMENTE EN SU GEOGRAFIA
ESTE CRUCERO EJERCE UN PODER DE ATRACCION Y DE DIFUSION
OCEANO PACIFICO

UN NUEVO EJE NORTE SUR
25
UNIVERSIDAD CATOLICA
FACULTAD DE ARQUITECTURA
INSTITUTO DE URBANISMO Y VIVIENDA
UN NUEVO EJE NORTE-SUR

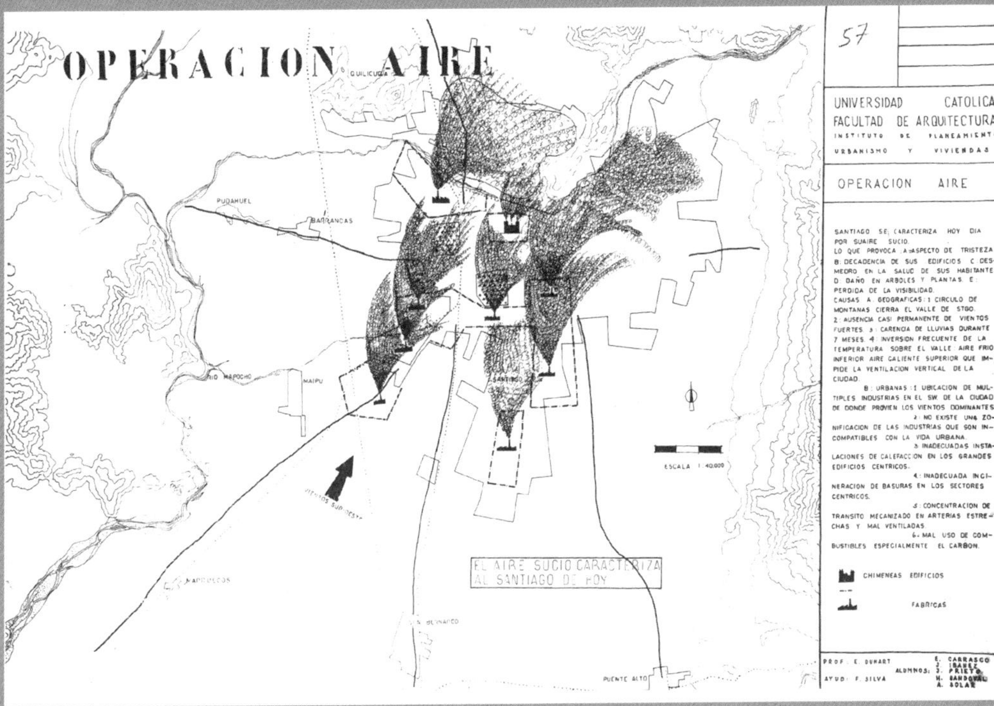
OPERACION AIRE
57
UNIVERSIDAD CATOLICA
FACULTAD DE ARQUITECTURA
INSTITUTO DE PLANEAMIENTO
URBANISMO Y VIVIENDAS
OPERACION AIRE
SANTIAGO SE CARACTERIZA HOY DIA POR SU AIRE SUCIO.
LO QUE PROVOCA A: ASPECTO DE TRISTEZA B: DECADENCIA DE SUS EDIFICIOS C: DESMEDRO EN LA SALUD DE SUS HABITANTES D: DAÑO EN ARBOLES Y PLANTAS E: PERDIDA DE LA VISIBILIDAD.
CAUSAS A: GEOGRAFICAS: 1 CIRCULO DE MONTANAS CIERRA EL VALLE DE STGO. 2: AUSENCIA CASI PERMANENTE DE VIENTOS FUERTES. 3: CARENCIA DE LLUVIAS DURANTE 7 MESES. 4: INVERSION FRECUENTE DE LA TEMPERATURA SOBRE EL VALLE: AIRE FRIO INFERIOR AIRE CALIENTE SUPERIOR QUE IMPIDE LA VENTILACION VERTICAL DE LA CIUDAD.
B: URBANAS: 1 UBICACION DE MULTIPLES INDUSTRIAS EN EL SW. DE LA CIUDAD DE DONDE PROVIEN LOS VIENTOS DOMINANTES.
2: NO EXISTE UNA ZONIFICACION DE LAS INDUSTRIAS QUE SON INCOMPATIBLES CON LA VIDA URBANA.
3: INADECUADAS INSTALACIONES DE CALEFACCION EN LOS GRANDES EDIFICIOS CENTRICOS.
4: INADECUADA INCINERACION DE BASURAS EN LOS SECTORES CENTRICOS.
5: CONCENTRACION DE TRANSITO MECANIZADO EN ARTERIAS ESTRECHAS Y MAL VENTILADAS.
6: MAL USO DE COMBUSTIBLES ESPECIALMENTE EL CARBON.
CHIMENEAS EDIFICIOS
FABRICAS
QUILICURA
PUDAHUEL
BARRANCAS
MAIPU
SANTIAGO
ESCALA 1: 40.000
EL AIRE SUCIO CARACTERIZA AL SANTIAGO DE HOY
PUENTE ALTO
PROF: E. DUHART
AYUD: F. SILVA
ALUMNOS:
E. CARRASCO
J. IBAÑEZ
J. PRIETO
H. SANDOVAL
A. SOLAR

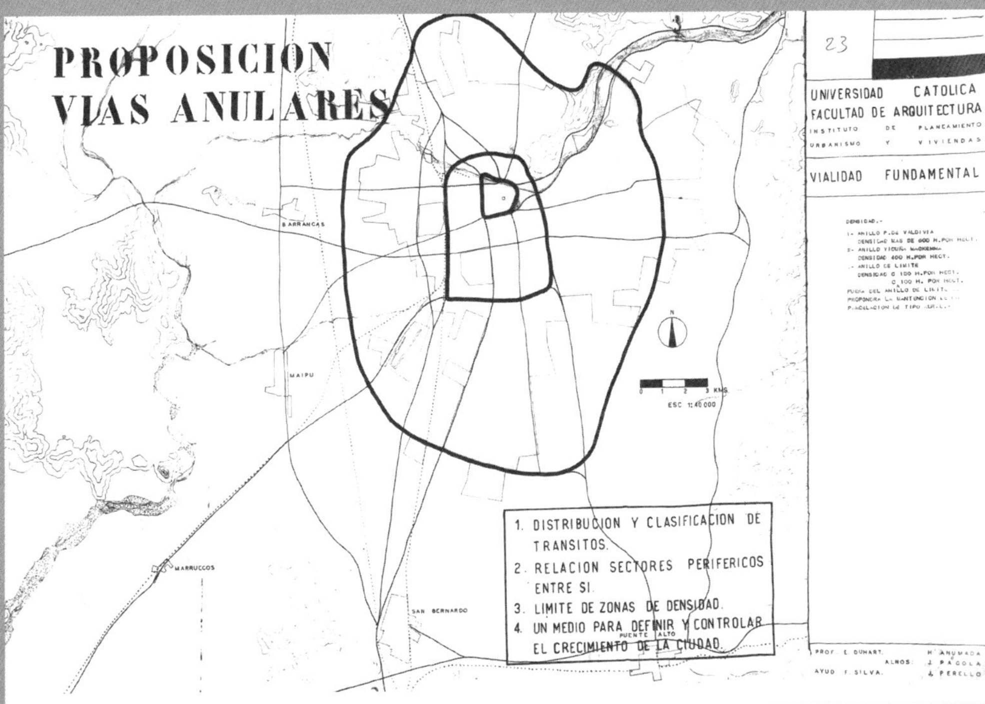
PROPOSICION VIAS ANULARES
23
UNIVERSIDAD CATOLICA
FACULTAD DE ARQUITECTURA
INSTITUTO DE PLANEAMIENTO
URBANISMO Y VIVIENDAS
VIALIDAD FUNDAMENTAL
DENSIDAD.-
BARRANCAS
MAIPU
MARRUECOS
SAN BERNARDO
ESC 1: 40.000
0 1 2 3 KMS.
1. DISTRIBUCION Y CLASIFICACION DE TRANSITOS.
2. RELACION SECTORES PERIFERICOS ENTRE SI.
3. LIMITE DE ZONAS DE DENSIDAD.
4. UN MEDIO PARA DEFINIR Y CONTROLAR EL CRECIMIENTO DE LA CIUDAD.
PUENTE ALTO
PROF: E. DUHART.
AYUD: F. SILVA.
ALMOS:

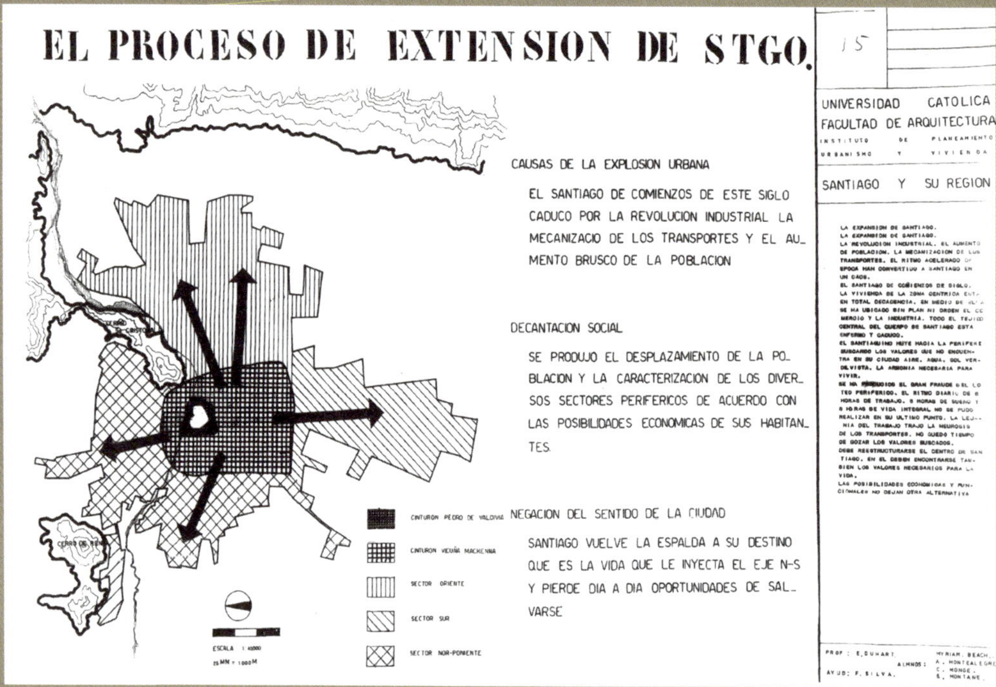
EL PROCESO DE EXTENSION DE STGO.
15
UNIVERSIDAD CATOLICA
FACULTAD DE ARQUITECTURA
INSTITUTO DE PLANEAMIENTO URBANISMO Y VIVIENDA
SANTIAGO Y SU REGION
CAUSAS DE LA EXPLOSION URBANA
EL SANTIAGO DE COMIENZOS DE ESTE SIGLO CADUCO POR LA REVOLUCION INDUSTRIAL LA MECANIZACIO DE LOS TRANSPORTES Y EL AU_ MENTO BRUSCO DE LA POBLACION
DECANTACION SOCIAL
SE PRODUJO EL DESPLAZAMIENTO DE LA PO_ BLACION Y LA CARACTERIZACION DE LOS DIVER_ SOS SECTORES PERIFERICOS DE ACUERDO CON LAS POSIBILIDADES ECONOMICAS DE SUS HABITAN_ TES.
NEGACION DEL SENTIDO DE LA CIUDAD
SANTIAGO VUELVE LA ESPALDA A SU DESTINO QUE ES LA VIDA QUE LE INYECTA EL EJE N-S Y PIERDE DIA A DIA OPORTUNIDADES DE SAL_ VARSE
CINTURON PEDRO DE VALDIVIA
CINTURON VICUÑA MACKENNA
SECTOR ORIENTE
SECTOR SUR
SECTOR NOR-PONIENTE
ESCALA 1:40000
PROF: E. DUHART
AYUD: F. SILVA
ALMNOS: MYRIAM BEACH, A. MONTEALEGRE, C. MONGE, S. MONTANE

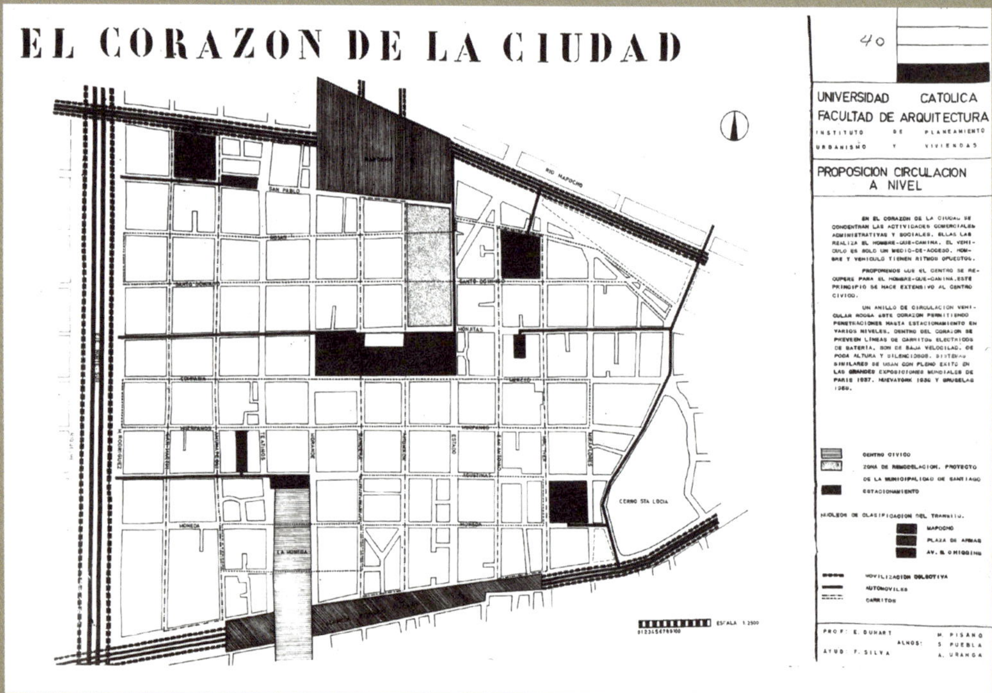
EL CORAZON DE LA CIUDAD
40
UNIVERSIDAD CATOLICA
FACULTAD DE ARQUITECTURA
INSTITUTO DE PLANEAMIENTO URBANISMO Y VIVIENDAS
PROPOSICION CIRCULACION A NIVEL
CENTRO CIVICO
ZONA DE REMODELACION. PROYECTO DE LA MUNICIPALIDAD DE SANTIAGO
ESTACIONAMIENTO
MAPOCHO
PLAZA DE ARMAS
AV. B. O'HIGGINS
RIO MAPOCHO
SAN PABLO
SANTO DOMINGO
MONJITAS
CERRO STA LUCIA
ESCALA 1:2500
PROF: E. DUHART
AYUD: F. SILVA
ALMNOS: M. PISANO, S. PUEBLA, A. URANGA

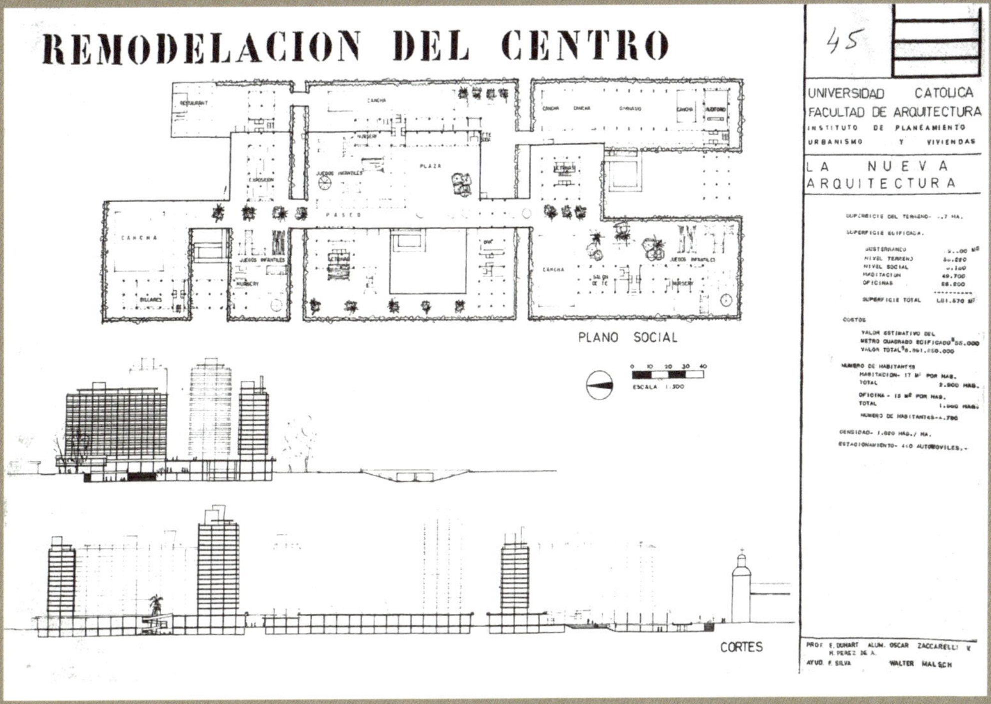
REMODELACION DEL CENTRO
45
UNIVERSIDAD CATOLICA
FACULTAD DE ARQUITECTURA
INSTITUTO DE PLANEAMIENTO
URBANISMO Y VIVIENDAS
LA NUEVA ARQUITECTURA
PLANO SOCIAL
CORTES

The University City of Concepción campus (1957-1970), was a grand-scale project commissioned to Duhart to diversify, reorganize, enlarge, and plan the grounds for the existing academic structure of the University of Concepción. Founded in 1919, the University is located in Concepción at around 357 miles to the south of the capital and is the first university campus in Chile and Latin America. With its multiple stages of construction, the project took over a decade to be completed. The master plan (pg. 258) was followed by additional commissions (fig. 139, 140 & 141), among which were the Institute of Chemistry Building (1958-61), the Open Forum Square (1958-61), and the Engineering Institute Building (1958-61). It also included the Institute of Mechanical Technologies (1961-63), the Central Meadow (1965-67), the Education Building (1966-69), the Social Sciences Building (1966-69), the Central Library (1967-71), the Student's House (1968), and the Sports Stadium (1971-72).

The Urban Master Plan of 1957 integrated the existing buildings. It evolved from the distribution of zones assigned rationally according to areas of knowledge such as technology, medicine, economics, social sciences, architecture, art, and design. In this commission the central focus of the design was to give priority to the human scale and pedestrian traffic. In this regard, Alberto Montealegre remarked that here "Duhart overcomes the schematic vision of CIAM urbanism in his conceptions of the spatial distribution of functions. He corrects the important flaw in its handling of the human scale."[87] Duhart reiterated many times that the campus had been designed for "the man who walks,"[88] one of his governing postulates.

The academic buildings were distributed to both sides of a rectangular and elongated central arena that cuts through the terrain and liberates the view toward the landscape, serving as the university city's heart (pg. 260). This open field is composed of the Open Forum Square (1958-61) and the Central Meadow (1965-67). It is the central and symbolic area of the University, a place for collective life for students, faculty, and the people of Concepción. Entering through the gate of the University (pg. 259), the Open Forum welcomes the passerby with a side-to-side set of stairs that reaches a campanile placed to the left, the symbol of the University. From this platform, one can observe the campus and the fields beyond. Standing at the campanile level, the Central Meadow follows the Open Forum. To the southwest the Institute of Chemistry (pg. 265) longitudinally surrounds the large square and to the northeast is the Central Library (pg. 262). The Plaza (pg. 261) is 253 feet wide by 319 feet long and consists of three levels. The Middle Plaza, at approximately 2-3/4 feet up, serves as the ground level connector to the campus's surroundings and as already mentioned, contains the campanile on one side. This preexisting feature was remodeled, simplified in its

87 Alberto Montealegre Klenner, "Cristián Berríos – Ciudad Universitaria de Concepción," unpublished manuscript.

88 Emilio Duhart, "El Foro Abierto: Corazón de la Universidad," *Boletín Informativo de la Universidad de Concepción* Nº6, 1958.

shape, and covered with polished gray granite. Then follows the High Plaza, from which the greater views of the complex can be appreciated. Down the stairs is the large Sunken Plaza, which is about six feet below ground level. The Forum's access stairs go up to the Middle Plaza, then up to the High Plaza, and then down again to the Sunken Plaza. The staircases stretch from side to side of the plaza serving as an auditorium for spectators, turning the space into a modern rectangular amphitheater. The eastern wall of the Sunken Plaza facing the audience has a water mirror at ground level and a wall with various water features, and lighting concentrated in that sector at night. Finally, there is a row of twenty flagpoles between the Open Forum and the Central Meadow on top of the eastern wall.

Duhart conceived this monumental plaza as the center of gravity of the university campus. The meadow area and the trees were integrated as a counterpoint to the rather austere and geometric architecture surrounding it. The Open Forum was designed as a congregation place for large groups (4,000 people seated in the auditorium) conceived for university ceremonies, cultural activities, performances, and movie screenings. To Duhart, the Open Forum was to become a favorite setting for the people of Concepción for evening walks and entertainment, free of vehicular traffic; a goal largely achieved given the still current appreciation of the place by the citizenry of Concepción. Duhart envisioned this monumental outdoor space as a place where "if [the university] is to meet its responsibilities as a cultural center … the school must abandon its traditional mold—a building that dies each afternoon at five."[89] He conceived the campus at all educational levels as "a 'house of culture' open to the entire community during the appropriate hours."[90] The Open Forum and the Central Meadow constitute "a place cleared and freed … a space … that has been made room for … within a boundary … from which something begins its presencing."[91] This major topographical man-made effort was to embody the representational construct of what the university would signify to the users; the students and faculty in ceremonial occasions, and the general public in their communal assemblies, to enhance in all of them their sense of community inclusion.

89 Marilyn E. Ludwig, "Technical Considerations – Health, Education and Recreation," *A.I.A. Journal* - 1965 Congress Convention (August 1965): 63.

90 Ludwig, "Technical Considerations – Health, Education and Recreation": 63.

91 Frampton, *Studies in Tectonic Culture*, 22.

The University City of Concepción represents one of Duhart's most outstanding works and one of the least known both nationally and internationally. However, the Open Forum presents itself as one of the capstones of Duhart's career. Furthermore, along with all the other urban planning projects, the Open Forum is a testament to this architect's interest in civic centers and in creating community, understanding architecture as a provider and facilitator of those functions. This interest, present since early on, was embodied throughout his work in urbanism. Humankind and its search for public contact and congregation are central motivations that were distinguished in his work.

University City of Concepción

UNIVERSIDAD
CONCEPCION
PERSPECTIVA INSTITUTO
QUIMICA Y FORO ABIERTO
E. DUHART ARQUITECTO
ABRIL 1958

UNIVERSIDAD
CONCEPCION
PERSPECTIVA FORO ABIER-
TO-
VISTA DESDE EL SUR-OESTE
E. DUHART ARQUITECTO
ABRIL 1958

CONCLUSION – A VISION OF A HUMAN, REGIONAL, AND ICONOGRAPHIC MODERNITY

From early in his career Emilio Duhart was an idiosyncratic, independent thinker who produced his own blend of modernist architecture, processing and translating international modernism in conjunction with elements proper to the Chilean local context. Before studying at Harvard's Graduate School of Design in 1941, many defining events in the life of the architect had already taken place. When young, his interests in aviation and navigation, drawing, and model making were the origins of the path he later pursued in life.

However, more critically, as a student and young architect, his thesis project and the adobe houses he devised prior to going abroad were crucial exercises in conceiving enduring professional models for himself. During that phase, he was acutely interested in modernism despite not yet having a formal education in it. This period of self-reflection on applying modern architecture and urbanism before studying at GSD remains one of the most conceptually fruitful and a highlight of his career. It was a singularly critical time in creating for himself a strong, self-made base from which to operate, collecting the distinctive traits he further displayed as an architect.

Being anchored in a faraway place, Chile, with the subsequent immersion into a remote type of reality and the cultural isolation that accompanied it, may have constituted a competitive advantage for Duhart and his envisioning of a more hybrid modern lexicon. Additionally, it is essential to stress how spread-out in time his encounters with Gropius and Le Corbusier were, namely a decade, which leads us to realize that the time between these decisive instances afforded him plenty of room to incorporate his learning autonomously and progressively.

From the onset, Duhart was endowed with the capacity of foreseeing that the local stratum could not be ignored. He was also a visionary who knew, albeit intuitively, that modernism was the inescapable movement of its era. This latter realization was a profound insight, given that this was understood by him when modernism was nascent, and time had not yet revealed its flaws.

A consequence of the lack of integration of neglected historical narratives is that a wealth of research in many new lights, both practical and theoretical, have been pending for decades. Duhart's multifaceted body of work, and the extent of his portfolio, still constitutes an open field in which many categories of projects could be independently analyzed, along the lines of the book by Cristián Berríos, which looks closely at a single project, the University City of Concepción. Analysis of categories of work as well as comprehensive surveys of single projects like the Central Library of the University City of Concepción, the Larraín, De la Fuente, and Andrade residences, the Hosterías Ancud, the Castro, the Ministerio del Trabajo Building, and the International Airport in Santiago are just a few prominent examples deserving detailed scrutiny.

Besides, and of no lesser importance, Duhart's study as a proto-ecologist could complete the vast array of topics he covered throughout his career. Duhart's predilection to emphasize the use of natural resources is embodied in his projects in many forms, such as the reuse of rainwater, the incorporation of pre-existing endemic flora, and the positioning of structures considered to grant the best perspective to contemplate the natural landscape. Moreover, he also produced iconographic images in homage to nature in, for example, the trunk of the walnut tree that crosses the surrounding outer walls of the Duhart House and the left-to-the-natural logs supporting the portico of the Labbé House. These examples tell the story of a transversal interest he found worth exploring in depth throughout decades of work.

Noticeably, from the start, Duhart was interested first in urbanism, being imbued on that pursuit throughout his career, and fundamentally inspired to help the dispossessed. Beyond recognizing the importance and value of his CEPAL Building and countless other projects, in his work on urbanism one encounters a legacy that is deeply relevant to our current times. It attests to his far-reaching thinking on the profound implication of urban arrangements. Moreover, Duhart focused on solving the housing problems for the economically disadvantaged in a country that remains plagued with negligence in these areas and where the profession could still produce significant social impact.

Perhaps more so than any other project, in his Fishing Base of San Quintín of 1941, he elegantly elaborates on four topics concerning urban planning that continue to be relevant to our contemporary society. The topics in question are centered around four themes: the concept of urbanism as a support system for existence, the consolidation of communities, the enhancement of people's economic opportunities, and an intuitive approach to localism.

Duhart profoundly rejected aestheticism in architecture and despised those professionals led by this inclination as their primary concerns, particularly in urban arrangements. By distancing himself from that position, he searched for another perspective. He thought that the architect had different roles to play, and in the case of urbanism, the architect's primary concern should be to attend to the needs of the masses through the reorganization and development of the existing regions and urban nuclei. In this sense, Duhart conceived of urbanism as a support system in which, through the carefully studied ordering of the urban components, the architect could assist in the betterment of life. The habitat where we live profoundly impacts our daily lives. If we live near a park, if grocery shopping is far away from home, if our environment is overcrowded, those are all elements that will shape our existence. Those elements are not necessarily under our control, but the urbanist is one of the agents that interact with them. Duhart foresaw the delicate implications of the urban fabric which needs to be threaded in a comprehensive way. A well-designed human settlement meant to him exhaustive holistic research that includes history, geography, topography, culture, people, economy, and so forth, all converging in a design that would respond to the contextual conditions.

Duhart was keen at devising urban formations with a sense of place where communities united by a shared existence and common attributes could interact and develop, advancing the possibilities of a thriving existence. Communities are understood here in the sense that "communities [are put into a] space and produce a place [, and] a place is a space endowed with meaning,"[1] that is, communities where the affective is contemplated. The assumptions common to Duhart's work in this area were his awareness of the human scale and experience, the provision of contact with nature, the parcellation of the expansion of the urban sphere, and the shielding of the citizenry from the alienating qualities of the city landscape. The human was always at the center of his proposals with the all-encompassing assumption that human well-being is closely related to the enhancement of human interaction and sense of belonging. These assumptions can also be found in the Achupallas Urbanization, the Jardin del Este Urbanization, and the Grand Santiago Seminar Proposal. In these projects, the practice of architecture and urbanism is emphasized through a well-studied formation of components that rationally channel human activity and enhance human encounters, interweaving work, recreation, leisure, family life, and so forth.

1 Ezio Manzini, *Politics of the Everyday* (Londres, Nueva York: Bloomsbury Publishing Plc, 2019), 24.

On the other hand, in his degree project Duhart exhibited a novel association between urban design, ethnography, and economic development. These interrelations evolved from the observation of customs and ancestral knowledge of an isolated community of fishermen, uniting and strengthening their inherited means of survival with the insertion of modern technology and its consequent possibilities of regional and national economic development. That community could not envision these prospects on its own, but as an urbanist and technocrat, Duhart could assist in imagining more elaborate connections. The realization that urban formations could give agency to economic development, so clearly outlined in the Fishing Base, is a proposition worth revisiting for existing low-income settlements.

As experienced during the COVID 19 crisis, the extreme global interdependence we live in today has revealed the ultimate contemporary vulnerabilities to which we are exposed. We live amidst an utmost complex system that constitutes a single fabric of interconnections where one event triggers the whole's unraveling. To balance such frailty and to create a more secure and stable subsistence, means that naturally the world will retract progressively towards the local. Many structures and components of our physical surroundings will have to be reengineered and re-thought. The Fishing Base project devised under the specifics of the local scene, its people, materials, ancestral knowledge and so on, could represent a template to be studied and to reflect upon on how to address possible solutions at a local and regional level to strengthen our chances of survival in our uncertain future. The Fishing Base, created in 1941, represents a remarkable example to pay attention to and expose to contemporary students of architecture and architects alike.

Finally, as one of the unifying principles of Duhart's practice, he was significantly invested in elaborating a local Chilean modern language, anticipating by decades what Kenneth Frampton called architectural regionalism. This particular focus represents a lesson for contemporary architecture in Chile, which for over a decade has increasingly gathered international attention and might benefit from reconsidering architecture's iconographic role in assisting society in creating a deeper sense of regional identity. Duhart had an extraordinary professional journey, with close contact with the creators of modern architecture and urban planning. Through his practice and academic career, he was a direct agent in bridging the original ideas of the modern movement in the professional field in Chile. As a consequence, architecture in the country inherited a crucial legacy originating from the imagination and precepts of this visionary architect.

BIBLIOGRAPHY

Abellaneda Manzanares, Miguel. "La Idea de Espacio en la Arquitectura de le Corbusier: La Villa Shodhan." PhD diss., Universitat Politécnica de Valencia, 2017.

Adamson, Glenn, Giorgio Riello, and Sarah Teasley. *Global Design History*. New York: Routledge, 2011.

Adriá, Miquel. *White Mountain: Architecture in Chile*. Santiago: Puro Chile & Germany: Hatje Cantz, 2010.

Aguirre, Beatrix and Salim Rabí. "La Trayectoria Espacial de la Corporación de la Vivienda (CORVI)." *Diseño Urbano y Paisaje*, Vol VI Nº 18 (2009): n/a. http://dup.ucentral.cl/pdf/18_trayectoria_espacial_b.pdf

Aguirre González, Max. *La Arquitectura Moderna en Chile (1907-1942)*. Santiago: Editorial Universitaria de Chile, 2012.

Akcan, Esra. *Architecture in Translation: Germany, Turquey & the Modern House*. Durham & London: Duke University Press, 2012.

Albrecht, Donald. "Introduction." In *World War II and the American Dream*, edited by Donald Albrecht, XVI-XXVII. Cambridge, Massachusetts: MIT Press, 1995.

Appadurai, Arjun"The Right to Participate in the Work of the Imagination." In *TransUrbanism*, edited by Arjen Mulder, 33-49. Rotterdam: V2_Publishing/NAI Publishers, 2002.

Aragón Godoy, Felipe. "Identidad Territorial de Emilio Duhart: El Viaje a Aysén como Origen para su Proyecto de Título." In *Taller de Investigación Primer Semestre 2017, Profesor Umberto Bonomo*, 1-34, Universidad Católica de Chile, Facultad de Arquitectura, Diseño y Estudios Urbanos, 2017.

Arancibia, Daniela. "El Lenguaje del Agua en el Edificio de las Naciones Unidas." In *Emilio Duhart Obra Completa, Taller VII de Investigación, Professor Fernando Pérez O.*, 2005.

AUCA. "Edificio de las Naciones Unidas en Vitacura." *Arquitectura, Urbanismo, Construccion, Arte, AUCA* Nº 3, 1966.

Bailey, Christopher. "The Global Future of Design History." *Journal of Design History*, Vol. 18 Nº 3 (Autum 2005): 231-233.

Ban, Shigeru. "Finnish Pavilion, New York World's Fair." In *Alvar Aalto Through the Eyes of Shigeru Ban*, ed. Juhani Pallasmaa and Tomoko Sato, 146-151. London: Black Dog Publishing in association with Barbican Art Gallery, 2007.

Barrientos, Marcos. "Terremotos, Arquitectura y la Norma Chilena NCh433. Of.72. Cálculo Antisísmico de Edificios (1959-1972.)" In Anales de Arquitectura UC, https://www.analesdearquitecturauc.com/terremotos-arquitectura-y-la-norma-chilena-nch433-of72.

Bayón, Damián and Paolo Gasparini. *Panorámica de la Arquitectura Latino-Americana*. Barcelona: Blume, 1977.

Berríos, Cristian. *Emilio Duhart, Elaboración de un Espacio Urbano: Ciudad Universitaria de Concepción*. Santiago: LOM Ediciones, 2017.

Bourillon, Florence. "Changer la Ville, la Question Urbaine au Milieu du 19º Siècle." *Vingtième Siècle, Revue d'Histoire*, Nº 64, Numéro Spécial: Villes en Crises? (Oct. – Dec., 1999): 11-23.

Browne, Alberto. "Casa Labbé: Un Modo de Pensar la Arquitectura." In *Emilio Duhart, Seminario de Investigación Fernando Pérez Oyarzun*, Chapter 1. Santiago: Pontificia Universidad Católica de Chile, 2005.

Bullrich, Francisco. *Nuevos Caminos de la Architectura Latinoamericana*. Barcelona: Blume, 1969.

Calvera, Anna."Local, Regional, National, Global and Feedback: Several Issues to Be Faced with Constructing

Regional Narratives." *Journal of Design History*, Vol. 18, No. 4 (Winter, 2005): 371-383. http://www.jstor.com/stable/3527242.

Camplá Lehmann, José R. "Modernidad y Contextualidad Regional: El Caso de Emilio Duhart." PhD diss., Universidad Politécnica de Madrid, 2012.

Candela Suarez, María. "Between Indian Tradition and Corbusian Modernity: The Case of the Villa Hutheesing- Shodhan." *Pombalina, Coimbra University Press*: 277-294. https://digitalis-dsp.uc.pt/bitstream/10316.2/41612/1/Between%20Indian%20Tradition%20and%20corbusian%20modernity..pdf

Caralt, David, and Verónica Esparza. "Conciencia de la Tradición y Proceso Creativo: Emilio Duhart y el Método Comparado como Herramienta de Proyecto Arquitectónico." *Dearq 22* (October 2017): 58-69. http://dx.doi.org/10.18389/ dearq22.2018.05.

Carranza, Luis E., and Fernando Luis Lara. *Modern Architecture in Latin America: Art Technology, and Utopia.* Austin: University of Texas Press, 2014.

Cartes Montory, Armando. *Bio Bio: Bibliografía Histórica Regional.* Santiago: Ediciones de la Dirección de Bibliotecas, Archivos y Museos; Centro de Investigaciones Diego Barros Arana; Editorial Universidad de Concepción, 2014.

Castedo, Leopoldo, *Latin American Art and Architecture.* New York; Praeger Publishers, 1969.

Castillo Buttinghausen, Carolina. "Base Pesquera en San Quintin." In *Emilio Duhart, Seminario de Investigación Fernando Pérez Oyarzun*, Chapter 1. Santiago: Pontificia Universidad Católica de Chile, 2005.

City of Richmond, California. "History of Richmond." Accessed July 9, 2020. http://www.ci.richmond.ca.us/112/History-of-Richmond.

Collier, Simon. *Chile: The Making of a Republic 1830-1865, Politics and Ideas.* Cambridge: Cambridge University Press, 2003.

Curtis, William J. R. *Le Corbusier: Ideas and Forms.* London: Phaidon Press, 1986.

Damaz, Paul F. *Art in Latin American Architecture.* New York: Reinhold Publishing, 1963.

Dias Comas, Carlos Eduardo. "Latin American Architecture at MOMA." *arq. urb*, Issue 20 (September- December 2017): 156-171.

Dickerman, Leah. "Bauhaus Fundaments." In *Bauhaus 1919-1933: Workshops for Modernity*, ed. Barry Bergdoll, Leah Dickerman. New York: The Museum of Modern Art, 2009.

Duhart, Emilio. "Architecture Parasismique." *Techniques & Architecture N°334*, March 1981.

Duhart, Emile. "Édifice des Nations Unies pour l'Amérique Latine." *Architecture d'Aujourd'hui*, December 1967 – January 1968.

Duhart, Emilio. "El Foro Abierto: Corazón de la Universidad." *Boletín Informativo de la Universidad de Concepción* N°6, 1958.

Duhart, Emilio. "En Búsqueda de la Tradición Viva." *Architectura y Construcción* N°16, September 1949.

Duhart, Emilio. Interview by Fernando Pérez Oyarzun y Pilar Urrejola. Interview part 1 of 8, audio. Archivo de Originales. Centro de Información y Documentación Sergio Larraín García-Moreno. Facultad de Arquitectura, Diseño y Estudios Urbanos, Pontificia Universidad Católica de Chile, 1993-1994.

Duhart, Emilio. "Recuerdos de Le Corbusier." *ARS #6*, September 1987.

Duhart, Emilio. Transcript of "Speech for the Reception of the National Prize of Architecture from the College of Architecture of Chile," August 18, 1977. Emilio Duhart Archive, Faculty of Architecture Pontifical Catholic University, Santiago.

Duhart, Emilio. "Tesis de Grado 1940." *Revista ARQ N° 23*, Santiago de Chile, 1993.

Duhart, Emilio. "Una Mirada al Estado Actual de la Arquitectura." *CA Revista Colegio de Arquitectos de Chile* 28, December 1980.

Eames Official Site. "Case Study House 8: The Eames House." Accessed 09/20/20. https://www.eamesoffice.com/the-work/eames-house-case-study-house-8/.

Eliash, Humberto and Manuel Moreno. *Architectura y Modernidad en Chile, 1925-1965.* Santiago: Ediciones Universidad Católica de Chile, 1989.

Esparza Saavedra, Verónica. "Emilio Duhart Harosteguy, Un Arquitecto Integral: 1935-1992." PhD diss., Universidad Politécnica de Cataluña, 2015.

Esparza Saavedra, Verónica. "Villa Presidente Ríos en Talcahuano,

1947-1951," Academia, accessed August 12, 2020. https://www.academia.edu/22618385/VILLA_PRESIDENTE_RÍOS_EN_TALCAHUANO_1947_1951_SERGIO_LARRAÍN_G_M_Y_EMILIO_DUHART_H.

Fisher, Matthew W. Prefabrication and the Postwar House: The California Manifesto. ScholarWorks @ UMassachusetsAmherst. Accessed 08/21/20. https://www.acsa-arch.org/proceedings/Annual%20Meeting%20Proceedings/ACSA.AM.97/ACSA.AM.97.50.pdf.

Foster, Hal. *The Anti-Aesthetic: Essays on Postmodern Culture.* Port Townsend, Washington: Bay Press, 1983.

Frampton, Kenneth. *Studies in Tectonic Culture: The Poetics of Construction in Nineteenth and Twentieth Century Architecture.* Massachusetts: MIT Press, 1995.

Fraser, Valerie. *Building the New World: Studies in The Modern Architecture of Latin America 1930-1960.* London & New York: Verso, 2000.

Friedel, Robert. "Scarcity and Promise." In *World War II and the American Dream*, edited by Donald Albrecht, 42-89. Cambridge, Massachusetts: MIT Press, 1995.

Fynn, Shaun. *Chandigarh Revealed: Le Corbusier's City Today.* New York: Princeton Architectural Press, 2017.

Fundación Vicente Huidobro, "El Oxígeno Invisible, Huidobro Visto por Otros", *Altazor Revista Electrónica de Literatur*a, nº1, Epoca/Año 3 (August, 2021).

García, Julián, Fernando Magdalena and Juan M. Medina. "Mid-20th Century Colombian Vaults, A Contemporary Tradition." ResearchGate (May 11, 2020): 124-134. https://www.researchgate.net/publication/330044857.

"General Panel Residence." Los Angeles Conservancy. Accessed July 7, 2020. https://www.laconservancy.org/locations/general-panel-residence.

Giedion, Sigfried. "Alvar Aalto," *The Architectural Review* (Archive: 1896-2005), Vol. 107, Iss. 638 (Feb 1, 1950): 77-84.

"History of Richmond." City of Richmond, California. Accessed July 9, 2020. http://www.ci.richmond.ca.us/112/History-of-Richmond.

Hitchcock, Henry- Russel. *Latin American Architecture since 1945.* New York: Museum of Modern Art, 1955.

Huppatz, D, J. "Globalizing Design History and Global Design History," *Journal of Design History*, Vol. 28 Nº2 (March 2015): 182-202.

Imperiale, Alicia. 'An American Wartime Dream: The Packaged House System of Konrad Wachsmann and Walter Gropius." Temple University Paper at the 2012 ACSA Conference.https://www.acsaarch.org/proceedings/Fall%20Conference%20Proceedings/ACSA.FALL.12/ACSA.FALL.12.8.pdf.

Ingold, Tim. *Being Alive: Essays on Movement, Knowledge and Descriptions.* London, New York: Routledge, 2011.

Izquierdo, Cristián. "Interview to Architect Cristián de Groote." In *Emilio Duhart, Seminario de Investigación Fernando Pérez Oyarzun.* Santiago: Pontificia Universidad Católica de Chile, 2005.

Jackson, Neil. *The Modern Steel House.* London and New York: Routledge, 2016.

Jackson, Neil. "Metal-Frame Houses of the Modern Movement in Los Angeles: Part 1: Developing a Regional Tradition." *Architectural History* 32, 1989. http://www.jstor.com/stable/1568566.

Jackson Turner, Frederick. *The Frontier in American History.* New York: Henry Holt and Company, 1920.

Jones, Colin. "Theodore Vacquer and the Archaeology of Modernity in Haussmann's Paris." *Transactions of the Royal Historical Society*, Sixth Series, Vol. 17 (2007):157- 183.

Junemann Gazmuri, Alfredo. *Jorge Aguirre Silva: Un Arquitecto del Movimiento Moderno en Chile.* Santiago: Ediciones ARQ, 1996.

Le Blanc, Aleca. "Palmeiras and Pilotis: Promoting Brazil with Modern Architecture." *Third Text*, Vol. 26, Issue 1 (January 2012): 103-116.

Le Corbusier. *The City of Tomorrow and Its Planning.* Cambridge, Massachusetts: The MIT Press, 1929.

Le Corbusier. *When the Cathedrals Were White.* New York: McGraw-Hill Book Company, 1964.

Legarraga, Patricio. *Los Vascos de Francia en Chile.* Santiago: Patricio Legarraga Raddatz, 2006.

Leone, Ilario. "Lo Studio di Le Corbusier nel Secondo Dopoguerra. Passaggi, Pratiche e Esiti," Parte I. PhD diss.,

Politecnico di Torino, Politecnico di Milano, 2013.

L'Esprit Nouveau: Revue Internationale D'Esthétique, n° 1, III. http://arti.sba.uniroma3.it/esprit/viewer/web/viewer.html?&file=Li4vLi4vcGRm L0VzcHJpdE5vdXZlY XUtRlRfMDEucGRm

Liernur, Jorge Francisco. *Escritos de Arquitectura del Siglo XX en América Latina*. Madrid: Tanais Ediciones, 2002.

Liernur, Jorge Francisco. "Forewords." In *Modern Architecture in Latin America: Art, Technology, and Utopia*, edited by Luis E. Carranza and Fernando Luis Lara, XI-XIII. Austin: University of Texas Press, 2014.

Los Angeles Conservancy. "General Panel Residence." Accessed July 7, 2020, https://www.laconservancy.org/locations/general-panel-residence.

Ludwig, Marilyn E. "Technical Considerations – Health, Education and Recreation. "*A.I.A. Journal - 1965 Congress Convention* (August 1965).

Macaya Bronstein, Francisca. "Dualidad Formal en la Casa Duhart: Entre el Arraigo y lo Foráneo." In Seminario de Investigación, Pontificia Universidad Católica de Chile, Primer Semestre, 2003.

MacCarthy, Fiona. *Gropius: The Man Who Built the Bauhaus.* Cambridge, Massachusetts: The Belknap Press of Harvard University Press, 2019.

Manzini, Ezio. *Politics of the Everyday.* London: Bloomsbury Publishing, 2019.

Mejía Vallejo, Clara Elena. "Rogelio Salmona y Le Corbusier: Sobre la Permeabilidad del Hacer." PhD diss., Universidad Politécnica de Valencia, 2015.

Meynard, Evelyn. "Interview with Alberto Montealegre Klenner." Video. Santiago, December 27, 2019.

Meynard, Evelyn. "Interview with Max Aguirre." Video. Santiago, January16, 2020.

Meynard, Evelyn. "Interview with Humberto Eliash." Video. Santiago, January15, 2020.

Molina Baeza, Cristóbal. "Alberto Piwonka: En el cruce de las ideas de la modernidad en Chile." PhD. Diss. Universitat Politecnica de Catalunya, Barcelona Tech, 2015.

Mongragón López, Hugo. "Project on Social Engineering: The Debate on Housing Plan in Journals, Santiago, 1930-1950." *AUS*, Volume 17, first semester 2015. http://revistas.uach.cl/pdf/aus/n17/art06.pdf.

Montealegre Klenner, Alberto. "Cristián Berríos: Ciudad Universitaria de Concepción." Unpublished manuscript.

Montealegre, Alberto. *Emilio Duhart, Arquitecto.* Santiago: ARQ Publishers, 1994.

Montealegre Klenner, Alberto. "Emilio Duhart y la Originalidad Posible." Unpublished manuscript.

Morshed, Adnan. "The Master Builder as Superman: Norman Bel Gedde's Futurama," *University of Minnesota Press*, (2015): 153-220. https://www.jstor.org/stable/10.5749/j.ctt1287nsj.7.

Mumford, Eric, "El Discurso del CIAM Sobre el Urbanismo, 1928-1960." Accessed August 21, 2020. http://www.bdigital.unal.edu.co/22070/1/18632-60516-1-PB.pdf.

"New York World's Fair 1939 and 1940 Incorporated Records." The New York Public Library, Manuscripts and Archives Division. Accessed April 1, 2020. http://archives.nypl.org/mss/2233.

Pallasmaa, Juhani, and Tomoko Sato. *Alvar Aalto: Through the Eyes of Shigeru Ban*. London: Black Dog Publishing, 2007.

Pearlman, Jill. *Inventing American Modernism: Joseph Hudnut, Walter Gropius and the Bauhaus Legacy at Harvard.* Charlottesville: University of Virginia Press, 2007.

Pelkonen, Eeva-Liisa, Eero Saarinen, and Donald Albrecht. *Eero Saarinen: Shaping the Future*. New Haven and London: Yale University Press, 2006.

Pevsner, Nikolaus. *Pioneers of Modern Design: From William Morris to Walter Gropius*. New Haven and London: Yale University Press, 1936.

Prinz, Ulrike. "La Herencia de la Bauhaus en América Latina." Deutschland.de. Accessed 09/15/20. https://www.deutschland.de/es/tras-las-huellas-de-la-bauhaus-en-america-latina.

Quantrill, Malcom. *Chilean Modern Architecture Since 1950*. College Station: Texas A & M University Press, 2010.

Quintana Guerrero, Ingrid. "La Colonie Latino-américaine dans l'Atelier Parisien de Le Corbusier." *Les Cahiers de la Recherche Architecturale Urbaine et Paysagère*, (February, 2018): 1-24. https://journals.openedition.org/craup/525.

Ragon, Michel, *Histoire Mondiale de l'Architecture et l'Urbanisme, Tome 2 Pratiques et Méthodes, 1911-1971*. Paris: Casterman, 1993.

Reed, Peter S. "Enlisting Modernism." In *World War II and the American Dream*, edited by Donald Albrecht, 1-41. Massachusetts: MIT Press, 1996.

"Report on Brazil." *The Architectural Review,* October 1954.

Roth, Alfred. *The New Schoolhouse*. New York, Washington: Frederick A. Prager, 1958.

Salingaros A., Nikos. *A Theory of Architecture.* Kathmandu: Vajra Books, 2013.

Spellman, Catherine and Karl Unglaub, eds. *Peter Smithson: Conversation with Students – A Space for Our Generation.* New York: Princeton Architectural Press, 2004.

Stewart, Ken. "Remembering Pei: Tracing the Architect's Legacy to the Harvard Graduate School of Design." Harvard University Graduate School of Design. Accessed July 10, 2020. https://www.gsd.harvard.edu/2019/07/remembering-pei-tracing-the-architects-legacy-to-the-harvard-graduate-school-of-design/.

Subercaseaux, Benjamin. *Chile o una Loca Geografía*. Santiago: Ediciones Ercilla, 1940.

The New York Public Library, Manuscripts and Archives Division. "New York World's Fair 1939 and 1940 Incorporated Records." Accessed 04/01/20. http://archives.nypl.org/mss/2233.

TMX. "Sliding Formwork." Accessed December, 2020. http://thm-holding.ru/en/sliding-formwork/.

Torrent, Horacio. "Otras Direcciones de la Vanguardia: La Revista ARQuitectura en Chile 1935-1936." In *Entre Puntos Cardinales: Debates sobre una Nueva Arquitectura (1920-1950)*, edited by Ana María Rigotti y Silvia Pampinella. Rosario, Argentina: Prohistoria Ediciones,

To Alfredo and Nicolas for your unwavering support.
To my mother who in her eternal silence still talks to me
and is my source of infinite love.

I would like to express my deepest thanks to:

Denise Duhart
Emile Duhart
Michelle Duhart
Monique Duhart
Solange Duhart

Ramon Prat
Marga Gibert
Felipe Sáez Contreras
Michael Corris

Ignacio Sánchez Díaz
Mario Ubilla Sanz
Fernando Pérez Oyarzun
Isabel García Perez de Arce
Emilio De La Cerda Errázuriz
Stephannie Fell Contreras

Alberto Montealegre Klenner
Humberto Eliash
Max Aguirre Gonzalez
Pablo Altikes Pinilla
Cristián Berríos
Cristóbal Molina Baeza

Rosita Lira
María Elena Comandari

Andrés Téllez Tavera
Leonardo Finotti
Cristóbal Caro

Francisca Cruz
Pablo Ciuminatto

Michele Faguet
José Molina Kock

Rory O'Dea
Jilly Traganou
Sarah Lichman
Jeremy Scott

Evelyn Meynard is a historian, researcher, and curator in the field of material culture. Her diverse interests span architecture, urbanism, sustainability, and design theory. She holds an M.A. in Design History and Curatorial Studies from Parsons School of Design and an M.A. in Design Research, Writing and Criticism from the School of Visual Arts in New York.

She believes strongly in the transformative power of unearthing critical and cultural perspectives that are underrepresented or neglected. She focuses on revisiting design histories, in the hope that their uncovering can contribute significantly to global and alter entrenched hegemonic narratives.

She has lectured on the work of Emilio Duhart H. at several architectural universities in Chile: Universidad Finis Terrae, Pontificia Universidad Católica de Chile, Universidad de Chile, and Universidad Diego Portales. She is currently expanding his research on Duhart by conducting an in-depth study of his furniture design, as well as that of his contemporaries, focusing on their influence on modern design principles and their cultural significance.

José Molina Kock is a freelance translator, proofreader and editor for scientific and specialized publications in the fields of architecture, the arts, and social sciences. He is an architect from the Pontificia Universidad Católica de Chile and holds a master's degree in architecture from Pratt Institute in New York. He has held academic positions and worked as a teacher and researcher at various Chilean universities, including the Pontificia Universidad Católica de Chile, Universidad Diego Portales, and Universidad UNIACC. He has participated in numerous editorial projects, being a regular contributor to scientific publications of the Universidad de Chile and the Universidad San Sebastián. He has also acted as external advisor in the preparation of texts, dossiers, and international applications for Chilean State agencies such as the Ministry of Culture and Heritage, Ministry of Housing and Urbanism, Undersecretary of Government, and others.

José Pérez de Arce holds a Ph.D. in Latin American studies from the University of Chile. He served as a museologist at the Museo Chileno de Arte Precolombino in Santiago, Chile from 1981 to 2014. Since the 1980s, he has focused on studying pre-Hispanic music in the Americas. His publications and presentations explore the history of Andean music from archaeological, historical, and ethnographic perspectives. In addition to his scholarly work, Pérez de Arce is also a musician and an accomplished illustrator of the indigenous peoples of Chilean territory.

Alfredo Jaar_pg. 221

Andrés Téllez Tavera, 1993_pgs. 170 above, 207 and 220

Antonio Quintana, c. 1950. Andrés Bello Central Archive of the University of Chile, Photographic Archive Collection, Antonio Quintana Conteras Sub-Fund_pg. 38 below

Antonio Quintana. Photographic Archive of the National Library of Chile_pg. 136

Antonio Quintana, c. 1955. Slide Collection. Archive of Originals. Faculty of Architecture, Design and Urban Studies. Pontifical Catholic Universitand of Chile_pg. 173 below

Archive of Enzo Costa. Courtesy of Pablo Chiuminatto_ pg. 189

Rio de Janeiro Museum of Modern Art Archive_pg. 20

Duhart Family Personal Archive_pgs. 15, 25, 32, 45, 64, 108, 114, 125, 157, and 162

Roberto Goandcoolea Infante Personal Archive_pg. 183, 263, and 264 below

Architectura y Construcción, no. 6, May 1946. https://quintanormalextrema.files.wordpress.com/2009/04/arquitectura-and-construccion-chile1.pdf. _pg. 139

Arquitectura y Construcción, no. 16, September 1949_pg. 140

Arts & Architecture, January 1944_pgs. 130, 131, and 179

National Library of Chile. Digital Archive_pg. 83, left

National Library of Chile. Chilean Memory. Code BN, MC0018550. https://www.memoriachilena.cl/602/w3-article-74701.html_pg. 202

Photography Collection, Medina Hall, National Library of Chile, Santiago. http://www.bibliotecanacionaldigital.gob.cl/visor/BND:314909_pg. 56 above

GSD History Collection: Student Affairs [Student Work], Folder CA113. Courtesy of the Frances Loeb Library, Harvard University Graduate School of Design_pgs. 122-124
Special Research Collection. Archive of Originals. Faculty of Architecture, Design and Urban Studies. Pontifical Catholic University of Chile_ pg. 38 above, left

José Perez de Arce Collection. Chilean Museum of Pre-Columbian Art, Santiago_pg. 50

Commons. Wikimedia.org. https://commons.wikimedia.org/wiki/File: Santiago_de_Chile_1930.jpg_ pg. 56 below

https://commons.wikimedia.org/w/index.php?curid=67871017_pg. 68 left

Cristián Berríos_pg. 261

Cristóbal Caro, 2017_pgs. 260-262

Emilio Duhart Arquitecto, book by Alberto Montealegre Klenner. Santiago, Chile, ARQ, 1994_ pg. 172 below

Ezra Stoller. Collection of history images, Finna Museum Agency. https://finna.fi/Record/museovirasto.80FC83754439F D58C007FEF 218A7E3EB_ pg. 68 right

Le Corbusier Foundation. © F.L.C. / ADAGP, Paris / Artists Rights Society (ARS), New Andork 2023_ pgs. 149, 152, and 167

Emilio Duhart Fund. Archive of Originals. Faculty of Architecture, Design and Urban Studies. Pontifical Catholic University of Chile_pgs. 72 -79, 89-95, 98-99, 101, 144, 146, 164, 166 right, 168, 170 below, 172 above,173, 174, 180, 181 above, 182, 190-191, 192 below, 195, 200, 210, 211, 224, 225, 230-241, 245, 246, 249-264 above, and 265

CA Magazine Fund. Archive of Originals. Faculty of Architecture, F.L.C. / ADAGP, Paris / Artists Rights Society (ARS), Nueva Andork 2023_pgs. 149, 152 above and below, and 167

Sergio Larraín García-Moreno Fund. Archive of Originals. Faculty of Architecture, Design and Urban Studies. Pontifical Catholic University of Chile._ pg. 245

Design and Urban Studies. Pontifical Catholic University of Chile_ pg. 38 above, left

Courtesy of the Denegri Family_pg. 198 below

Courtesy of the Echeverría Baeza Family Succession_pg. 166 left

Guy Wenborne_pg. 48

Leonardo Finotti_pgs. 212-219, 222, 223, 226, and 227

Luis Ladrón de Guevara, Santiago. National Historical Museum Collection_ pgs. 173 above, 176, 181 below, and 199

Harvard Art Museums / Busch-Reisinger Museum, a gift of Walter Gropius, BRGA.98.14._pg. 133

Norberto Seebach_pg. 28

Pablo Altikes Pinilla_ pgs. 192 above, 198 above, 208, 209, 213 below, and 228

Roberto Dávila, 1936. CA Magazine Fund. Archive of Originals. Faculty of Architecture, Design and Urban Studies. Pontifical Catholic University of Chile_ pg. 38 above, right

Tom Dempsey. https://www.bibliotecanacionaldigital.gob.cl/bnd/631/w3-article-331590.html_pg. 83 right

CEPAL Repository_pgs. 193, 206, and 225 above

Re-Imagining Modern Architecture
Emilio Duhart, 1940-1970

Published by
Actar Publishers, New York, Barcelona
www.actar.com

Author
Evelyn Meynard

Editor
Evelyn Meynard

Graphic Design
Ramon Prat, Marga Gibert

Translation
Michele Faguet
(Foreword and Preface)
Evelyn Meynard
(Original Spanish notes)

Copy Editor
Walter Ancarrow

Printing and Binding
Arlequin SL

Distribution
Actar D, Inc. New York, Barcelona.

New York
440 Park Avenue South, 17th Floor
New York, NY 10016, USA
T 212-966-2207
salesnewyork@actar-d.com

Barcelona
Roca i Batlle 2
08023 Barcelona, Spain
T +34 933 282 183
eurosales@actar-d.com

Indexing
ISBN english : 978-1-63840-179-7
LCCN : 2025931814

Printed in Spain

Publication date: March 2025

Cover image: ©Leonardo Finotti